Multiethnic Australia

Multiethnic Australia

Its History and Future

CELESTE LIPOW MACLEOD

McFarland & Company, Inc., Publishers
Jefferson, North Carolina, and London

LIBRARY OF CONGRESS CATALOGUING-IN-PUBLICATION DATA

MacLeod, Celeste Lipow, 1931–
    Multiethnic Australia : its history and future / Celeste Lipow MacLeod.
      v.   cm.
    Includes bibliographical references and index.
    Contents : Before the British — Convicts and colonists — Class conflicts with unexpected outcomes — Spreading across the land — Dispossessed : the indigenous people — A place in two cultures — Immigrants and "White Australia" — A multiethnic nation — Diversity and dissent — Embedded legacies — Turbulent times — Asian connections — Which way ahead?

    ISBN 978-0-7864-2522-8
    softcover : 50# alkaline paper ∞

    1. Australlia — Ethnic relations — Government policy.
    2. Australia — Race relations — Government policy.
    3. Multiculturalism — Australia.   4. Australia — Emigration and immigration — Government policy.   5. Immigrants — Australia — History.   6. White Australia policy.   I. Title.
DU120.M325   2006
305.800994 — dc22   2006010760

British Library cataloguing data are available

©2006 Celeste Lipow MacLeod. All rights reserved

No part of this book may be reproduced or transmitted in any form or by any means, electronic or mechanical, including photocopying or recording, or by any information storage and retrieval system, without permission in writing from the publisher.

On the cover: large portrait photograph ©2006 Corbis Images; background by Sarah Sanders

Manufactured in the United States of America

McFarland & Company, Inc., Publishers
  Box 611, Jefferson, North Carolina 28640
    www.mcfarlandpub.com

In memory of
Netta Burns, Australia
Jenny Johnston, Scotland
John Ruymaker, USA

Table of Contents

Acknowledgments — ix
A Note to the Reader — xii
Introduction — 1
Prologue — 5

ONE • Before the British — 11
TWO • Convicts and Colonists — 18
THREE • Class Conflicts with Unexpected Outcomes — 32
FOUR • Spreading Across the Land — 48
FIVE • Dispossessed: The Indigenous People — 66
SIX • A Place in Two Cultures — 79
SEVEN • Immigrants and "White Australia" — 97
EIGHT • A Multiethnic Nation — 113
NINE • Diversity and Dissent — 128
TEN • Embedded Legacies — 139
ELEVEN • Turbulent Times — 153
TWELVE • Asian Connections — 166
THIRTEEN • Which Way Ahead? — 185

Chapter Notes — 203
Selected Bibliography — 217
Index — 221

Acknowledgments

First, special thanks to John S. Conroy of Sydney, a friend since the days we both lived at the International House in Berkeley, California, as students. He read and commented on several drafts, found answers to a bevy of questions about his country, and he and his wife Una Conroy provided hospitality in Sydney, letting me use their home as a base. Next, I am grateful to Ethel Ruymaker, an American friend who taught at two Australian universities: she gave me the names of several people there who proved helpful, read the manuscript and assisted in too many ways to list.

Some of the numerous Australians who helped me with this book also arranged interviews or sent me lists of people to contact. For this I am grateful to the late Netta Burns in Canberra, Ilsa Sharp, Sandra Theseira and Ramdas Sankaran in Perth, and Janet E. Durling and Judith Ventic in Darwin. Many thanks also to James Jupp, Director of the Centre for Immigration and Multicultural Studies at Australian National University in Canberra, who was ever ready to answer my research questions, and who read some chapters.

Several people who read my manuscript and gave me feedback also did editing. Dorothy Witt and Eva Goodwin were thoughtful readers and ace editors. Jean Pauline, Maggie Walker and Mark Walker read more than one draft and offered helpful comments and editing, while Emmy E. Werner read some chapters and gave me sound editorial advice. Stephen Cole and Arthur Lipow read and commented on the manuscript and also sent me relevant material about Australia. Nils Gunnar Nilsson and Kerstin Stjarne of Sweden gave the manuscript a careful reading and made valuable suggestions. Others who read some version of the manuscript include Elias Abu-Saba, Hilde Burton, Pascal Destandou, Sharleen Harty, John R. Hill, Allan Hoben, Val Honey, Ellen Huppert, the late Jenny Johnston, John Johnston, Herman Lipow, Emilia Bolin Ransom, Demi Rasmussen and Anton Schouten. Some chapters were read by Mary Abu-Saba, Gae Canfield, Gerard

Colby, Estelle Jelinek, Doris Linder, Betty Anne Lipow, Rita Maran, and Ros Pesman. I am grateful for all their help,

In Australia I interviewed Sandy Atkinson, Hakan Akyol, Isaac Brown, Carolyn Cherett, Elizabeth Chong, David Coles, Beth Davies, Eric van Dissell, Joe DeLuca, Janet E. Durling, Sol Encel, Diana Encel, Rita Erlich, Hugh Garsden, Don Grimes, Ann Gruen, Fred Gruen, Tony Haritos, Gary Highland, Sandra Krempl-Pereira, Brij V. Lal, Bob Lewis, Lewis Lloyd, Edna McGill, Irwin Minjott, Barbara Overbury, the late Edith Phillips, Dennis Pryor, Ramdas Sankaran, Laurie Shears, Peter Smith, Edmund Teo, Janet Seah Teo, John Theseira, Sandra Theseira, Barbara Shore, Charles See Kee, and Mary E. White. I thank them all.

For help with research I want to thank several libraries and librarians in Australia: Marg McCormack and others at the State Library of Victoria, John Schembri, librarian of the Ethnic Affairs Commission of New South Wales; Alex di Montis and others at the former Bureau of Immigration and Population Research, and staff at the National Library of Australia and the State Libraries of New South Wales, the Northern Territory, and Western Australia. In the United States thanks to librarians at the University of California at Berkeley, the Berkeley Public Library and the Sonoma Public Library.

Librarians in Australia also helped me find and order photographs in their collections and gave permission to use them. Thanks to Jennifer Broomhead, Helen Harrison and others at the Mitchell Library; Sylvia Carr, Marika Tolgyesi, and others at the National Library of Australia; Angelo Comino of the Oxley Library; Gerard Hayes and others at the State Library of Victoria; and Mawghan Elverd of the Battye Library. Thanks also to James Jupp and Elizabeth Gilliam for help in obtaining photos.

Other people in Australia, the United States and elsewhere helped in various ways: my thanks to Bonnie Britt, Alden Bryant, Daniella Bagozzi, Harry Baker, Gwen Baker, Ed Beecher, Bob Canfield, Anne-Marie Catalano, Phillipa Challis, Pat Cody, Crispin Conroy, Nancy Dutcher, Edna Finkelstein, Leland Finkelstein, Meg Grimes, Bruce Grimshaw, Gary Highland, Stan Jacobsen, Marian Kassovic, Delphine LeDain, the late Anne Lipow, Marie Lynch, Lorien Milligan, Margaret Murfett, Rex Murfett, Larry Noye, Maurice Perera, Caroline Pincus, Jacquie Reed, Margaret Reynolds, the late John Ruymaker, Harvey Schwartz, Lucy Taska, and Sayre van Young. For hospitality in Melbourne I am grateful to Rita Erlich and to Dennis Pryor. If I have inadvertently omitted someone, my apologies and thanks.

A collective thanks to people in groups I belong to where I gave work-in-progress presentations on this book and got useful suggestions: the Women and Work Group in Berkeley, and the Institute for Historical Studies, an organization of historians and history buffs in the San Francisco Bay Area. Another collective thanks to the many Australians I met and had long conversations with over breakfast and dinner when I stayed at the Macquarie Hotel in Canberra on a research trip.

I am indebted to the Howard Gotlieb Archival Research Center at Boston University for permission to quote from a letter in the Emma Goldman Collection, and to John S. Conroy, John Hill, and Kay Lawson for permission to quote from parts of their letters to the author. Pia Courtis, Media and Information Officer at Uluru-Kata Tjuta National Park gave permission use a photo taken at the Park and also provided information about the indigenous people there. Terry Milligan gave permission to use his photograph of Mick Dodson, and Mick and Lucy Catalano gave permission to use a photo of them supplied by Ethel Ruymaker. My thanks to all of them. I thank cartographer Ben Pease of Pease Press in San Francisco for the fine maps.

My two sons and their wives helped in many ways but I am especially grateful for their ongoing computer-related assistance: thanks to Peter MacLeod, Debbie MacLeod, David MacLeod and Leila Abu-Saba. Thanks also to Herman Lipow and Sally Skanderup for computer help.

Spending time with my grandchildren—Stuart, Catherine, Joseph, and Jacob MacLeod—provided a pleasant respite from research and writing. Their parents, mentioned above, along with my extended family and friends, were all remarkably patient and supportive during the many years when my mind was focused primarily on Australia.

A Note to the Reader

    Indigeneous Australians are advised that Chapters Five, Six, and Eleven of this book include images or names of people now deceased.

Introduction

When riots broke out on a beach in Sydney in December, 2005, people around the world were stunned. Television pictures and Internet descriptions of blond young men bashing dark-haired young men did not fit the usual images of Australia.

For some viewers, part of the surprise came from seeing people with dark hair and complexions—identified by the media as Middle Eastern or Lebanese immigrants—on the beaches. These viewers still thought of Australia as a British nation in the antipodes whose population was essentially white except for a sprinking of indigenous Aborigines who lived in remote outback areas. Who were these immigrants, they wondered, and what were they doing on a surfers' beach?

For many others abroad, the beach riots fit into what they already believed. They were aware that after once trying to restrict immigration to people from Britain, Ireland and Western European nations, Australia ended that policy decades ago and that people from many places lived there now. But they still thought of Australians as opposed to a multicultural society, so they shook their heads and told each other the beach riots were what one would expect to happen there.

There was a third reaction as well, by people who knew that Australia is among the world's most multiethnic countries and that it made the transformation to that status with remarkably little violence. They knew that from 1947 to December 10, 2005, there were no race riots in Australia although the country took in five million immigrants during this period and they came from every continent. Among this third group the reaction was sadness.

My response fell into the third category. More than a decade earlier, on my first visit to Australia, I was impressed with its multiethnic society, the services it provided for its people and the relative lack of physical violence there compared with my own country, the United States. I decided to write a book about the country. This took longer than I expected, in part because so many changes kept occurring, both in Australia and in the part of the world where it is located.

One part of my research involved studying Australia's past to help me understand how and why the country developed as it did. Hence Chapters Two through Four are about British settlement during the colonial period, Chapters Five and Six are about the indigenous people the British displaced, and Chapters Seven through Nine cover the rise and fall of the White Australia policy and the transformation into a multiethnic nation. Chapter Ten looks at lingering British influences. The last few chapters focus on the present, especially the years 1995 to 2005. The Sydney beach riots erupted just before the publication of this book, so I was able to include a short section about them near the end of the last chapter.

For readers who know little about Australia, the historical chapters provide a loose overview of the past; but they don't cover everything because this is not a general history of the country. Rather my aim here is to lay the foundation for the story of multiethnic Australia in order to help readers understand the country today.

The book also brings in related material that is essential to this understanding: Australia's relationships with countries in its region, and a description of where it is located. Many Australians view their country as isolated from the rest of the world. This perception has been projected abroad: Australia is thought of as sitting right next to New Zealand, the two countries huddled together in the Pacific Ocean far from all other nations.

A look at a map or globe, however, shows that the country is more than 1600 miles from New Zealand but less than 450 miles from East Timor, (map on page 167 shows Australia's location in the Asia Pacific). Papua New Guinea is considerably closer. Australia, which has 20 million people, is also closer to parts of Indonesia (population 232 million) than to New Zealand (population under four million). Above Australia and Indonesia is the Philippines, and a little to the west are Brunei, Singapore, Malaysia and the continent of Asia. Geographically Australia sits at the tip of Southeast Asia and is part of the Asia Pacific region.

Modern Australia, founded as a British penal colony, became a nation that defined itself as a distant satellite of the British Empire. But after World War II, as the empire gradually dissolved, Australia's ethnic makeup changed, and several countries in its region became important players on the global market (and major trading partners of Australia), the question of the country's identity came to the fore. Is Australia a displaced Western nation with binding ties to the old homeland, is it part of the region where it sits, or is it a combination of the two? To this day the issue has not been fully resolved.

Introduction

In popular usage, in Australia, the United States and some other countries, the term "multicultural" has come to mean the inclusion of nonwhite people who don't speak English as their first language and are part of a minority group. But this book includes everyone, the British/Irish majority as well as minorities. I called the book *Multiethnic Australia* to get away from the more restricted definition, though within the book I sometimes use the two terms interchangeably.

The name of one of Australia's political parties may cause confusion because the country's conservative party is called the Liberal Party. The country's liberal party is the Labor Party.

While Britain has a Labour Party, Australia has a Labor Party—but otherwise Australians use the spelling "labour." In this book I generally follow American usage but in quotations, titles and the names of organizations and institutes, I retain the Australian spelling, which in most cases is also the British spelling.

Prologue

King William Street was closed for a parade. Children and parents in red folk costumes marched down the main street of Adelaide, South Australia's capital city, flanked by the banner of the Macedonian Ethnic School. Close behind came the Maltese Guild Language and Folk Dancing School with its own band.

Group upon group followed, each identified by its banner: Korean Ethnic School, Punjabi School Adelaide, Alliance Française de l'Australie du Sud, Vietnamese Community in Australia, Uzbek Ethnic School, the Arabic Language School, Greek Schools of Adelaide. The insistent sound of Scottish bagpipes filled the air as a band of young pipers in kilts went by. What was the occasion?

To find out I joined the edge of the parade. We crossed the bridge that spans the narrow Torrens River, went by the city's performing arts center and stopped at a park whose grassy slopes descended to the water. A woman handing out programs told me what was happening: this was the fifth annual Parade and Concert of South Australia's Ethnic Schools Association, she said. Children of immigrants attended these schools on Saturday morning or after school to learn the language and customs of their people. After the parade ended the children would dance and sing for their families and each other.

A few minutes later as I watched a group of young Ethiopian dancers in white, I was struck by the changes in Australia. After once seeing itself as an Anglo-Saxon preserve and trying to exclude people of color, at least a third of its citizens now have ancestries other than British or Irish. They come from some 240 countries and places, with the largest numbers coming from Asia in recent years. Australia absorbed this new population in less than half a century and did it so peacefully and uneventfully that people in some parts of the world are unaware that it happened.

Nor were these the only changes. By the early 1990s increasing numbers of Australians were reassessing their national identity. Although some still saw Australia as welded to the British crown, others were leading a movement to become a republic. The country was also busy forging ties with nearby Asian nations it had once ignored.

Watching that parade in 1994, Australia seemed to me a model of how a country could adapt to changing circumstances and thrive. Yet two years later a series of ethnic and political troubles erupted. They continued through the final years of the century and spilled into the next, bringing to the surface a deep-seated conflict that has long bedeviled the nation.

Two opposing factions are fighting for political dominance there. Those on one side see their country as a Western nation — displaced in the East by historical happenstance — that must cling to its British heritage for cultural and political survival. These days they worry that refugees from the Middle East might inundate the country. Their opponents on the other side see Australia as a country of the Asia Pacific region and want to participate actively in its affairs. For them, the nation's multiethnic population is an asset.

This book also explores the related conflicts over Australia's identity and its place in the world. The narrative centers around the nation's peoples, with several chapters telling the stories of its three main groups: the large base of citizens of British or Irish descent; the small numbers of indigenous people whose nomadic way of life was decimated after the British arrived and who are trying to make it economically while also maintaining their traditional cultures; and all other immigrants, who continue coming in from around the globe.

Two events changed the course of modern Australian history. The first was the penal colony Britain set up at Botany Bay (Sydney) in 1788. The second was the discovery of gold in Australia in 1851. People poured in from around the world but the large numbers of gold seekers from China set off the panic button. Fears that hordes of desperately poor Chinese peasants would swoop down and engulf Australia if it didn't watch out — and that poor people from other Asian nations might follow suit — led the colonies to enact legislation barring people of color from coming to Australia. When the colonies became a federation of states in 1901, its new Parliament passed the restrictive law that became known as the White Australia policy.

After World War II the country gradually opened its doors to peoples from around the world and became a model of multiculturalism. But memories of the old restrictive law remain fixed in minds around the world. Nor is this the only misconception. Although Australia became a social innovator in the late nineteenth and early twentieth centuries, passing legislation in several areas that improved the lives of its people, the country's progressive social heritage is little known abroad or has been forgotten. Yet the egalitarian tradition established in colonial times helped immigrants and the indigenous people in the second half of the twentieth century. Later chapters fill in the details: the brief account below gives the gist of what happened.

During the penal period, British jailers assumed that prisoners who finished their sentences would remain at the bottom of Australian society, forming a low-paid workforce with neither stature nor clout. But former prisoners, finding themselves in a spacious land with a labor shortage, refused to stay down. They joined force with poor immigrants and turned the country into the "fair go" society. This meant that every person should have the chance for a pleasant life. For the most part workers did not expect to become rich, but they wanted to be comfortable and to make sure that old age would not plunge them into poverty as in the old country.

Australia was among the first nations to provide old-age pensions and set a "fair and reasonable" wage. By the early twentieth century, Australian workers enjoyed a rate of pay and standard of living that made labor groups in Europe view the country as a workers' paradise. Australia had the first secret ballot in the world. Women were given the vote in 1902.

These benefits were for whites only at that time. Australia began to change in this regard in 1947 when it inaugurated a massive immigration program, centered at first on war-torn Europe. In the ensuing years the scope of the program expanded to include nations from other continents, including Asia. The country did more than just open the door to peoples of every background. Drawing on the strong tradition of a fair go for all, it extended that mandate to recent immigrants and devised practical services to help them make the transition. It also promoted a national multicultural policy that encouraged immigrants to retain their cultural traditions while becoming loyal Australians.

This new policy included the indigenous people. For nearly two centuries the government had denied them the basic rights of other Australians. It also tried to force them to live like Europeans. But starting in the 1960s Australia did a turnaround on this and other policies that affect the Aborigines. Along with now encouraging them to follow their traditions, the country set up programs, run mainly by indigenous people, to try to help improve their peoples' lives and economic prospects. But the indigenous people, currently 2.4 percent of the population, are still the poorest Australians.

From 1973 through 1995, four successive governments encouraged acceptance of Australia's increasingly mixed population. Many citizens

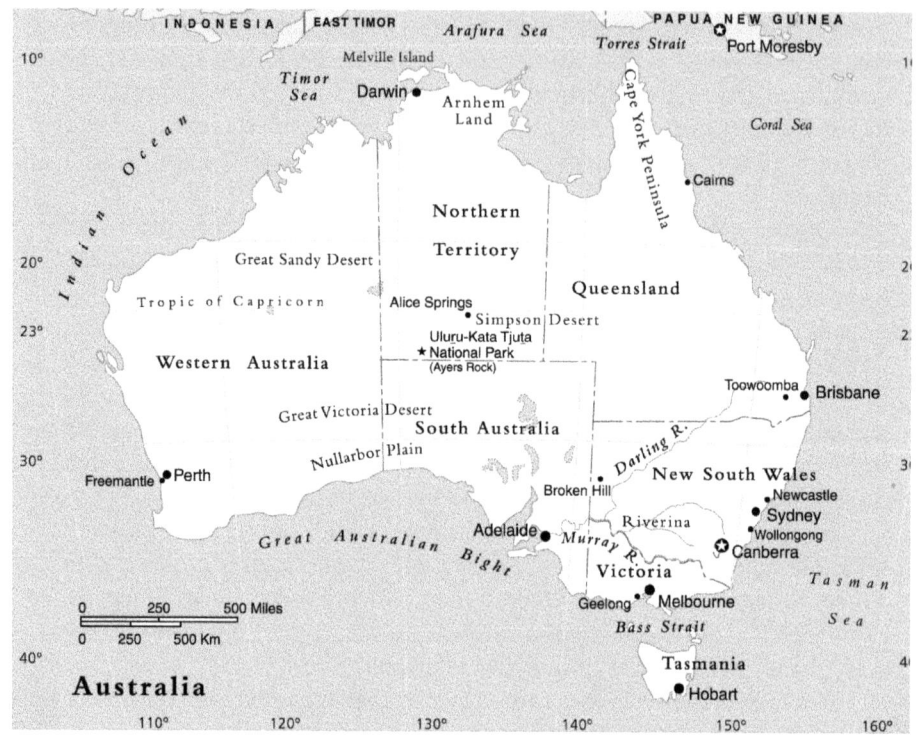

Australia (map by Ben Pease, Pease Press).

applauded the change but others were dismayed and wanted the country to go back to the way it used to be. After a coalition of two conservative parties came to power in 1996, the new prime minister and his administration reemphasized ties with Britain and the West. In 1999 they helped defeat a referendum measure that would have made Australia a republic. Two years later the prime minister refused to let a boatload of refugees from Afghanistan and Iraq land on Australian soil. The country was so swamped by refugees, he declared, that it had to stop illegal boats from coming.

At the same time, events closer to home were moving the country in a different direction. China has emerged as the powerhouse of Asia. Its industrial success is helping other countries in the region as well. Australia has benefited as a major supplier of the iron ore and several other raw materials that China needs for its development. By the beginning of the twenty-first century nearly two-thirds of Australia's exports were going to countries in Asia.

The belief that Australia was isolated gave its citizens a sense of security, because it meant that the country was far from violent conflicts in trouble spots like the Middle East. Likewise, recent immigrants and refugees viewed Australia as a quiet safe haven. That illusion was shattered in 2002 when bombs exploded on the tropical Indonesian island of Bali. Investigations led to members of Jemaah Islamiah, an organization with a link to Al Qaeda, operating in Malaysia, Indonesia and the Philippines. Of the 202 people the bombs killed, 88 were Australians. In the aftermath of the tragedy, officials from both major political parties stressed the importance of building closer relationships with nations in the region.

A handful of leaders and analysts abroad with detailed knowledge of Australia have suggested it might play a larger role in its region. So have a few within the country itself. Noting the nation's connections with both East and West, along with its location, development and multiethnic population, they see Australia as a potential negotiator that might help ease tensions between nations with different cultures and outlooks. But to do this effectively, Australians need to recognize their assets and reconcile the opposing views that divide the nation.

The roots of the controversy are embedded in the past so the narrative reaches back in time and then moves forward to concentrate on recent happenings. We start with the period before the British arrived. This in turn takes us to two distant continents.

ONE

Before the British

With tropical islands nearby for the taking, who needed an arid land? Dutch and English explorers who reached the dry west coast of Australia during the seventeenth century declared the place worthless. The Dutch, who later explored the western and northern coasts, christened the land "New Holland" just in case they should want to claim it one day.[1] They never did.

In 1770, a British ship, the *Endeavour*, approached New Holland from the east. Captain James Cook, returning from an exploratory trip to South Pacific waters, found a bay along the east coast that would do for a layover. The land looked more inviting than the desolate wasteland described by visitors to the opposite coast: its gently rolling hills of bluish hue were covered with woods, grasses, and a myriad of plants and shrubs.[2] Cook was pleased and one group onboard — the botanists — became ecstatic.

Young Joseph Banks of England and his Swedish colleague Daniel Carl Solander were overwhelmed by the profusion of unfamiliar plants.[3] For eight days they rushed around collecting thousands of specimens to take home; at least half belonged to species never seen before by Europeans. In honor of their work, Cook named the port Botany Bay.[4]

The indigenous people's reaction was another surprise. Cook's instructions had directed him "to endeavour by all proper means to cultivate a friendship with the Natives, presenting them with such Trifles as may be acceptable to them."[5] The assumption was that native peoples of every country were essentially alike — childlike individuals who would be entranced by gifts of colorful trinkets and baubles. The Tahitians had already reacted on cue.

Tahiti had been the *Endeavour*'s prime destination. There Cook and staff set up their quadrant and telescopes, observed the transit of the planet Venus across the sun and then determined the distance of the earth from the sun.[6] (Their figures were wrong because equipment and methods for measuring the distance accurately had not yet been developed.) The men enjoyed their stay because local people, including the young women, were friendly.

The Tahitians "were delighted to greet these fascinating strangers with their great sailing ship, their extraordinary clothes, their wonderful trinkets and gadgets."[7] They smiled in wonder at the smallest European trifle; in fact, the Tahitians were so taken with European objects that they walked off with several of them, including the quadrant — but their chief helped Cook get it back.

The natives of Botany Bay reacted differently. Even before the crew disembarked, two Aboriginal men standing on a rock with spears gestured frantically for the ship to leave. When it remained they threw their spears at it. As Cook and his men came ashore in rowboats, people fishing in small canoes paid no attention to the huge ship with its tall masts and many sails. On shore, Aboriginal men treated the visitors as alien intruders. Women and children were kept safely in the background. Cook and his officers took out their trinkets as peace offerings, only to find that these people showed not the slightest interest in their gifts. "They seem'd to set no value upon anything we gave them," Cook wrote later, "nor would they part with anything of their own."[8]

To Captain Cook the indigenous response was puzzling and frustrating. Early on he fired a warning shot over their heads. The first shot made no impression: apparently the Aborigines had never heard gunfire before. But after Cook fired lower to the ground they realized this weapon might kill, and they ran off.

From Botany Bay the *Endeavour* continued up the east coast. At one stopover Cook held a ceremony where he declared the eastern half of the country for the British crown, naming it New South Wales. Then he turned west and headed for England. Cook had been on a scientific voyage of discovery, but like most such voyages at the time, it had hidden agendas as well.

From the days of the ancient Greeks, philosophers had postulated the existence of a huge southern continent below the equator named Terra Australis Incognito — the unknown Southland — thought to be necessary to balance the great northern land mass of Europe and Asia. In people's minds this vast continent was filled with fabulous treasures. The country that discovered it would become rich beyond compare.

But getting there was a major obstacle, until the fifteenth century when improvements in ships and their navigational instruments made long exploratory sea voyages possible. The Portuguese led the way, with navigator Vasco da Gama finding the first sea route to India. Word of such feats caused a rash of European explorers to head for Asia seeking treasures. Some ships ventured further south in search of the great southern continent.

During the 1500s, Portugal established several trading posts in Asia and on Pacific islands south of the mainland. Italian traders had also made inroads in Asia, while Arab and Chinese merchants had traded in these islands for centuries. Portuguese traders concentrated on the Malay Archipelago (now Indonesia), especially a cluster of islands called the Moluccas, or Spice Islands. The cloves, nutmeg, and mace that grew there in abundance then fetched astronomical prices on European markets.[9] Spain tried to wrest control of the spice trade from the Portuguese and failed. But the Dutch, who built the fort of Batavia (Jakarta) on Java in 1619, succeeded. They drove the Portuguese out of most of the region, including the Spice Islands, and became rulers of the Malay Archipelago. For the next few centuries it was known as the Dutch East Indies. The Portuguese, however, managed to hold on to the eastern half of Timor Island.

The Dutch in turn soon had to watch out for the English, whose ships were plying these waters. In 1603, England, which wanted in on the lucrative spice trade, occupied Run, a tiny island in the southern Moluccas that was full of nutmeg trees. Soon these two European contenders were fighting over Run and other nearby islands. Finally in 1667 they signed a treaty where England gave Run to Holland in exchange for a small island in North America. It was called Manhattan.[10]

European countries were also trading with China by then at the port city of Canton (Guangzhou), buying tea and silk, and selling their goods. But traditional trade alone could not bring the profusion of riches they sought. Instructions given to navigator Abel Tasman by the Dutch East India Company in 1642 express the expectations that kept European ships heading for the South Pacific. Referring to Portuguese and Spanish conquests, the Dutch company wrote: "With what valuable treasures, profitable trade connections, useful commerce, excellent territories, vast powers and dominions the said kings have by this discovery and its consequences enriched their kingdoms and crowns." In light of such rewards the Dutch "determined no longer to postpone the long contemplated discovery of the unknown South-land."[11]

No explorer thought New Holland was the fabled southern continent. They were right. Mary E. White, a paleobotanist in Sydney, puts their quests in perspective: "The early European explorers looking for the giant land mass Terra Australis were on the right track," she says. "They just got there 100 million years too late."[12]

Ages ago our planet was one major land mass, but about 200 million years ago it split into two parts. The split was caused by the shifting of tectonic plates on which the continents ride. (Most volcanic activity today occurs at the edges of such plates.) In time the northern and southern parts themselves broke apart. The southern land mass, which concerns us here, was called Gondwana. It was once made up of present South America, Africa, India, Antarctica, Australia, New Zealand, and numerous smaller countries and islands.[13]

While Australia was still part of that giant land mass, it was covered with rainforests and had abundant rivers and lakes. The wet, fertile land was hospitable to dinosaurs who ate the large green leaves of plants and trees that grew in profusion. But further cataclysms kept splitting the big mass until around forty-five million years ago, scientists believe, the continent we know as Australia broke off and went its own way.

It drifted northward slowly, less than three inches a year — a rate imperceptible in terms of human lifetimes or even the recorded histories of nations. But in time this movement changed the land dramatically. Because Australia was below the equator, its climate became hotter as it drifted further north. Over tens of millions of years most of the lakes and rivers dried up, the formerly green land became parched, and desert or grasslands gradually replaced most of the rainforests. Only on a few coastal edges did the old forests survive.

Australia's flora and fauna adapted to the change. Hard-leafed (sclerophyllous) plants that required little water gradually became dominant except in a few moist rainforest areas. More than 600 species of Eucalypts and nearly 1000 of Acacias developed, to name two of the most successful plants.[14] Likewise animal species that could cope with the dry climate proliferated. The kangaroo, whose sturdy back feet and upright stance enabled it to hop with alacrity in search of food, was one of numerous creatures that thrived and multiplied there.

By the time the first human beings arrived, the present flora and fauna were basically in place, although some changes were still in progress. When did people come? Past estimates were in the thirty to forty thousand year range; but as technological breakthroughs have led to more accurate dating techniques, scientists are pushing the date back to sixty thousand years ago or even earlier.

The last Ice Age was still in progress when the first people set foot on Australian shores. This meant that water levels were lower then because of ice caps, so it was possible to complete more of the journey by land. These original inhabitants, long known as Aborigines (and now often called the indigenous people) probably came by way of China and Indonesia over long periods of time, moving from place to place in search of unoccupied land where they could settle. They entered Australia from the north and gradually spread across the entire continent, dividing into several hundred groups over time. Each group claimed a specific territory as its own. Within groups, smaller bands traveled together within their own territory over established routes, stopping annually at places where they knew from experience they would find food and water during certain seasons.[15]

How many indigenous people lived in Australia when the British arrived? Estimates vary from 300,000 to 1,000,000, but whatever the number there was plenty of space for their nomadic life. The Aborigines had no reason to fear that it would ever change. On the other side of the world in North America, however, the consequences of a war in the late eighteenth century would lead to a change in Australia that destroyed the Aborigines' nomadic pattern of life.

Britain had been shipping convicted felons to its North American colonies since the days of Queen Elizabeth I. Jailers in England sold them to ships' contractors who in turn brought them out from England and sold them to colonists as indentured laborers. Planters in Virginia and Maryland bought the most convicts but South Carolina and Pennsylvania also took a goodly number. (The colony of Georgia, founded to help debtors languishing in English prisons, was quite a different arrangement: debtors were free on arrival and received small land grants.)

This system of "transportation"—as the practice of sending convicts abroad was called—relieved the British of the expense of feeding and housing its felons, made tidy profits for shipping companies and provided colonists with a supply of servants who spoke English and came from their own culture. Prisoners were indentured for the term of their sentences, usually seven to fourteen years, and then became free.[16]

During the fifty years before the American Revolution, about 100 convicts a month arrived in the colonies. Far more settlers came out voluntarily as indentured servants: poor people would sign up to work without wages for a number of years in exchange for sea passage to North America. But the presence of convicts in their midst upset many colonists. In 1670, for example, an official in Charles Town, South Carolina, prohibited ships carrying "jail birds" from landing there, citing "the danger to the Colony caused by the great number of felons and other desperate villains sent over from the prisons of England."[17]

A century later when the Americans complained that their rights as Englishmen were being denied in the colonies, Samuel Johnson in London declared: "The Americans are a race of convicts and ought to be thankful for anything we allow them short of hanging."[18] But instead of being grateful, the Americans asserted their independence, went to war — and refused to accept more convicts.

The refusal caused a crisis in London. Crime was soaring in Britain and prisoners were packed into hulks in Portsmouth and London harbors waiting to be shipped off. Where could they be sent instead? One place mentioned was Botany Bay in the South Pacific, which Captain Cook had visited seventeen years earlier. Although Cook had been killed on a later voyage by natives of the Sandwich Islands (Hawaii), Joseph Banks and others from the *Endeavour* were still around to extol the merits of New South Wales. But it was halfway around the world from Britain. Why did they choose such a distant spot? Some say they wanted to make sure the convicts could never return home. Others believe that economic and political considerations were involved in the decision. A port at Botany Bay where British ships could refuel and pick up fresh food and water would facilitate trade in the region. It would help Englishmen bringing back cargoes such as sea otter pelts from the coast of Northwest America, and it would benefit British whaling ships as well.[19]

Clipper ships had begun to appear in South Pacific waters from a new competitor, the Yankees of New England. But their threat paled in comparison with that from Britain's archrival, the French. Britain and France had long fought each other in Europe and would continue doing so through the Napoleonic Wars that ended in 1815. In North America, the French had teamed up with Indian tribes to try to keep the British from gaining more land in the new world. To Britain, the possibility that its hated opponent might gain a foothold in the Far East was unthinkable. Recently the French had sent a scientific expedition to the South Pacific and the British knew what that could mean: it was probably a cover to hunt for lands they could take over. Having a British outpost in that part of the world could help keep the French at bay.

Whatever the reasons for choosing Botany Bay, its distance from Europe had a strong impact on the colony and future nation. In those days before the Suez Canal was built, the voyage from Britain to Australia took more than three times as long as trips to the United States or Canada. The prisoners who arrived in Botany Bay felt they had come to the ends of the earth.

In 1787 a group of eleven convict ships, now called the First Fleet, left England for Botany Bay. They went by way of Rio de Janeiro and the Cape of Good Hope. The voyage took nine months. Passengers included Captain Arthur Phillip, newly appointed governor of the prison settlement, with his staff of nine, 568 male and 191 female convicts, some 200 marines to keep order, and a sprinkling of accompanying wives and children.[20]

The new land gave them a shock. Cook's party had visited Botany Bay during the autumn in what must have been a rainy year; eighteen years later Phillip's fleet arrived in January — mid-summer in that part of the world — during a typical dry spell. Not only was the land parched and the climate hot, but also the supply of fresh water at Botany Bay could not begin to meets the needs of so many people. Phillip and a few officers set out to look for a better site. They were in luck. About ten miles away they discovered a capacious, landlocked harbor with a good supply of fresh water in an inlet near the shore. The delighted Phillip named the harbor Port Jackson and the inlet Sydney Cove, the latter in honor of the home secretary.

Just as their ships were ready to move, they noticed two ships in the distance approaching Botany Bay. Could it be reinforcements from England? Or the Dutch coming to claim New Holland? As the ships came near they realized it was the French scientific expedition led by explorer Jean-François de La Pérouse. The British, although polite, extended few courtesies. Captain Phillip gave orders that the French must not be told of the existence of Port Jackson or of British plans to move there. The next morning "at first light" Phillip's ship slipped out of Botany Bay and headed for Port Jackson.[21] The following day, January 26, 1788, he held a ceremony on the shore near Sydney Cove and formally claimed the port for Britain.

Phillip had succeeded in obtaining "the finest harbour in the world" for the British crown.[22] But he would have few other triumphs in the years ahead.

Two

Convicts and Colonists

Avoiding starvation was the first challenge. Weevils had rotted much of the seed grain on the long trip out, but even healthy seedlings withered and died in the sandy, parched soil around Sydney Cove. The supply of tools was inadequate and the convict workforce scarcely knew which end of a hoe went into the ground.[1]

Captain Phillip kept looking for the arrival of more ships filled with provisions but none came for more than two years. As crops failed and the food they had brought with them dwindled, Phillip tried to stretch the existing supplies: he put convicts and marines on the same rations, kept cutting their daily portions, and added his private supply of flour to the general store. He sent a ship to the African port of Cape Town to buy supplies from the Dutch; the ship ran into storms and barely came through, but returned seven months later with enough wheat and barley to sustain the colonists for four months.[2]

Meanwhile the colony was taking shape. The flat shore adjoining Sydney Cove was reserved for growing crops while the penal settlement was built on sandstone hills nearby. Prisoners assigned the job of removing enough boulders to erect basic shelters dubbed the area "The Rocks," a name that stuck.

Phillip decreed that there would be no slave labor in the new land.[3] Instead, convicts were put to work building sheds for the precious food supply and a few one-room huts for the officers and staff. Whatever makeshift shelter the prisoners had, they devised in their spare time: no prison barracks would be constructed to house them for thirty years. Building tools and skilled carpenters were in short supply. Even more distressing to the governor, most convicts would only work if forced to.

Bred in poverty-stricken villages or squalid city slums, the prisoners had been cooped up in overcrowded jails and hulks for years, and then endured an agonizing sea journey below deck in chains. The prisoners emerged to find themselves in a desolate spot on the other side of the world with no hope of ever seeing their families or homeland again. It is little wonder that they proved uncooperative.

To make the prisoners work and behave themselves, a gallows, stocks and flogging post were speedily erected. The first man hanged, 17-year-old Thomas Barrett, had stolen some dried peas, salt pork, and a bit of butter.[4] Some prisoners fled into the bush, but either they returned starving and perishing with thirst, to be flogged and put back to work, or their speared bodies were found months later. The indigenous people, pushed out of their best sites for fresh water and fishing, took their revenge where they could. They made a determined effort to drive out the intruders but spears and boomerangs were no match for guns.

Female convicts also faced constraints. For the first two weeks the women were confined to the ships while the men began building the settlement. Then tents were put up for the women and they were allowed to disembark. But heavy winds and rain that evening blew down the tents. Male convicts, along with sailors who asked their captain for extra rum "to make merry with upon the women quitting the ship," and got it, spent the night pursuing the women and raping them on the rocks in the mud.[5] In later years the women were blamed for that riotous evening and were said to have incited the men by their lewd behavior.

After several months, fertile land was found some miles upstream along the banks of the Parramatta River. Removing the thick bush without adequate tools proved a challenge but by using prisoners in chain gangs as draft animals, the colonists succeeded in clearing the land and planting crops. By the second year the colony had a small supply of vegetables. Later another fertile area was discovered along the Hawkesbury River, thirty miles to the north. The first farmers settled in these areas.

Ships of the Second Fleet finally arrived in June of 1790. They brought the first letters from Britain, news of the French Revolution and a middling supply of food. But their human cargo was a disaster. More than a thousand convicts had been sent out but a quarter had died on board, and two-thirds of the rest were sick. "To provide room for profitable cargo, they had been overcrowded; to save money, they had been underfed."[6] The prisoners had been locked into shackles with short, rigid bolts between the ankles; anyone who tried to move in them risked breaking both legs.[7] One convict who lived through the eleven-month voyage described his ordeal in a letter to his parents, which was later published as a broadsheet in England.

He and the other prisoners were "chained two and two together and confined in the hold during the whole course of our long voyage ... we were scarcely allowed a sufficient quantity of victuals to keep us alive, and scarcely any water; for my own part I could have eaten three or four of our allowances, and you know very well that I was never a great eater.... When any of our comrades that were chained to us died, we kept it a secret as long as we could for the smell of the dead body, in order to get their allowance of provision.... I was chained to Humphrey Davies who died when we were about half way, and I lay beside his corpse about a week and got his allowance."[8]

There was another reason why so many died: jailers had used the voyage as an opportunity to get rid of their sick prisoners. The furious governor wrote to the authorities protesting that the colony could not become self-sufficient if they kept sending him prisoners too sick to work. But the Third Fleet was already on its way. Only one in ten had died en route this time, but those who landed were "so emaciated, so worn away," Phillip protested, that they were unfit to work.[9]

Shipping companies could shortchange these passengers without consequences in those days, because in the eyes of society their human cargo belonged to the "criminal classes," the lowest of the low. Few voices spoke up for them. It was widely believed that the poorest people inherited the tendency to steal. They formed a despicable underclass, depraved by nature, who lived by preying on their betters instead of working for their bread.

This "inborn" moral deficiency was thought to explain why children of criminals in the slums became lawbreakers themselves and why alcoholics begat babies who grew up to be drunkards. It was useless to try to change such people, the upper classes believed; all one could do was to get rid of the worst of them if possible, by sentencing convicted offenders to hanging or transportation. When crime rates soared, Parliament responded by passing laws with stiffer penalties.[10] The cause of increased lawlessness, conventional wisdom decreed, was a further breakdown of morality among the criminal classes.

With historical hindsight we can identify other reasons for the increased crime rate. Britain's fledgling Industrial Revolution was changing employment patterns, shifting jobs from small workshops in villages to large factories that were usually located in cities. Subsistence farmers faced stiff competition from large farms using new machinery. In addition, farmers who had grazed their few animals on a village common now found themselves fenced out by new Enclosure Laws.

People whose ancestors had lived in the same village for centuries flocked to the cities in search of factory jobs or other ways of making a living. The cities could not begin to provide jobs for all, nor were there enough dwellings to house the newcomers. Those who became destitute found themselves in a bind: under the Poor Laws of 1601 all charity was tied to church parishes where they had been born, so they were not entitled to any relief in the cities.

The poor learned to survive in cities by whatever means came to hand. A subterranean economy of crime and black-market trading grew in slum areas of British cities, with the largest network in London. For some, theft became a full-time occupation. Others found jobs but with wages so low that they stole to supplement their incomes.

The government coped by gradually increasing the number of offenses meriting the death penalty from around fifty to more than 200.[11] Most were offenses against property. The population of England doubled between 1805 and 1842 but criminal prosecutions increased by 600 percent in that period, peaking in recession years. Despite tougher laws, crime increased.

Hanging was a common penalty even for stealing a loaf of bread, but the sheer numbers of convicted criminals made this remedy impracticable. More than half sentenced to hang probably were transported to Australia instead, a punishment considered merciful. Seven or fourteen years were typical sentences, whether the crime was petty theft or aggravated assault.

A sprinkling of "gentlemen" convicts from the middle classes were also transported, usually for white-collar crimes such as forgery. They provided some of the earliest professionals for the colony. Francis Greenway, an architect sent out for forgery, designed many of Sydney's first public buildings, for example.[12] A few upper-class men were transported for political offenses, especially from Ireland during periodic uprisings against the English.

But Irish convicts, who were at least 20 percent of those transported, came predominantly from the peasantry and were the poorest of the poor. Prejudice against them was strong, in part because most were Catholics while all the judges, in Ireland as well as in England, were Protestants. A British visitor to Australia during the 1840s summed up his observations about who got transported: "A man is banished from Scotland for a great crime, from England for a small one, and from Ireland, morally speaking, for no crime at all."[13] The Scots sent out the fewest convicts in proportion to their numbers because their legal system was more lenient; it allowed the plea of mitigating circumstances and handed out moderate punishment for theft until the third offense.

Women, who accounted for 15 percent of all convicts, were reputed to be mainly prostitutes. In fact around 80 percent had been domestic servants at home.[14] They were transported for crimes such as stealing a pewter plate from their employer or a piece of cloth from a shop. In Australia most were assigned as servants in private homes, although a women's factory run with Dickensian severity was set up in Parramatta for those who committed further crimes or behaved in a manner deemed lewd.

With theft the most common crime for which both sexes were transported, one might have expected Sydney to become a huge black market for stolen goods, its street overrun with pickpockets, its homeowners in constant danger of being burglarized. Instead, crime rates were consistently lower there than in England. A different situation produced quite a different outcome. As Robert Hughes put it in *The Fatal Shore*: "Here was a community of people handpicked over decades for their 'criminal propensities' and for no other reason, whose offspring turned out to form one of the most law-abiding societies in the world."[15]

The availability of jobs was a prime factor in keeping the crime rate low. Penal Australia had a severe ongoing labor shortage. Prisoners were the main labor force but there were not enough of them. Arriving immigrants who started businesses, farms and sheep stations (ranches) also needed workers. But poor laborers in Britain lacked money for the long sea voyage to Australia; if they emigrated, it was more often to Canada or United States.

To meet the demand for labor, prisoners in Sydney were permitted to take second jobs in the private sector after finishing their daily stint for the government. In addition, those who stayed out of trouble might be given a "Ticket of Leave," enabling them to work full-time for wages while serving out their sentences.[16] Convicts were also sent to the country (called the bush or outback) as assigned laborers or servants to farmers and sheep raisers.

The early "emancipists," as prisoners who finished sentences were called, might be granted 40 acres of land, more if they were married.[17] Few emancipists succeeded as farmers: poor soil, bad weather, lack of equipment or access to credit, and little farming experience were among the factors that brought them down. But they could usually find work back in Sydney at higher wages than the going rate in Britain.

Not every convict had the opportunity to take a second job, however, nor could they all look forward to being emancipated. A system of closed prisons gradually was established in remote areas to house convicts who committed further crimes and misdemeanors. One of the largest and most infamous was at Port Arthur in Tasmania (then called Van Diemen's Island).

Governor King had rushed a schooner to the island in 1802 after he heard rumors that a French expedition planned to found a settlement there. King's men hoisted the Union Jack and stayed until the French departed.[18] The next year Britain founded Hobart City on the southeast coast of Tasmania; it was Australia's second city. Port Arthur, the largest closed prison in the system, was built in the vicinity. At times convict ships brought prisoners there directly so it was not used only for troublemakers.[19]

Closed prisons were established in several locations such as Newcastle, Port Macquarie, Moreton Bay (Brisbane), and Norfolk Island. Only a small percentage of convicts were sent to these prisons, but they became infamous: "Legend has perhaps exaggerated the quantity, but not the severity, of the inhumanly cruel and often illegal tortures inflicted on prisoners at these places."[20]

Once the penal system ended, citizens tried to block out the memory of such hellholes and forget that Australia had been founded as a dumping ground for convicts. This proved impossible, in part because a sensational novel about the enormities of the system, *His Natural Life* (1870), became a best seller and has remained in print to this day (usually as the later, shorter version entitled *For the Term of His Natural Life*).[21] Its author, British-born journalist Marcus Clarke, used materials he found in the Melbourne Library to fashion the story of Richard Devine, son of an English lord, who is transported for a murder he didn't commit. Convict Devine assumes the name Rufus Dawes to hide his real identity. A passive saint-like figure, he is sent in turn to the colony's worst prisons where he is subjected to diabolical punishments. His nemesis, a sadistic penal official named Maurice Frere, is said to be closely modeled on John Price, the hated commandant of Norfolk Island.

Sydney, where most prisoners were sent, was the center of the colony. For the men sent out as guards, the new city offered opportunities they could only have dreamt about back home.

The Corps

The Second Fleet, crammed with prisoners too sick to work, brought an even bigger headache for Captain Phillip. This was the New South Wales Corps (the Corps), a contingent of soldiers and officers sent out to keep order. Several Corps officers proved less interested in military service than in amassing personal fortunes. The Corps had free rein after Captain Phillip left and their commander, Major Francis Grose, was put in charge until a new governor arrived. Grose preferred hunting to governing and let his most ambitious officers run the colony, a duty they were happy to assume. They became so powerful that the next three governors could not restrain them.[22]

Within a few years a ring of Corps officers cornered the market on goods entering Sydney, especially liquor, and sold them at profits of 300 percent or higher. When an American cargo vessel from Rhode Island arrived in 1793 with foodstuffs and 7600 gallons of raw spirits and its captain refused to sell the food without the liquor, for instance, a group of Corps officers bought the lot. Where did officers on regimental salaries get so much money?

The colony had no currency system then so the Corps was paid by Treasury bills from regiment funds sent to their paymaster in Sydney. The paymaster, a young officer named John Macarthur, "paid" for the goods by charging them to some account of the Corps (later honored by an official in London with no knowledge of the particulars) or against their future salaries. The officers made so much money from the Rhode Island cargo and other deals that they soon bought all shipments that arrived, assisted by the creative financing of Macarthur, who was a member of their distribution ring.

John Macarthur, son of a linen draper in Devon, came from the same middle-class background as most Corps officers. But he soon stood out as "the most able business man, the most imaginative, and the one who could best turn the wheels of colonial power to his economic benefit."[23]

Most officers, including Macarthur, had been granted land by Grose, so they raised sheep as well as running their "Rum Ring." By 1769 Corps officers owned "72.5 per cent of the livestock in the lands of private settlers, including all the horses, oxen and cattle, together with 97.7 percent of the sheep."[24]

Convicts taking second jobs were often paid in rum rather than with money (all hard liquor was called rum) because cash was in short supply. The convicts are not known to have protested, but visiting clergymen were shocked by the amount of drunkenness in the colony, and by the huge profits officers made from demon rum.

By the time Captain John Hunter arrived as governor in 1795, the Corps had "entrenched itself as the ruling elite of New South Wales."[25] Farmers in Parramatta and the Hawkesbury complained of exorbitant prices and favoritism shown to Corps officers. But when Hunter tried to quell them, he clashed with a formidable opponent. Macarthur wrote letters to the Duke of Portland, the secretary for the colonies, complaining about Hunter's administration and blaming him for the "licentiousness and drunkenness which prevailed throughout the colony."[26] Portland, who was also receiving petitions from colonists seeking relief from the "growing extortion of monopolists and dealers" must have concluded that the job was too much for Hunter. He was recalled.

The next governor, Lieutenant Philip Gidley King, also clashed with Macarthur and the Rum Ring but was unable to break the Corps' grip on power. After fighting them for six years he returned to England in a state of physical collapse and soon died. By this time the British were determined to find a governor strong enough to clean up the rum scandal. They thought they had their man when they appointed Captain William Bligh. But he found his match in John Macarthur.

Ambitious, intelligent, truculent, and vindictive, Macarthur went after his opponents relentlessly and was rarely without one. Earlier, after Macarthur had feuded with a top Corps officer and seriously wounded him in a duel, Governor King had dispatched him to England for trial, perhaps as a way of getting rid of this troublesome man. But the resourceful Macarthur used his time in London to promote Australian wool — and himself. Invited to give testimony before a Privy Council committee, he assured its members that "from the unlimited extent of luxuriant pastures with which that country abounds, millions of those valuable animals may be raised in a few years, with but a little expence than the hire of a few shepherds."[27]

Macarthur returned to Sydney triumphantly in 1805 with the charges dismissed, a land grant of 5,000 acres, and some merino sheep from a private flock belonging to King George III. He resigned his commission and turned his energies to his sheep station at Camden and other entrepreneurial ventures.[28] Macarthur was in the midst of several when Captain William Bligh arrived.

Outside of Australia, Bligh is remembered for an incident that occurred some fifteen years earlier in Tahiti. While he commanded the ship *Bounty*, his men mutinied. Bligh and those loyal to him were put into a small boat. His navigational skills enabled him to guide the open boat 3600 miles through difficult seas and bring all but one person to safety on the island of Timor.

William Bligh has been portrayed as a ruthless flogger but flogging was standard practice in those days for a slight infraction of rules. In tongue lashings, sarcasm, and temper tantrums, however, few could match him.[29] His fractious personality apparently doomed him in Sydney despite the genuine efforts he made to dismantle the monopoly of the Corps and champion the rights of ordinary citizens.

Bligh's confrontational style alienated so many potential allies that by the time he clashed with John Macarthur no one came to his aid. When Bligh interfered with several of Macarthur's commercial ventures, including importation of illegal liquor stills into the colony and a plan to "open up a Sydney-Calcutta-Canton trade link in defiance of the East India Company," Macarthur decided that the governor must go.[30] After Bligh arrested Macarthur over a land dispute in Sydney, Macarthur convinced other Corps officers to take the lead in unseating Bligh.

On January 26, 1808, while Macarthur sat in jail, a group of armed

Corps members forced their way into the governor's mansion, arrested Bligh and declared their leader, Major George Johnston, to be lieutenant governor. In the aftermath of the Rum Rebellion, as it became known, Johnston and Macarthur left for London to give their version of the coup. Bligh also left town so Corps officers once again ran the colony.[31]

Meanwhile officials in London tried to figure out what happened. Johnston, although roundly criticized and dismissed from the Corps, was allowed to return to Sydney. But Macarthur, by then seen as a troublemaker, was prevented from going back for several years. Britain also prohibited the importation of liquor into Australia, disbanded the New South Wales Corps, and sent out a new governor.

Bligh's successor was Lieutenant-Colonel Lachlan Macquarie, a Scot who arrived in 1810 with his own regiment of 73rd Highlanders to keep order. Macquarie soon saw the country's future as a permanent colony of free settlers rather than just a penal settlement. He laid the foundation for this transformation. During Macquarie's tenure the colony's first currency system and bank were created; buildings for public services such as law courts and government offices were erected; and the frontiers of the settlement were pushed beyond the Blue Mountain barrier, some forty miles west of Sydney, opening up the vast ranges beyond for farming and sheep raising.[32] Also significant in terms of national identity, Macquarie urged people to call the country "Australia" instead of New Holland. (Matthew Flinders, who in 1803 became

Portrait of Lieutenent-Colonel Lachlan Macquarie, governor of New South Wales from 1810 to 1821. He saw Australia as more than a penal colony and thought "emancipists" (prisoners who finished their sentences) should have the rights of other citizens unless they committed further crimes. This angered the new pastoral elite who wanted to keep the emancipists down. Their campaign against Macqarie led to his being recalled, but history has exonerated him (Mitchell Library, State Library of New South Wales).

the first person to circumnavigate the continent, is credited with coining the name.)

In Macquarie's day large numbers of prisoners had completed their sentences and become emancipists. For a few decades they and their families still outnumbered the immigrants who kept arriving. Macquarie tried to integrate emancipists into the colony: he believed they were free citizens and should be treated as such unless they committed more crimes.

This view brought him into sharp conflict with the "exclusives," as the emerging upper echelon were called. Their base came from former Corps members and other penal officials, and men raising sheep in the outback (also known as "pastoralists") along with affluent immigrants from Britain. The exclusives enjoyed considerable social status in the new colony and they were not about to share it. They followed an unwritten social code that classified emancipists as pariahs. The handful of former prisoners who started businesses that prospered and became rich were rigorously excluded from the exclusives' social set.

Macquarie broke that social code early in his tenure when he invited four successful emancipist entrepreneurs to dine with him in the governor's mansion.[33] He further enraged the exclusives by appointing emancipists as members of civic committees and upholding their right not only to serve on juries but also to have a trial by jury if arrested. But when he began restricting the number of convicts any citizen could receive as free labor—so there would be enough for new settlers and emancipist farmers as well—Macquarie came too close to the pastoralists' pocketbooks. Their prosperity was predicated on unlimited free convict labor. The exclusives, with pastoralists in the lead, set out to destroy Macquarie.

They besieged London with letters complaining about Macquarie: he was squandering money on elaborate, unnecessary buildings, they claimed, to glorify his own administration; he showed such favoritism to the emancipists that he was destroying the livelihood of the colony's productive, morally upstanding citizens (themselves), who were the hope of the future. He was coddling criminals.

Macquarie, accustomed as a military officer to issuing orders and being obeyed, saw the exclusives as a selfish, petty lot who cared for nothing but their own enrichment. He in turn wrote long letters to London describing his accomplishments and criticizing his opponents. After receiving such conflicting reports, confused officials decided to find out what was really happening in faraway Australia. They sent out a commissioner, John Thomas Bigge, to examine Macquarie's administration and evaluate the penal system.

Bigge spent three years in Australia collecting evidence. No doubt he thought himself impartial because he talked to many people; but he listened more closely to those whose opinions reflected his own. One person whose opinions he valued was John Macarthur. After an eight-year exile in England, Macarthur was able to return home in 1817. He arrived in time to convince Bigge that Australia's future lay in wool production.[34]

When the Bigge Report appeared in Britain, some of its recommendations sounded as if they had been dictated by Macarthur. The government should give land grants of not less than 10,000 acres to established men of substance, Bigge said, and stop parceling it out in dribbles to immigrants of limited means. Emancipists should get 10 acres at most.[35] Landholders, with large tracts of land should also be given as much free convict labor as they requested; this would enable the sheep industry to prosper and would also help reform convicts by removing them from city vices.

Bigge reflected the exclusives' view when he advised against giving emancipists the right to trial by jury or the ability to serve in local government. It was important not to make the emancipists' lot too pleasant, he cautioned, or the threat of being transported to Australia would no longer serve as a deterrent to crime in Britain. His report gave credence to the exclusives' complaint that Macquarie was soft on criminals.

One of Bigge's findings, however, was at odds with then-current beliefs. He described what he had seen and heard, setting it down in amazement because it contradicted what people in his class assumed — that the children of convicts in Australia would likely grow up to be criminals as well. To the contrary, Bigge found emancipists' children to be sober and hardworking. "The class of inhabitants that have been born in the colony affords a remarkable exception to the moral and physical character of their parents," he wrote. These children, taller and slender, "are capable of undergoing more fatigue and are less exhausted by labour than native Europeans ... and I only repeat the testimony of persons who have had many opportunities of observing them, that they neither inherit the vices nor feelings of their parents."[36]

Bigge believed this second generation had miraculously developed the moral fortitude to be appalled by their parents' vices. More likely the change reflected a buoyant labor market. Compared with Britain at the time, wrote historian Russel Ward: "Australian conditions offered a very good living to anyone able and willing to work. There was an almost continuous labor shortage — even children could command good wages — and did."[37] With plenty of jobs, space, and sunshine, the children of emancipists flourished.

Women sent out as convicts also became law-abiding in Australia. Professor Portia Robinson of Macquarie University, who has studied the records of every woman transported, found that although most had committed some crime at home (typically petty theft), and a few continued the practice abroad, most women's names never again appeared in court records.[38] They became wives and mothers in the city or outback, quietly raising the law-abiding children that amazed Commissioner Bigge. Records also show that many emancipist women worked at paid jobs or ran their own businesses.

But for almost two hundred years female convicts were regarded mainly as prostitutes, a picture that fit the stereotype of "bad" lower-class women. This image was reinforced by the work of Reverend Samuel Marsden, a Sydney clergyman, magistrate and entrepreneur. In 1806 Marsden compiled a Female Register that listed all woman in the colony, classifying them as either "married" or "concubine."[39] He found that 395 women were married while 1035 cohabited out of wedlock. When a copy of the Female Register reached England, people were shocked by such immorality.

Robinson found errors in Marsden's work: some widows and married women were listed as concubines by mistake.[40] More significant, large numbers of women labeled concubines were living in stable relationships with men and raising families. Their circumstances often precluded marriage. Convicts had been forced to leave their wives and husbands behind and few were allowed to join them later despite pleas and petitions. But if emancipists remarried while they had a living spouse in Britain, they could be prosecuted for bigamy. Catholic couples could not be united by a priest in the early years because the only clergy were Protestants. Such couples often lived as common-law husband and wife.

Marsden gave testimony to Commissioner Bigge on a related matter: the immoral behavior of women in the Parramatta Factory. He blamed everything he disapproved of on Governor Macquarie. The frustrated governor, finding himself criticized on all sides after he had done so much for the colony, wrote an angry letter of resignation while Bigge was still collecting testimony. Once authorities in London began reading Bigge's reports, they accepted Macquarie's resignation with alacrity. He returned to Britain and spent his remaining few years trying to clear his name.[41] History has exonerated Lachlan Macquarie, but he received little recognition in his own time.

In the decades that followed, Sydney's residents began agitating to end transportation. They did not want a prison colony in their midst or a continuous influx of the "criminal classes." Only pastoralists favored the system, which ensured them a steady supply of free convict labor; but by the 1830s pastoralists were outnumbered by city folk. In England many people were also having second thoughts about the efficacy of the penal system. Conservatives (Tories) believed the Australian prison colony made life too sweet for convicts, while Liberals (Whigs) were convinced that the system was monstrous. In 1837 the Liberal faction set up a committee to investigate, headed by Sir William Molesworth. Testimony to the committee provided documentation of the system's inefficiency and injustices.[42] (Marcus Clarke drew heavily on material in the Molesworth Report for the novel *His Natural Life*.)

After 1840 convict ships no longer came to Sydney and the prison colony there was dismantled a few years later. Closed prisons were gradually phased out. Tasmania stopped receiving convicts from abroad in 1850, although Port Arthur remained open in skeletal form for another three decades.

Western Australia was the coda of the transportation system. Its coast was settled after another French scare: in 1826 when Lord Bathurst in London heard that a French expedition was headed to the west coast, he wrote three letters in one day to the governor instructing him to rush out some men and claim the region for England.[43] They established the port town of Albany, which became a sleepy backwater. Three years later Sir James Sterling founded the western settlement of Perth along the banks of the Swan River, named for the black swans there. Perth and its nearby seaport Fremantle were both hard-pressed to survive, because settlers could not entice workers to the dry, isolated area. So in 1850, just as transportation was ending on the east coast, Western Australia requested convict labor. Prisoners were sent there for about fifteen years and constructed some public buildings. By the late 1860s transportation to Australia was over.[44]

Today only a few physical remnants of the old prison system remain. Port Arthur in Tasmania is one of them. Fragments of its main buildings, ravaged by periodic bushfires, have been preserved and some smaller cottages restored. Visiting the Port Arthur Historical Site today, it is hard to reconcile the beauty of the place with its dark history. Skeletal, yellow-gold sandstone walls stand out like sculptures on emerald-green lawns, surrounded by a tranquil bay and rolling hills.[45] But old photographs on display show a cluster of grim buildings that faced one another for security. Except when convicts were chained in work gangs or marched to chapel on Sunday, they saw little of the natural beauty around them.

In Sydney the downtown prison barracks that Governor Macquarie commissioned in 1817 is now a museum. Designed by emancipist Francis Greenway, the handsome rectangular building of red sandstone bricks is a far cry from the gloomy structure that felons usually live in.[46] A few miles away at The Rocks, where the main prison colony was located, no original buildings remain.[47]

After the penal settlement closed in 1843, The Rocks became home to newly arrived immigrants from many nations. The first Catholic Church in Australia was built there, as was the first Chinatown. The narrow winding streets and stone boulders made it difficult to build housing and sanitation facilities, so the quarter deteriorated into Sydney's worst slum. The flat area below became the commercial hub of the shipping industry, while streets near Sydney Cove formed a honky-tonk district of flophouses, taverns, and brothels serving sailors in port.

When an epidemic of bubonic plague erupted in The Rocks in 1900, the city razed many of its buildings, including all remnants of the old penal settlement, to eradicate the disease-carrying rats. More buildings came down later to make way for the Harbour Bridge, and at one time there were plans to build high rises on the old site. But a strong movement of Sydney preservationists, determined to save The Rocks, fought the developers and won. The part of The Rocks adjoining Sydney Cove was restored as an historic area, retaining its cobblestone lanes and courtyards.[48] Like Port Arthur, it is now a popular tourist attraction that likely provides jobs for some people whose forebears arrived in chains.

Charles Darwin visited Sydney in 1836 when the *Beagle* stopped there on the way home from its three-year voyage. In his journal Darwin remarked that as a place of punishment and moral reform the colony had failed, but as a means "of converting vagabonds, most useless in one hemisphere, into active citizens of another, and thus giving birth to a new and splendid country ... it has succeeded to a degree perhaps unparalleled in history."[49] In time these active citizens, with help from the far greater numbers of immigrants who followed, would take the nation in a new direction.

Three

Class Conflicts with Unexpected Outcomes

"Caste in Hindoostan is not more rigidly regarded than it is in Australia," said a visitor to Sydney in 1843.[1] Long after transportation ended, the class divide continued. Exclusives at the top strove to keep a tight grip on their new power and wealth by keeping their former charges at the bottom.

The arrival of new immigrants did not upset this dichotomy because they joined forces with their own kind. Affluent immigrants who started businesses in cities or pastoral ventures in the outback became part of the exclusive faction while the much larger numbers of impoverished immigrants joined emancipists in the working classes.

At first it looked as though the exclusives would triumph: Australia would not fulfill the age-old dream of poor people that a new land would offer them a better life. But this conclusion proved premature. While the exclusives were busy consolidating their positions, those at the bottom were building power bases of their own. They organized trade unions and then formed a political party geared to their own needs. By the end of the nineteenth century, labor had emerged as a political force in Australia.

More than social class was involved in the fights that ensued. As in national conflicts elsewhere, religious and ethnic differences also came to the fore. The hatred and prejudices that had festered for centuries in the old countries arrived intact. Convicts and then immigrants docked at Sydney, settled in, and continued their battles in the antipodes.

British Protestants versus Irish Catholics was the religious conflict of the nineteenth century. One denomination, the Anglicans, initially stood above the fray. At home this was the official state religion — the Church of England — so its bishops in Sydney assumed it would likewise become the Church of Australia. Government officials agreed; in 1825 they handed the bishops control over primary school education.

Cries of outrage went up. Scottish Presbyterians, Methodists, and other dissenters including Baptists and Congregationalists attacked the Anglican monopoly, as did Catholics, whose priests were now allowed to practice. In order to defeat the Anglicans, Protestant sects formed an uneasy alliance with the Catholics. And defeat them they did, as frustrated officials suspended and finally revoked the Anglican franchise.[2]

The fight for children's souls continued. In 1836 a new governor, Richard Bourke, tried to solve the problem by setting up secular schools for all but allowing ministers and priests to come in and instruct children in their various faiths. A storm of protest broke over the governor's head.[3] This time Anglican and Presbyterian clergy were united in their outrage at the idea of priests in the schools. Next, funds were given to religious groups that wanted their own schools, but pressure from Protestant sects led the government to revoke all state funding for religious education in 1880.

Catholics set up their own parochial schools. So different was the view of Britain presented in history classes within the two systems that their teachers might have been talking about separate planets: "In the government schools children were taught the glories and virtues of the British Empire," says historian Geoffrey Sherington, "while Catholic children learnt that British tyranny was oppressing Irish freedom. Such contrasting views of the world would influence those who came of age not only in the late nineteenth century but also well into the twentieth."[4]

Irish convicts were followed by a stream of Irish immigrants whose numbers swelled in the years following the potato blight of the 1840s, when starvation was rampant in Ireland. Regardless of what brought them to Australia, they remembered the past.

Britain sent troops to Ireland in 1171 and occupied the country. As English settlers arrived and took over, Irish chieftains rebelled periodically but were unable to drive out the conquerors. Around the time of Queen Elizabeth I, the English began confiscating the estates of Irish rebels, giving them to British immigrants. Gradually the Anglo–Irish formed an aristocracy; they kept their distance from the peasant masses, who became increasingly poor.

Religion further divided them. The English became predominantly Protestant after Henry VIII broke with Rome in 1534, while the Irish remained overwhelmingly Catholic. When Catholics were denied the right to serve in the Irish government or attend universities, this excluded most of the populace.[5] When Britain started transporting prisoners to Australia, Irish Catholics viewed the process as yet another abomination by their oppressors.

The enmity was mutual as a letter from Governor Hunter in Sydney makes clear. His Irish charges, he wrote in 1798, were "so turbulent, so dissatisfied with their situation here, so extremely insolent, refractory, and troublesome that without the most rigid and severe treatment it is impossible for us to receive any labour whatsoever from them. Your Grace will see the inconvenience which so large a proportion of that ignorant, obstinate, and depraved set of transports occasions in this country."[6]

Soon Hunter's letters complained about another kind of Irish convict, "bred up in genteel life or a profession unaccustomed to hard labor."[7] These men were political prisoners. As restrictive laws in Ireland against Catholics mounted, some people in the upper and emerging middle classes formed a movement to drive out the English. After a rebellion in 1798 failed, at least 500 insurgents were transported to Australia, where in prison "their political commitment found common cause and sympathy with their fellow countrymen."[8]

Irish Protestants also emigrated to Australia, coming mainly from the northern counties. In many cases they were middle class—as were some Irish Catholic emigrants. But the vast majority who came from Ireland were Catholic and poor.

By the twentieth century Irish Australians made up nearly a quarter of the nation's population; after the English they were the country's largest ethnic group. They shared an ancient heritage with emigrants from smaller countries and regions of Britain — Scotland, Wales, and Cornwall: all had Celtic roots and many spoke Gaelic languages. Thus a portion of the early immigrants and convicts could not speak the English language and found English culture alien to their way of life.

These differences caused friction, but the greatest divider was land ownership. Commissioner Bigge, as we saw in Chapter Two, had recommended giving large parcels of land to people with capital. When the government followed his advice, men who qualified rushed out to take advantage of the big land giveaway. Where else on earth could one get such a deal — not only huge tracts of land gratis but also free convict labor to do the work? For those with money but middling social status at home, Australia also offered an opportunity to join the upper class.

The parceling of land into enormous sheep stations brought "a change in the social status of those who owned land and an obvious bias against the small man without capital, whether he was a former convict, a native born, or a free immigrant," wrote historian F. G. Clarke.[9] There was "an apparently deliberate attempt to create artificially a colonial equivalent of the British landed gentry."[10] The land giveaways ended in 1831, but, as the next chapter describes, a new policy that allowed ranchers to lease vast amounts of land for a pittance perpetuated these social divisions.

Families that had a station in the outback, or several such holdings, often kept mansions in Sydney as well. City dwellers with connections to the wool trade also became rich and prominent, be they bankers supplying capital, ship owners, or merchants whose warehouses near the docks stored bales of wool until they were shipped to England. These men, along with others who opened mines, built businesses, or held top positions as judges, government officials and military officers, formed the core of the country's elite.

While the men were busy making their fortunes, their wives worked equally hard to establish homes where Queen Victoria would feel at ease should she visit Australia and take tea with them. She didn't. Along with well-polished floors and frequently starched curtains, they took equal pains to admit into their drawing rooms only those whose social standing was indisputable — and to relentlessly exclude all others.

In 1838, reports Jan Morris, "a citizen was ejected from the Queen's Birthday Ball at Government House on the grounds that during his military service he had been only a sergeant-major; he argued in vain that his wife's father was a lieutenant." In that period, "many shoots of snobbism took root, from a general toadying to visiting nobility to a preoccupation with suitable dress. The apparatus of visiting cards and proper introductions was rigorously upheld."[11]

The new land enabled many to get rich quickly, but frequently that was not enough. Half the sweetness would come from being accepted by the upper-class British who had excluded them at home. But a curse hovered over their heads to block their entry — the dreaded "convict stain" of Australia's penal origins. At a time when people still believed that the "criminal classes" were inherently inferior, the upwardly mobile found themselves in a quandary. The base of the population initially came from the despised underclass; this fact, they learned to their dismay, caused the British to look down on all Australians.

To offset this disadvantage the exclusives felt driven to preserve class distinctions more rigorously than in England. They rejected everyone even remotely tinged with the convict stain. By their genteel way of life the exclusives hoped to show that they had no connection with the rabble; they were respectable upper-class Britons who just happened to be living on the other side of the world.

This drive for social status was seen among the newly rich in colonies throughout the world but in Australia it became more pronounced. Exclusives also felt diminished by the land itself. They revered the green fields and spreading chestnut trees of England while categorically viewing the grasslands and gum trees of Australia as ugly. A few individuals living on the land did come to see beauty in their surroundings, but the trend was to import oaks, elms, and chestnuts, along with plenty of rose bushes, to try and make Australia look like England.

Sydney was the undisputed social capital — until the gold rush of the 1850s turned Melbourne into a rival. Bendigo and Ballarat, the sites with the most gold, were each less than 80 miles from the port of Melbourne. As a result, that city grew so quickly in population and wealth that it soon caught up with Sydney. Adelaide in South Australia and Brisbane in Queensland likewise developed apace though neither city could match the opulence or populations of the two giants.

In their efforts to be accepted by the English upper classes, the exclusives rejected everything Australian. In 1826 a newspaper editor scorned the general populace as "a poor grovelling race, who cannot be inflamed because they no longer think nor feel like Englishmen ... they are no longer Britons but Australians."[12] To be called an Australian was an insult, an indication that you had capitulated to the lower standards of the masses. The more the exclusives tried to replicate Britain in Australia however, the greater the disdain for Australia they engendered back home. Perhaps Britons believed that if the people who lived in Australia considered it such a terrible place, then it must truly have no redeeming features. A joke in George Bernard Shaw's 1907 play *Major Barbara*, reflected this attitude: "He is a very nice fellow, certainly nobody would ever guess he was born in Australia."[13]

The exclusives who copied the lifestyle of upper-class Britons never got the recognition they sought. Their problem was compounded by the numbers of poor immigrants who kept arriving on every ship. These newcomers joined emancipists and their progeny and together formed a strong working class.

From 1788 to 1856 about 156,000 convicts had been transported but far more free workers emigrated during the nineteenth century. A large portion came out through an arrangement called "assisted passage." To meet Australia's pressing need for labor, the government either paid the cost of the long sea voyage or gave workers a low price and usually a loan to cover it, payable after the worker found a job in Australia. These assisted immigrants, combined with emancipists and skilled workers who paid for their own passage, formed strong trade unions during that century.

Two categories of workers were eligible for assisted passage: male rural laborers and female domestic servants. The assisted passage plan began in 1831 and extended far beyond the convict period; in one form or another, the practice of paying British workers to emigrate to Australia did not end completely until 1982.[14]

Although assisted immigrants came from every part of Britain and Ireland, 80 to 85 percent of them were English. Why so many? One reason relates to size: England had almost four times the population of Scotland, Wales, and Ireland combined. A second reason was the plight of rural English workers then; a third was the fact that the Poor Laws of 1601 made local parish churches responsible for helping the destitute there.

Wages for rural laborers fell in nineteenth-century England. In parts of southern England, even farm workers with jobs could not earn enough to feed their families. "The solution seen by many parishes in southern England was to reduce their populations by paying laborers and their families to emigrate," says immigration specialist James Jupp in *The English in Australia*.[15] When the Poor Laws were reformed in 1834, some provisions made it easier to get rid of the poorest people and many parishes used them. For example, "Altogether, 34 East Sussex parishes and 46 Kent parishes used the new Poor Law to unload surplus people between 1836 and 1847. Nearly all were agricultural laborers and their families."[16] The parishes paid for transport to waiting ships while Australia covered the cost of the long sea voyage, using money from land sales. "Public policy deliberately encouraged the immigration of a manual working class for at least a century after settlement," says Jupp.[17]

Gradually the role of the parishes in assisted emigration tapered off, as some in England "denounced pressures to emigrate as inhuman."[18] But assisted passage continued. The Colonial Land and Emigration Commission had a network of agents, mostly "in agricultural districts and some in large villages."[19] In addition, some other individuals started organizations to assist immigrants. Caroline Chisholm, an English-born reformer, set up the Female Immigrants' Home in Sydney in 1841 where newly arrived single women could stay until they were settled.[20] She provided loans to families seeking to emigrate to Australia and sometimes accompanied young women to small outback communities where they usually married bachelors seeking wives.

The colony of Queensland initiated its own program to help fill up its vast spaces, often chartering its own ships because immigrants who docked at Sydney rarely went that far north. "Among the first free passages granted were to 1781 unemployed cotton textile workers from Lancashire with their families during the crisis caused by the American Civil War in 1863."[21] When ships carrying cotton from U.S. southern plantations were unable to reach English ports during that war (1861–1865), cloth manufacturing in Lancashire came to a halt. Workers soon faced starvation. The contract for the ship bringing out Lancashire workers stipulated that half of them must be taken to North Queensland to help develop remote towns there.

Along with a dearth of workers, Australia also had a shortage of women to marry these laborers and produce the next generation of workers. After

1852 immigration commissioners made special efforts to recruit single young women; some came out in "bride ships." Not enough English or Scots women would come, however, so commissioners turned to young Irish women; facing worse poverty than in the other two countries, these women were more ready to emigrate. Ships of female Irish immigrants were sent out in the 1850s and 1860s until a colonial governor became concerned about the number of Irish women coming in; he stipulated that "all unmarried females should then be recruited from elsewhere in Britain."[22]

Assisted immigrants, like convicts, had scant reason to look back on their old country with nostalgia. One provision of the 1834 Poor Law reforms especially rankled: it specified "lesser eligibility," that is, conditions in workhouses, "should be worse than for the lowest paid labourer outside,"[23] reflecting the view of wealthy lawmakers that poor people were inherently shiftless and lazy. Conditions in workhouses were deliberately harsh, with husbands and wives separated in the dormitories. As one young woman told Chisholm: "Oh, what a difference there is between this country and home for poor folks. I know I would not go back again. I know what

Six hundred Irish women arrive on a "bride ship" in 1866. Colonial Australia had a shortage of women, so whole ships of young women were sometimes sent out to provide wives for male immigrants. From the French travel book, *Voyage Autour du Monde*, 1878 (by permission of the National Library of Australia).

England is. Old England is a fine place for the rich, but Lord help the poor."[24] Immigrants who were literate wrote letters urging relatives back home to join them in Australia where wages were higher and food cost less.

Workers were likely to embrace their new identity as Australians with enthusiasm, seeing the country as a passport to the good life that had been out of their reach at home. And a number of them — often skilled workers who paid for their own passage — came out with something else. They had experience in the emerging trade union movement in England or in a reform group such as the Chartists.

By the second half of the nineteenth century, labor unions were flourishing in Australia: "building, engineering, printing and mining were all unionised in England and soon became so in Australia."[25] In small crafts unions in cities, members of the same skilled occupation banded together not only to bargain over wages and hours but also to maintain the standards of their trade. Melbourne formed a Trades Hall Council in 1860, mainly composed of skilled artisans. By 1871 Sydney had a Trades and Labour Council. The word "labour" indicates that unskilled workers as well as skilled craftsmen were organizing in cities by then.[26] Women also organized. In 1872 women in the clothing trade (called tailoresses) went on strike in Melbourne, won higher wages, and soon formed a tailoresses' union: "this was the first strike and the first union of women workers in Australia, and perhaps in the world," says historian Ian Turner.[27]

Many jobs were outside the cities and it was here that the larger industry-wide trade unions took shape. Men who worked on ships formed a Federated Seamen's Union in 1874. Coal miners in the Hunter Valley had organized as early as 1850; by 1884 miners established "the first truly national union," the Amalgamated Miners' Association, which sought to unite all gold, silver, copper and coal miners in one body. Its membership reached 25,000 by 1890.[28]

W. G. Spence, the miner who was instrumental in forming that union, soon found that no mine owner would hire him because he was tagged as a troublemaker. Spence, a Scottish immigrant, turned his energies elsewhere and began organizing sheep shearers, the predominantly itinerant workers who found seasonal employment on large sheep stations. In a booklet he later wrote, Spence included a copy of an agreement that workers had to sign before they were hired.[29]

Except for setting 20-minute "smokos" (breaks) for workers, the contract was wholly in the employer's favor. A basic rate per sheep was specified, but if the employer found one sheep in a pen not shorn to his satisfaction, he would pay the shearer a "second price" (lower rate) for every sheep in the pen. According to Spence, "Men have often been discharged during the last week of shearing and paid off at the lower rate, though the whole of their previous work had been fully approved."[30] The agreement further specified that if the employee brought liquor on the premises or got drunk, "all moneys due him for shearing may be forfeited."[31] Likewise, in the event of a strike on the sheep station "the employee shall have no claim whatever on the proprietor in respect of any sheep already shorn by him."[32] By signing the contract the employee agreed to remain until all sheep were shorn — he could not quit if dissatisfied — and he was also bound by the terms of the agreement. But, said another clause, "The manager to have the right at any time to make any changes he may see fit."[33]

With such one-sided conditions, Spence and other organizers had little trouble recruiting sheep shearers. After they set up the Amalgamated Shearers Union in 1886 it grew to more than 9000 members within a few months. "Unionism came to the Australian bushman as a religion," said Spence.[34]

Workers wanted higher wages and more control over their lives, but they also sought dignity. In Britain those at the bottom were treated with contempt. The Duke of Wellington, hero of the Battle of Waterloo, later characterized the men in his army as "composed of the scum of the earth — the mere scum of the earth."[35] Nurse Florence Nightingale encountered this attitude during the Crimean War. Soldiers were denigrated as drunks but she found they had no place to relax except drink shops. When she proposed opening a recreation room, officers scoffed: the men would not use it, they would steal the note paper to buy drink. Nightingale persisted and soldiers flocked to use the room she set up. No one stole the note paper.[36]

A legal case in Australia underscores this class bias in the military and shows why Australia was so attractive to the poor. Joseph Sudds and Patrick Thompson were young British soldiers stationed in Australia in 1826. In Sydney they found that convicts were treated better than rank-and-file soldiers, and that emancipists earned higher wages than people from their class could make at home. They staged a clumsy robbery so they could be arrested, serve their term — and remain in Australia. When their motive came to light, Governor Ralph Darling, a former British general with a reputation as a martinet, feared that if the men were not punished severely other soldiers might follow suit. He disgraced them at a public ceremony. The two were drummed out of their regiment to the tune of Rogue's March, "wearing massive spiked collars linked to their leg-fetters by 13-pound chains."[37]

A few days later Private Sudds died. The case became a *cause célèbre* when two crusading Sydney editors— W. C. Wentworth of the *Australian* and E.S. Hall of the *Monitor*— used Sudds's death to unleash a campaign against the autocratic governor. They accused him of murder and pressed for an end to the governor's absolute power. Darling had some rough months but managed to retain his post.

Workers wanted to make sure they would never be treated as scum in Australia. The need for their labor gave them an edge they lacked at home. Unions provided a way to capitalize on it. By the 1880s, "trade unionism in Australia was stronger than in any other country at that time," says Ward. When London dock workers went on strike in 1889, Australian unions sent 30,000 pounds to their strike fund, "not without some feeling of condescension to the 'backward' English workers," says Ward. Their gift "had a decisive effect on the strike's success."[38]

But when Australia's economic picture changed in the 1890s, it affected the bargaining position of unions. After a speculative land boom where money flowed in freely from investors in Britain and demand for Australian wool remained steady, the market collapsed in 1888. The downturn was worldwide, caused in part by unsound investments: expecting quick profits, bankers had lent money to speculators without reserves or collateral to cover losses. When the financial bubble burst, its effects caused a severe recession.

During the same years that workers had been organizing into unions, their employers had been forming associations to combat them. When a massive strike erupted, employers were prepared to fight back, aided by the high unemployment rate during the recession.

The Great Maritime Strike of 1890, as it is called, was touched off by an unlikely cause: ships' officers, who had formed their own unions, decided to affiliate with the Trades Hall Council in Melbourne. Employers protested publicly that "it would be impossible to maintain that discipline essential to safety of life and property if maritime officers and men serving under them were allied by union."[39] Privately they saw another aspect to the strike. As the chairman of the Steamship Owners' Association explained: "All the owners throughout Australia have signed a bond to stand by one another.... They are a combined and compact body, and I believe that never before has such an opportunity to test the relative strength of labour and capital arisen."[40]

Employers saw themselves as fighting for the principle of "freedom of contract"—the right of employer and employee to negotiate contracts individually without union interference. Workers had a different view, believing that as individuals they had little chance of negotiating: either they accepted their employer's terms or they were out of a job.

The strike soon spread to many unions, including the sheep shearers, now 16,000 strong, who were fighting their own battles with management.

Dock workers refused to load wool sheared by nonunion labor, the miners struck in sympathy with the maritime workers, and a general strike ensued. As the situation deteriorated, the workers' unions called for a conference between representatives of workers and management, but the employers, smelling victory, refused. In Melbourne, Chief Justice George Higinbotham sent 50 pounds to the strike fund and promised more "while the United Trades are awaiting compliance with their reasonable request for a conference with the employers."[41] But Higinbotham's attitude was the exception. Most citizens in the upper echelons sympathized with employers, as did the government. "By and large, the governments of all the colonies opposed the strikers, and used troops and police against the workers."[42]

British trade unions reciprocated by sending money to the workers' strike fund, but they were able to collect only 4000 pounds, less than a seventh of what they had received from Australian unions the year before. Although strike Defence Committees in Sydney and Melbourne raised upwards of 70,000 pounds, this was not enough to sustain the more than 50,000 workers on strike. With the recession in full force and unemployment high, the unions could not continue the strike. Before the end of 1890 all workers had returned to the job on their employers' terms.[43] Their bosses were confident that they had crushed the unions. For a while it looked as if they were right, because workers continued to lose virtually every strike through 1893 — or as long as the economic downturn lasted.

Meanwhile the defeated unions did a postmortem on the strike. They decided that strikes alone could not bring workers the gains they sought because the two sides were unequal: their opponents had more power and financial resources. But workers had the vote and their numbers were larger. If unions concentrated on electing more workers to the parliaments in their colonies, they could help push through legislation that was favorable to working people.

This was not a new idea. After workers got the vote in the 1850s (the property qualifications that had excluded them were lifted), they tended to pass over candidates with a background of wealth and privilege and chose people more like themselves. Union members also began participating in government and later some were elected as members of parliaments (MPs) in Queensland and South Australia. Their influence played a role in helping to make Australia an innovator in social services.

Anthony Trollope noticed the trend when he visited Australia in 1871: "One cannot walk about Melbourne without being struck by all that has been done for the welfare of the people generally," the English author reported in his book on Australia. "There is no squalor to be seen."[44] He was told that squalor existed in the Irish and Chinese districts: "But he who would see such misery in Melbourne must search for it especially. It will not meet his eye by chance as it does in London, in Paris, and now also in New York."[45] What Trollope saw also applied "not only in reference to Melbourne and Victoria but as regards the colonies generally — that a care for public things predominates."[46]

After the Maritime Strike, one labor leader wrote in his diary that the strike "teaches the workers another lesson and that is they will have to get their Reforms another way through the Ballot Box by sending some of their own Labor men into the Parliament to get the Reforms for them and it will be done at the first election."[47]

Not all union leaders agreed. As in several other countries at this time, two outlooks emerged. Characterizing them by their beliefs, they could be called the pragmatists and the utopians. The pragmatists focused on winning specific gains for workers such as higher wages and better working conditions as well as seeing a role for unions in making government provide help for circumstances that workers' salaries could not cover. The utopians went beyond these goals: the government was so inimical to workers' needs and the power of the rich so entrenched, they believed, that nothing but sweeping changes in the fabric of society could give the workers a fair go in life.

The utopians were influenced by theorists in other countries — the works of Europeans, including Karl Marx, and two books written by Americans: *Poverty and Progress*, by Henry George (who visited Australia in 1890), and *Looking Backwards*, by Edward Bellamy.[48] The utopian aspect of the latter, which envisioned a perfect society in the future, was part of its attraction.

William Lane, a radical journalist from England, helped spread the utopian view. Arriving in Australia in 1885, he started a newspaper, *Boomerang*, was active in the labor movement and later edited *The Worker*, where he serialized Bellamy's *Looking Backwards*. After the defeat of the Maritime Strike, Lane became disillusioned with Australia. He decided to found a communal agricultural colony in Paraguay where he could put his beliefs into practice. In 1893 Lane sailed with a few hundred people to Paraguay, where they set up "New Australia."[49] But like utopian communities in the United States during that period, his colony ultimately failed, brought down by "arduous conditions, inadequate labour and capital, and internal rivalries."[50]

Australia was also influenced by the Chartists, a working-class political movement that was active in England from 1838 to 1848. Its Charter called for reforms to make Parliament more democratic: property qualification for voters to be abolished, every male adult given the vote, a secret ballot, and pay for members of Parliament so workers could afford to serve. Its demands seem moderate today but the English government of the time made vigorous efforts to suppress it, and succeeded. Some Chartist leaders were transported while others emigrated to Australia or New Zealand.[51]

Under Chartist influence, New Zealand, before the turn of the century, gave women the vote and provided old-age pensions for workers. By 1911 New Zealand offered other reforms such as low-interest loans to farmers from the state, and compulsory arbitration for strikes.[52] Australia adopted most of these reforms. American historian Peter J. Coleman, who has studied the antipodean influence on early twentieth-century America, found that "Australasia" (meaning Australia and New Zealand) became a model to early social reformers in the United States such as Henry Demarest Lloyd. America's "struggles to limit working hours drew heavily on Australasian progress for inspiration and strength," says Coleman.[53]

In turn some Australian workers formed a branch of the "Wobblies," the Industrial Workers of the World, a radical union founded in the United States in 1905. Twentieth-century Australia had a number of political parties to the left of the Labor Party, including a small but active Communist Party. But most workers focused on practical matters such as the size of their paychecks. Historian B. K. de Garis wrote that after the Maritime Strike, "the decisive factor [in the direction of labor] was probably the pragmatic attitude of most trade unions which wanted improved wages and conditions rather than the reconstruction of society."[54] Or as Jupp put it: "Australia was known for the strength of its unions and parliamentary Labor parties, but not for its socialist ideology."[55]

In Queensland workers formed one of the first Labor Parties in the world in 1891.[56] Other colonies soon followed suit. In New South Wales that year the new party elected 35 members to the colony's parliament. Once the recession ended, the Labor Party gained a foothold in colonial legislatures; soon the unions recouped their losses and started winning strikes again. In 1894 W. C. Spence organized shearers and several smaller unions of country or "bush" workers—from drovers taking livestock to market to railway workers— into the Australian Workers Union.[57]

In the final decade of the century, labor representatives in colonial parliaments teamed up with reform-minded middle class MPs in cities who likewise wanted to improve the lives of their constituents, and were also determined to curb the power of the pastoralists. Together they passed laws to improve working conditions: "minimum standards were enacted controlling wages, employment of juveniles, hours of work for women, and the conditions of apprenticeship. Maximum working hours for shop assistants were specified."[58]

A larger change also was gaining momentum in those years: the drive to unite the Australian colonies as states under a federal government. By the 1890s there were six colonies—New South Wales, Victoria, Queensland, South Australia, Tasmania and Western Australia (as well as the sparsely populated Northern Territory). As in the United States a century earlier, some colonies initially balked at federation, fearing a loss of autonomy and power. But on January 1, 1901 the Commonwealth of Australia was established. The colonies became states and the new country got a written Constitution and a federal Parliament.

The country retained some official ties with Britain, whose queen was designated Australia's head of state and sent a governor general there to represent her. But as in most parliamentary democracies based on the British model, it was the head of government — the prime minister — who actually ran the country.

With many Labor representatives serving in earlier colonial legislatures, workers' concerns were reflected in the 1901 Constitution. It gave Parliament the power to make laws with respect to "invalid and old-age pensions" as well as "the provision of maternity allowances, widows' pensions, child endowment, unemployment, pharmaceutical, sickness and hospital benefits ... benefits to students and family allowances."[59] Such social benefits were designed to cover situations that working people often could not afford on their wages. In the decade after federation, Parliament passed national laws in several of these areas. "One striking fact is the extent to which Australians had come to expect their governments to play an active part in the economic and social life of the country," says de Garis.[60]

Here a caveat is necessary. Benefits such as invalid and old-age pensions went to white people only then. The indigenous people, the Chinese, and other "coloured" people were excluded. Several other countries—the United States, Canada, Peru, Panama, Ecuador and New Zealand—also passed racially restrictive legislation during this period, aimed primarily at the Chinese; but in Australia the exclusion was broader and lasted longer.[61] Eighty years later multiculturalism would flourish, as we will see in Chapter Eight; but in 1901 that day was a long way off.

Australia was also in the vanguard in labor-management relations and workers' rights. The new Constitution empowered Parliament to provide a mechanism for mediating disputes between labor and management; in 1905 the country set up a Court of Arbitration and Conciliation under the leadership of Justice Henry B. Higgins.[62] Former prime minister Alfred Deakin had spoken of the need for a "fair and reasonable" wage for workers, in connection with protective tariffs but didn't define the term. That task fell to Higgins when he presided over a case on the issue in 1907. For wages to be fair and reasonable, Higgins ruled, they must be sufficient to support a worker, his wife and three children — a typical family of the day.[63]

To reach his decision Higgins figured out how much money workers would require to "satisfy the normal needs of the average employee regarded as a human being living in a civilized community."[64] Along with food and shelter, he said they must also have enough money for "light, clothes, boots, furniture and utensils, rates [taxes], life insurance, savings, sickness and accidents, fares, unemployment, union fees, school requisites, holidays and amusements, tobacco, alcohol, religion and charity."[65] His ruling was overturned later on technical grounds but it influenced labor policy: "eventually need became the basis for wage fixation throughout Australia," says historian Charlie Fox.[66]

Among industrialized nations, Australia and the United States rank at opposite ends of the spectrum in terms of worker participation in labor unions and public acceptance of unions. This had been the case for most of their histories. At first glance this seems strange because workers in both countries initially came from Britain. But their situations and expectations soon diverged. In Australia emancipated prisoners and immigrants could usually find jobs because of the labor shortage. Not so in the American South, the region where indentured immigrants, as well as convicts, were often sent. Once free, their unskilled labor was not in demand as long as African slaves were readily available. In the northern U.S. states, which industrialized earlier, however, there *was* a need for labor.

But American workers had other options as well in both regions. They could migrate and become farmers in areas with fertile land and regular rainfall. They could start a business in one of the myriad of small towns that were springing up in newly settled regions west of the Atlantic coast. Dissatisfied laborers had less motivation to organize when an independent life beckoned on the frontier. Workers in Australia also dreamed of becoming farmers but as the next chapter will show, for most it proved illusory.

People's expectations were also different in the two countries. In the United States immigrants who arrived hoping to escape poverty were soon caught up in the American Dream that said each generation would become wealthier than their parents in an endless upward spiral. By the mid-nineteenth century getting rich had become a national obsession. A stream of books instructed Americans on how to go from rags to riches.[67] In such a heady climate, labor unions seemed irrelevant. The idea of success was to climb out of the working class, not to improve conditions for people in it. In the United States, unions did attract a strong following in certain regions such as some highly industrialized states of the Midwest and a handful of cities on either coast; but nationally, unions and workers in the United

States were disparaged while businessmen who made millions were idolized.

In Australia, by contrast, a preoccupation with wealth did not characterize most working people then. As Ward explains: "The plain fact is that the typical Australian frontiersman in the last century was a wage-worker who did not, usually, expect to become anything else.... By loyal combination with his fellows, he might win better conditions from his employers, but the possibility of becoming his own master by individual enterprise was usually but a remote dream."[68]

Ward was talking about workers in the bush but the same held true in cities. Most wage earners identified with the working class and expected to remain in it, so they were motivated to form strong unions that would work to help improve their lot. Their successful fights helped give Australian workers a comfortable standard of living by the early twentieth century, with benefits that workers in few other countries yet enjoyed.

But in one respect Americans in the nineteenth century had an advantage over Australians. The United States was already an independent nation whose government could pass laws to suit its own needs while Australia was still a group of British colonies. Officials in London granted the colonies self-rule in local matters but retained control in certain areas. Land policy was one of them. That control, combined with the aridity of the interior and other circumstances, resulted in unusual patterns of settlement.

Four

Spreading Across the Land

Anthony Trollope noticed the urban tilt: "the city populations of Australia are excessive," the English author wrote in 1872.[1] "The proportion of urban to rural population — or I may perhaps better say metropolitan to non-metropolitan — is very much in excess of that which generally prevails in other parts of the world."[2] Trollope expected this situation to reverse itself as rural wages caught up with those in the cities. Instead it intensified. Small towns in the bush kept losing population while coastal cities swelled.

This trend has continued to the present day. Nearly 90 percent of Australians live in cities on the coast or in towns less than a hundred miles inland. Of these, two-thirds live in the southeastern coastal arc that stretches from Brisbane to Adelaide and includes Sydney and Melbourne. The parched condition of the interior is usually cited as the defining reason why all big cities are on the coast. This was certainly a significant factor; but it was not the only one. In other parts of the world large cities exist in dry regions. This chapter looks at settlement patterns — what caused them and how they helped shape the nation.

Who Received Land

Governors gave out land with a liberal hand in the first decades after the British arrived. They could afford to be generous because there was so much of it. Penal officers and well-connected immigrants received the largest parcels but emancipists and free settlers of limited means were also given some land in the colony's early years.

The first land grants were in Sydney and environs because the Blue Mountains to the west formed a seemingly impassable barrier to the interior. But after a party of explorers crossed those mountains in 1813, and then convicts built a road over them, the colonists went further afield and staked out their own land. Governors soon issued orders to restrict settlement to a defined area, to retain control over the colonists and to avoid problems with the indigenous people, who had already been pushed out of Sydney.

But there was no stopping land-hungry men who now had a way to reach endless stretches of land where they could establish farms or sheep stations. There was no stopping them, that is, when you lacked personnel to police the interior and had far more pressing problems to deal with in Sydney. The pioneers continued westward or headed north with their livestock. In the process they displaced indigenous people who had lived on the land for tens of thousands of years. (The next chapter describes the devastating effects this had on the Aborigines.)

Sheep, which were brought to Australia soon after the first convicts arrived, proved able to survive on land that defeated many other plant or animal species. Their wool provided a valuable annual cash crop that found a ready market in the new British woolen mills. As a result, large sheep stations developed quickly. But their owners faced a familiar problem: the lack of enough skilled workers. Even though free convict labor was available in the early decades, these unwilling workers often were not adept at the essential operations of birthing lambs and shearing sheep.

Immigrants kept arriving from Britain and Ireland but most took jobs in the city or wanted their own land. They did not line up to take jobs in hot, isolated areas, especially seasonal jobs that required long hours but paid little. "We must have Labour in some Shape or other," said one pastoralist. "Free Labour if we can get it — if not, then Prison Labour and failing either, Coolie Labour."[3]

Edward Gibbon Wakefield came up with a solution. His 1829 "Letters from Sydney" to a London newspaper (later published as a book) outlined a plan for "systematic colonization."[4] As long as laborers and mechanics could obtain land in Australia free or for a pittance, he said, they would not work for wages. The answer, first, was for the crown to stop giving land away and start selling it for a "sufficient price," thus putting it beyond reach of the working classes. Second, they must use the money from land sales for assisted immigration; that is, pay ship passage out for poor people who could not afford to come on their own. This scheme would bring people to Australia who would work for wages wherever they were needed.

In theory it sounded perfect; but theory was all that it was. Wakefield never set foot in Australia. He wrote "Letters from Sydney" from Newgate jail in London, where he was serving a three-year sentence for abducting a young heiress in order to marry her and gain possession of her fortune. A follower of Adam Smith, whose work he had edited, Wakefield was an attorney who wanted, writes historian Michael Roe, "to create societies wherein the pursuit of self-interest led to ineffable social harmony."[5] Some of his theories led to the formation of a new colony, South Australia, with creditable results. But when his ideas for land sales were adopted for all the colonies, they had unforeseen consequences.

Although some land in Australia was sold at higher prices and the money generated was used to pay sea passage for impoverished immigrants, the results were mixed. Station owners complained that England was sending them the dregs from its poorhouses, people who were not much better as workers than convicts. But often owners could not even entice such people out to the bush. Assisted immigrants tended to stay in the cities where their ships docked and look for work there.

The most noticeable result of raising land prices was to switch the direction of land possession from sale to lease, and usher in the era of the squatters. A tradition grew up where enterprising graziers would settle their flocks on large areas of unoccupied crown land and pay the government a small annual fee for their leases. These men were called "squatters," because they "squatted" on the land instead of owning it. The squatters became a prosperous class who typically kept increasing the size of their holdings. In time the term "squatter" became a generic label used to describe the proprietor of any sheep or cattle station, whether it had been obtained by land grant in the early 1800s, by lease — as most were initially — or as happened later in the southeastern colonies, by purchase.

Along with the growth of the wool industry this system caused more mutton and beef to be grown for consumption in the colonies and increased wheat production. But wool, which was light to transport and fetched a high price in London, became the country's dominant export.

What all squatters had in common was possession of capital or access to credit from a bank or merchant. Even with free land they needed money to buy and maintain their flocks and stations, and to survive while they waited for payment to arrive from London. Emancipists and assisted immigrants could not afford to become squatters; neither could the many people who paid their own way out but brought little money with them and found no way to borrow any.

Classes developed in the outback just as they had in the cities. The Australian Agricultural Company, formed in the 1820s after the Bigge Report appeared, and floated on the London stock exchange, provided money for squatters whose growth potential seemed likely to generate a high return on investment. Some entrepreneurs acquired multiple land holdings.

The landless usually could find jobs in the cities. But when a deep recession hit the country in the early 1840s and unemployment soared in

Sydney, people began to flock to the country in search of a living. They were an addition to all the emancipists and poor settlers who had already gone "up country." For a decade or so more people lived in rural areas than in cities.

The discovery of gold in 1851 attracted people to Australia in record numbers, nearly tripling the population in ten years. They came from all over the world, including California, where miners who had failed to strike it rich there boarded ships for the newest El Dorado. Most miners did not get rich in the goldfields and eventually moved on, usually to the nearest city. But some stayed in the bush.

Norwegian sailor Peter Larsen jumped ship at Melbourne to go to the digs nearby, then moved on to the goldfields of west-central New South Wales. Eventually he stopped panning for gold and became a carpenter, building houses for other recent settlers whose incomes were typically as modest as his own. He later anglicized his name to Lawson. His son, Henry Lawson, who helped his father on jobs from the age of 12, grew up to write stories and poems about the hardships of people he knew in childhood.[6] He became one of Australia's best-known writers.

Many dreamed of becoming prosperous farmers but few achieved their goal. "One of the recurrent themes in Australian political life," wrote Jill Ker Conway, "was the longing of the landless for the independence of the family farm, and their hatred of the privilege they saw accruing to the owners of huge grazing properties."[7] Reformers in Sydney and Melbourne who thought of Australia as a haven for Britain's poor and downtrodden, a place where people of modest means could rise and prosper on the land through hard work, likewise found it galling that "the richest and most accessible land of the colony had been permanently placed out of the people's reach."[8] They vowed to bring about change.

In 1861 the reformers succeeded. Legislators in New South Wales, led by John Robertson, passed the bill that became known as the Selectors' Act. Designed to give the little man a chance, it enabled anyone — any white person, that is — to select from 40 to 320 acres of land, paying five shillings per acre as down payment, with the remaining fifteen shillings per acre due within three years. The buyer could select unsurveyed crown land, or he could choose crown land that was being occupied by a squatter who leased it. He could not, however, select that part of a squatter's land that had improvements on it, such as his home and wool sheds, and there were also restrictions on how much of a squatter's holdings could be selected. Victoria, Queensland, and South Australia also passed versions of this act during the 1860s.[9]

The acts seemed revolutionary to both sides. The squatters protested that the legislation would put them out of business and cause the downfall of the country. The poor and their supporters were ecstatic. A folk song of the time expressed their elation:

> No more through the bush we'll go humping the drum,
> For the Land Bill has passed and the good times have come.
> No more through the bush with our swags need we roam,
> For to ask of the squatters to give us a home:
> Now the land is unfettered and we may reside
> In a place of our own by some clear waterside.[10]

They should have waited to celebrate. Although tens of thousands of people would become "selectors" over the next few decades, in practice squatters benefited most from the Selectors' Acts. This was because squatters, too, could select land at these prices. By claiming 320 acres of their own sheep runs and then selecting additional 320-acre parcels of their holdings in the names of their wives, each of their children, all of their relatives and employees, and anyone else they could bring into the scheme, sometimes as paid "dummies," squatters were able to buy the land they had leased, at bargain prices. Once paid for, it was easy to transfer title to their own names.[11]

The best land stayed in the hands of the squatters. The acts did help some small-scale farmers, especially those in areas near the coast with higher than average rainfall. But successful selectors were in the minority. Although these families worked long and hard to succeed, often enduring lives of grinding poverty, most of them ultimately failed.

Henry Lawson left an account of his own childhood among the selectors: "I grubbed, ringbarked, and ploughed, in the scratchy sort of way common to many native-born selectors round there; helped fight pleuro and drought; and worked on building contracts with Dad, who was a carpenter. Saw selectors slaving their lives away in dusty holes among the ridges … saw how the gaunt selectors' wives lived and toiled. Saw older sons stoop-shouldered old men at thirty."[12]

Lawson's work portrayed selectors and bushmen with grim realism. Another writer coated hard times with humor in depicting the life of a poor selector family. Steele Rudd, whose real name was Arthur Hoey Davis, grew up as the eighth child in a family of thirteen on a farm at Emu Creek in the Darling Downs area of Queensland. His Welsh father and Irish mother fought an endless battle for survival on their selection, causing Rudd to leave school at twelve and work as a bushman and stockman before moving to Brisbane at age sixteen.[13]

Rudd found a job in the government and began writing stories at night about his family's experience on their farm. The Sydney *Bulletin* published them and in 1899 brought out some of the stories as a book, *On Our Selection*.[14] Readers loved the comic scenes (including the bashing of recalcitrant domestic animals), the irrepressible character of gruff Dad who plunged into one unworkable scheme after another with renewed enthusiasm, and endlessly supportive Mother who nurtured everyone. Readers were also drawn to the values of the Rudds, who held on to their concertina even when there was nothing for dinner but dry bread and sugarless tea, and danced through the night with their neighbors on special occasions such as daughter Kate's wedding.[15]

But underlying the merriment ran a thread of futility. In a year when Dad successfully harvested a corn crop and took it triumphantly to the local store, after the storekeeper subtracted the money the Rudds owed for groceries, Dad's check was a pittance. Another year when he had a bumper crop, by the time he paid railway charges for getting it to market, he was again left with virtually nothing.

In the leanest times, Dad kept the family from starvation by going up country for a few months—that is, he worked for rich squatters. When son Dave "wanted to know why Dad didn't take up a place on the plain, where there were no trees to grub and plenty of water, Dad would cough as if something was sticking in his throat, and then curse terribly about the squatters and political jobbery. He would soon cool down, though, and get hopeful again."[16] Another Rudd son, Dan, "implored Dad, over and over again, to go shearing, or rolling up, or branding—*anything* rather than work and starve on the selection."[17] But the Rudds stayed put. The achievement of owning land may have overshadowed all else, or perhaps they saw no other option.

Countless people like the Rudds struggled on, as poor when they died as on the day they arrived at their selection. "One of Australia's tragedies in the second half of the nineteenth century," says historian Geoffrey Blainey, "was the failure of the tens of thousands of farmers and their families to make a living from small farms after slaving for years."[18] Their grown children did not stay around to repeat the pattern. They swarmed into cities and found jobs that paid year-round wages. Their descendants, for the most part, have clung to the cities.

Depictions of dirt-poor selectors and wealthy squatters do not give the whole picture; many people fell between these extremes. Not only did some selectors manage to prosper, but, conversely, not all squatters were rich. Some settlers with modest capital were able to start small sheep or cattle stations and hold on to them, passing the property on to their children.

Other small-scale squatters tried and failed. Fred Trollope was one of them. In England young Fred decided to seek his fortune in Australia. With his father's help in securing a loan he bought Mortray, a sheep station of

27,500 acres and 10,000 sheep in New South Wales near Grenfell. We can read descriptions of life there because his father, novelist Anthony Trollope, came out to visit Fred and wrote about it.[19]

Anthony had visited a few enormous sheep stations before he spent a month at Mortray with Fred and family, so he was familiar with the gradations among squatters: "The number of sheep at these stations will generally indicate with fair accuracy the mode of life at the head station," he wrote with wry humor. "A hundred thousand sheep and upward require a professional man-cook and a butler to look after them; forty thousand sheep cannot be shorn without a piano; twenty thousand is the lowest number that renders napkins at dinner imperative." With ten thousand sheep there was plenty of meat and tea, along with brandy and water "but do not expect champagne, sherry or made dishes."[20]

Fred's ten thousand sheep put him at the bottom of the squatter hierarchy. In time he and wife Susie had nine children, so they needed a good income. But floods the first year rotted part of his hay and after that came a drought which lasted for several years. Given the variable prices for wool, competition from large station owners who were friends of bankers and wool exporters in Sydney, the scarcity of labor, the high cost of transport, and the stiff interest rates charged by bankers, Fred became weighted down with debt. After seven years Fred realized that he could not make it no matter how hard he worked.[21]

Mortray was sold. His father Anthony lost several thousand pounds but did not blame Fred; he had seen how hard his son worked and his earlier research made him aware of the odds against success. "Fred seems to me to have more troubles on his back than any human being I ever came across," he wrote to a friend, a comment applicable to thousands of selectors and small-scale squatters.[22]

Through a contact of his father's, Fred obtained a post inspecting the lands chosen by selectors, a difficult job that entailed long treks on horseback through the hot bush, as well as frequent transfers. But most failed squatters or selectors lacked access to such jobs. Some stayed in the bush by working for wealthy squatters or trying some other region; but the more common option among families down on their luck was to head for the city. There they found jobs or went into business and except for recession years managed to make a living.

By the 1890s far more people were living in a handful of coastal cities than in the rest of the country combined. Compared with Britain, Continental Europe, the United States, indeed most of the world, Australia's settlement patterns were anomalous. Country towns did not disappear, but on the whole they failed to thrive. Something was impeding their growth.

Four • Spreading Across the Land

On more than half of the country's land it is unlikely that cities could have developed because of sheer physical limitations: the Simpson Desert, the Nullarbor Plain, the Great Sandy Desert and the Great Victoria Desert are among the regions that fall into this category. But several other regions proved more hospitable to agriculture. Most were in belts of land within 100 to 150 miles of the coast: the Darling Downs in Queensland as well as the sugar-cane growing areas above it, the New England region in New South Wales, the fertile plains of Victoria, the rich Barossa Valley of South Australia where German immigrants started a wine industry in the 1840s, and patches of coastal area below Perth in Western Australia. In addition, a few inland areas along rivers such as the Riverina district also had the potential to develop cities.

The policy of centering Australian economic life around the export of wool, and encouraging enormous sheep stations, helped stifle the growth of inland towns. Historian Manning Clark called the owners of such estates "the ancient nobility of New South Wales" to poke fun at their pretensions.[23] Some stations did resemble feudal estates in size but not in other ways.

The lives of the old feudal lords of Europe were interconnected with those of their peasants and vassals. They depended on each other. Not so in nineteenth-century Australia where squatters on large stations had minimal contact with people in the nearest country towns. The bulk of their workforce was often seasonal itinerant workers, so they had scant reason to concern themselves with nearby schools and community facilities. Their own children were sent to boarding schools in Sydney, Melbourne, or Geelong — or to England if they were rich enough. Some squatters owned sheep stations in several places and hired managers who might have no connection with the area. And the owners of a few large stations lived in Britain. Thus for all their wealth, these squatters did little to stimulate the local economies. Nor did they use their political connections to help towns near their stations prosper.

"In the fifties, and for decades afterwards, most squatters spent little money in the country towns near their stations," wrote Ward. "Generally their drays took the wool clip to the colonial capitals each year and carried back flour, tea, sugar, tar, tools, and other station supplies bought from wholesale importing houses near the wharfside."[24] In other words, they bought British-made products from large suppliers.

A hundred years later a British journalist working in Sydney saw signs of this same division between wealthy squatters—also called graziers—and country townsfolk. John Douglas Pringle, who visited some of the largest stations in the mid–1950s, approved of the people he stayed with. "On the whole, they form an admirable class," he wrote. But Pringle was concerned about one characteristic: "Unfortunately they have one fatal weakness—they are selfish. Content with their pleasant prosperous existence, they refuse to take part in public life and local government. They do little or nothing for the country towns which, in spite of the enormous wealth around them, are often little better than country slums—dreary, hideous, unspeakably dull."[25]

Residents of country towns yesterday and today would object strenuously to Pringle's description, with some justification. Details of Fred Trollope's life show that even towns of a few hundred had a strong community life. In Hay during the 1890s, for example, Fred served as president of the Horticultural Society and vice president of the Cricket Club while his wife Susie sang in the Hay Operatic Society's production of the *Mikado* and contributed to the local Benevolent Society.[26] But more than cricket clubs and operatic productions are needed to spur economic growth. Most country towns like Hay did not have the sufficient capital, infrastructure, amenities or consumer base to thrive.

The fact that land policy was controlled by people halfway around the globe further contributed to the urban tilt. From the earliest days, exclusives unhappy with the governor's rulings besieged officials and other influential people in London with letters of protest. Colonial governors became frustrated when workable policies they had put into place from firsthand knowledge of the situation were reversed after officials in London received several complaining letters. For example, in 1844 George Gipps, the governor of New South Wales, learned that although three million acres of crown land were leased to squatters, the government received only £7,000 a year for it. He issued new regulations that significantly increased the cost of leasing land, a move likely to decrease the size of individual holdings.

"Pandemonium broke loose in the squatting community."[27] Some people threatened to revolt like the Yankees. The British government, facing strong protests, reversed Gipps's ruling. Not only did new laws give squatters the use of land for practically nothing, but they also extended their leases to fourteen years. These changes helped perpetuate the pattern of immense holdings by relatively few people.

Limited self-government was well established by Gipps's time. A legislative council for New South Wales had been set up to deal with local matters during the 1820s. Initially its members were all appointed by the crown, but under pressure from the colonists this was modified in 1842 so twenty-four council members were elected and only twelve appointed. But property requirements for council members meant that wealthy squatters predominated—the lawmakers' body was known as "The Squatters' Council."

As a result, good roads and railways were likely to be developed in areas where the largest landowners had holdings. In Thomas Keneally's novel, *The Chant of Jimmy Blacksmith*, Jimmy's employer complains: "Yer get a town like Walcha — thousands of people — does the train go there? No, it goes to a place where there's no town, fifteen miles away. Just so some bloody squatter in parliament don't have to haul his wool any distance to a railhead. They're scandalous, those blokes."[28]

Those whose district lacked a railway, or a decent road, found the cost of getting their products to market prohibitive. In 1861, "it was still much cheaper to transport a ton of wheat across the Pacific from Valparaiso to Sydney than to carry it about 150 miles by bullock-dray from the vicinity of Goulburn on one of the main bush 'roads' of the period."[29] Thus wheat, which weighed ten times as much as wool and fetched lower prices, took a back seat on the market.

Anthony Trollope saw that lack of adequate transportation was hurting farmers and small-scale squatters alike. In his book on Australia he described the problem in a chapter on the Riverina, a pastoral district of 28,000 residents that he called "the Mesopotamia of New South Wales," because it was bounded by rivers: the Murray, the Murrumbidgee, the Lachlan, and the Darling. The Riverina, located in the far western corner of New South Wales, was several hundred miles from Sydney. But the closest railway to Sydney started at Goulburn, more than two hundred miles from the Riverina. With roads poor or nonexistent, drays loaded with wool typically took more than a month to reach Goulburn. Riverina residents had tried in vain to get a railway or even an adequate road in their district.[30]

In addition, Trollope was appalled to find customs houses along both sides of the Murray River, which served as the border between the colonies of New South Wales and Victoria. No product could go in either direction without payment of a tariff. A town on the Victorian side of the Murray had a railway that went straight to Melbourne, which was much closer to the Riverina than Sydney. Riverina growers did use that railway because the high transportation costs to Sydney wiped out any profit they might have made. This meant they had to pay customs duties, however, which put them at a disadvantage with competitors in other regions.

"The Riverina and Victoria," wrote Trollope, "instead of being to each other as are Lancashire and Yorkshire, or as New York and New Jersey are in reference to their custom house laws as are France and Germany.... Great Britain forbids her colonies to send the produce from one to another, except on payment of such duties as are levied on the same articles when imported from foreign countries."[31] This law abetted parochial business interests in the various colonies, Trollope pointed out: "the jam-makers of Victoria, for instance, objecting to the free introduction of Tasmanian jam."[32] The result was to impede the country's growth. In America, each state had its own legislature and made its own rules, he pointed out, "but they do not declare war against each other by border tariffs and internal custom duties."[33]

As a loyal Englishman, Trollope was careful to show that he was not advocating "what we at home call 'American institutions'" and to be circumspect in his criticism. He argued that "it is for the advantage of England and of Englishmen ... that Australia should be well-governed and prosperous."[34] Trollope implied but did not spell out that, as long as Victoria and Tasmania slapped tariffs on each other's jams, the market for British marmalade would remain vibrant.

Given the legitimate grievances of Australian growers at that time, it seems surprising that no strong rural protest movement emerged there as it did in the United States. During this same period many American farmers were being driven into bankruptcy by the high prices charged by the railways to bring their products to market. A few railway owners had kept lowering their prices until they drove their competitors out of business. Once the winner had a monopoly, prices skyrocketed.

But the American farmers fought back. In Kansas their manifestos reviled the monopolists as "robber barons."[35] Protests from farmers and small businessmen in many Southern and Western states, coupled with action from those up north who also were being ruined by outrageous prices, helped bring about the first antitrust legislation in 1890.

Why did selectors and small-scale squatters in Australia fail to organize and press their joint claims? Many were descended from the same stock as the American homesteaders and brought with them from the old country the growing Western tradition of protesting against injustices. As we have seen, itinerant bush workers did band together through labor unions and improve their lot. But farmers and small-time squatters mainly went down to their individual defeats.

The regions where American farmers organized were honeycombed with small towns, thriving country communities supported by the families in the district. The roads connecting them might seem primitive by today's standards, but they provided a way for people in different places to stay in touch. Equally important, American farmers could ship their goods freely from state to state. Had there been customs houses collecting tariffs at every state border, American farmers and their towns also would have been hampered.

Britain used its colonies to obtain needed raw materials, then sent manufactured goods back to the colonies, providing its factories with captive markets abroad. Once wool was established as Australia's most profitable commodity, this was all that mattered to people in Britain who grew rich from the trade. From their vantage point, the country might have contained nothing but enormous sheep stations in the outback plus a couple of ports where bales of wool could be loaded onto ships bound for England.

Despite the setbacks of those in the bush, in one arena the country cousins triumphed — or at least some of them did. Today when Australians look for the values that shaped their national character, they turn to the outback, not the cities. A legend of heroes has grown up, men who are seen as representing the essence of what is best in the national character. (There are no women in the legend.) These heroes of old are portrayed in literature, film, and television to the present day, carrying the underlying message that these stalwart forebears were imbued with moral qualities that have been lost in the urban industrial wastelands of our modern cities.

The United States likewise has a frontier myth that idealizes some of its pioneers, endowing them with virtues the nation holds dear. Although the first British colony in North America was founded 180 years earlier than Botany Bay, their main eras of territorial expansion occurred at roughly the same time. The nineteenth century was the period when settlers both in the United States and in Australia spread across the land in great numbers, pushed the indigenous peoples out of their way and, by their settlements, helped their governments establish control from coast to coast. In this regard the two countries have much in common.

But when we examine the two histories, a surprising fact emerges: their heroes are different. Furthermore, each country disparages the group which forms the hero class of the other. In Australia, seasonal itinerant bushworkers became the frontier heroes, as we will see ahead. Small farmers, scorned in their day, have now been forgotten. The Rudd family, divorced from their historical context and romanticized, stand out as a colorful exception.

Americans, by contrast, deified small, individual farmers on the frontier while scorning the itinerant workers who took seasonal jobs and moved from place to place as the Australian bushmen did. In the United States these workers were called "hoboes," a term that has come to mean wandering loafers who tried to avoid an honest day's work. In fact most men falling under that rubric picked fruit and vegetables, cut lumber and ice — in the days before refrigeration — and filled the need for temporary workers on building projects. They once formed an important part of the American workforce although they have not received much recognition.[36]

In comparing the two national myths, we need to define the American frontier: initially it meant all land west of the original thirteen colonies. In 1775, Daniel Boone, one of the earliest frontier heroes, led a group of settlers into Kentucky, which borders Virginia. The country they found was incredibly green and lush. A small acreage could sustain a large family. With no towns or infrastructure at first, these early farmers did need to be self-reliant. But once they cleared the land and planted crops, the rich soil nourished them and the skies cooperatively provided rain. In time, towns developed, along with roads that took their products to ready markets in eastern cities. The success of small farmers in Kentucky and neighboring states surely played a role in the apotheosis of the independent little guy on the frontier.

Australian author Mary Durack believed that differences in the physical terrain of the two countries affected their national characters. The Australians who strove to make it on their isolated frontier developed "a great deal of initiative, resourcefulness, and self-reliance," she wrote, "but these were generally expended in the sheer struggle for survival that fostered collective security rather than the competitive individualism of the United States."[37] Durack's book *Kings in Grass Castles* recounted her own pioneering family's hardships in the nineteenth century, including their overland trek with cattle in the 1880s from Northern Queensland to the Kimberly ranges of Western Australia.

During the nineteenth century, American pioneers who reached the arid lands west of the 100th meridian faced hardships similar to those of Australians. For example, the family of writer Hamlin Garland, who homesteaded in South Dakota, had no better luck than the Rudds, what with poor soil, droughts, and grasshopper plagues. The Garlands abandoned their farm and headed east. So did most of their neighbors.[38]

Geologist John Wesley Powell explored the regions of the Rocky Mountains for the federal government in the 1870s. He concluded that the 160 acres granted individuals under the Homestead Act for farms was not appropriate in these arid lands. Instead he proposed granting homesteaders there 2560 acres or more for sheep and cattle ranches. This brought cries of outrage from Congressmen who thought his plan "would destroy the time-honored ideal of a society of yeoman subsistence farmers."[39] The comforting theory then in vogue that "the rain follows the plough" was also advanced to defeat Powell's proposal. Although in 1910 Homestead grants were increased to 310 acres, this was still insufficient to support a family in some regions. To this day, the areas Powell surveyed are among the least-populated parts of the United States.[40]

Most early American farmers, however, lived on verdant lands in the eastern part of the country. These were the people celebrated for their pluck and rugged individualism. The later cowboy legend that made heroes of ranchers and sheriffs in the far West who spent their days pursuing "bad guys" was mostly myth: real ranchers and cowboys led difficult, often lonely, lives while taking care of their cattle.

In Australia, small farmers got no kudos for trying to eke out a living on poor soil in regions with uncertain rainfall. Even itinerant bushworkers disparaged them. Russel Ward explained why in *The Australian Legend*. Shearers and other seasonal workers needed overnight shelter and food as they moved between sheep stations on foot, but there were few inns or restaurants. Owners of large stations depended on the seasonal labor of these men, so a tradition grew up where squatters would provide traveling bushmen with free dinner, breakfast, and a space to lay their "swag" (bedroll) for the night.[41] Dinner was usually meat, bread and tea — monotonous fare to today's palates — but emancipists and poor immigrants appreciated any food in abundance.

Small selectors like the Rudds, who rarely had meat at their own tables, could not match the hospitality of wealthy squatters. "Until federation an honest selector was usually extremely poor and wretchedly over-worked," says Ward. "With the best will in the world he could not afford to issue, as the squatters did, free rations to every passing swagman. Nor could he afford to pay such comparatively high wages."[42] As a result, selectors were derisively called "cockies," meaning stingy old roosters. By the 1890s, "the 'cocky' had become, at least in the mythology of the migratory bushman, a byword for meanness and stupidity. He was mocked for his very virtues: providence and a considerable capacity for back-breaking toil.... At bottom it was the small farmer's grinding poverty which gave rise to the pastoral worker's contempt for him."[43]

Itinerant bushmen, rather than farmers, became the heroes of the Australian frontier. Ballads, poems, and stories about, and sometimes by, bushmen brought them to national attention. These writings filled a void. At that time the very idea of a distinctive *Australian* literature seemed laughable to most upper-class Australians.

The Bulletin, a Sydney-based magazine, played a key role in spreading the writings of the bushmen. We have seen that it published Steele Rudd's stories about his farm family, but more of the magazine's literary works were about itinerant bushmen. Some pieces grew out of tales sung around the campfire. Men on the isolated frontier devoured the weekly *Bulletin*. Reading stories and poems about lives like their own encouraged those of literary bent to take up their pens and send the results to Sydney.[44]

Henry Lawson and A. B. "Banjo" Paterson, who wrote "Waltzing Matilda," were two *Bulletin* contributors whose work "built the bushman into a legendary, often heroic figure."[45] Another contributor was Joseph Furphy, who "traveled the Riverina as a bullock driver with a small edition of Shakespeare's plays in his pocket."[46] Furphy sent a draft of his manuscript about life on the frontier to the *Bulletin* in 1897. "I have just finished writing a full-sized novel," he explained, "title, *Such Is Life*; scene, Riverina and Northern Vict.; temper, democratic; bias, offensively Australian." The editors encouraged Furphy and in 1903 published his novel, which became an Australian classic.[47]

Bushmen also helped shape other attitudes that became ingrained in the Australian character. Mateship was one of them. This concept, which means strong friendships among men, also includes fierce loyalty to members of one's group. The earlier experiences of some bushmen in the harsh closed prisons outside Sydney probably contributed to their hatred of authority and their camaraderie with other men of their class. Emancipists, the earliest itinerant workers in the outback, were later joined by immigrants whose dreams of making it in the city or on their own farm had been dashed. They banded together against a harsh world.[48]

"The greatest good is to stand by one's mates in all circumstances, and the greatest evil is to desert them."[49] These strictures of mateship led to the national attitude called the Tall Poppy Syndrome: namely, if a mate became rich and successful, his peers could hardly wait to cut him down to size. Unlike the United States, where self-made millionaires were cheered and worshipped, in Australia they were seen as traitors to their class.

The Work of Women

Mateship was a male phenomenon. Women were not only outside the fraternity but also, many Australian women felt, they were disparaged as nuisances. Men had lived without women by necessity in prisons and as itinerant workers, and some came to like it that way. The nineteenth-century view of women as guardians of Victorian morality may have increased their reputation as killjoys. Even when men married they did not necessarily look to their wives for companionship.

Anglo–Kenyan author Elspeth Huxley gave a vignette of such a marriage in her book on Australia. At a party in Alice Springs in the 1960s, Huxley met a woman who told her this was the first time she had ever had a night out away from the children. Was her husband babysitting, Huxley asked? "'*Him?* Not he! He's over there.' She nodded towards the bar.... 'It started on our wedding night. We stayed in an hotel. "You go off with the girls," he said. "I'm staying with the men." It was after midnight when he showed up, full of beer. Now we've got four kids. Oh, well. He's been a good husband, I suppose.' She laughed and fetched another whiskey and did not seem to mind."[50]

"And what indeed, had she to mind about?" Huxley continued. "Her man paid the bills, did not ill-treat her, gave her babies—though one might suppose their procreation to be a little perfunctory—and did not chase other women."[51] But others saw the situation of women differently. During the 1970s two Australians published books that said women did mind and should mind, because they were denigrated in their own country.

In *The Real Matilda*, Professor Miriam Dixon argued that it was women, more than the itinerant bushmen immortalized in "Waltzing Matilda," who got a raw deal in Australia.[52] Dixon bolstered this perspective by including the views of several observers, including Norman MacKenzie, a British author who was invited to Australia in 1958 to study the position of women there. In his resultant book, MacKenzie said, "It is felt by many Australians and by overseas visitors that women have a less significant role in the professions and public life, that they encounter more formal and informal discrimination, and that, in short, Australia is more a 'man's country' than any other industrial democracy."[53]

Writer and feminist Anne Summers agreed that Australian women were downgraded but put the problem in a somewhat different context. In *Damned Whores and God's Police* she argued that the nineteenth-century dichotomy of "bad" women (prostitutes) and "good" women (virtuous wives who acted as "God's Police," enforcing morality) still influenced Australia. Women, expected to be "dutiful wives and bountiful mothers," were stymied by "the absence of any cultural tradition which approved of women being anything else," said Summers.[54]

But in 1988 Professor Portia Robinson challenged the view that most women in colonial Australia were either neglected wives or prostitutes. At least during the penal years, she documented in *The Women of Botany Bay*, numerous women ran their own businesses: "Mrs. Smith of 21 Castlereagh Street, Sydney, was a stationer; Mrs. Stuart of Brickfield Hill sold 'ladies wear and groceries'; while Mrs. Weavers of 19 Pitt Street was 'in business with her mother, Mrs. Reynolds.'"[55] Some women obtained licenses to distill or sell liquor: "By the 1820s almost every street of Sydney Town had at least one public house, tavern or inn of which the proprietor was a woman."[56] Outside the city some women were farmers.

Which view of Australian women is accurate? All these books describe a segment of women there. It is hard to discount the evidence that women in some quarters were overlooked or disparaged. But when you look at lives of actual Australian women, quite a different picture emerges. In the collection *200 Australian Women*, for example, instead of passive women drowning their frustrations in whiskey, there is an abundance of dynamic, active women whose achievements from colonial days to the present in education, the arts, literature, journalism, business, labor unions, medicine, law, science, religion, and sports and other pursuits left their mark on the country.[57]

Many of these women were political activists. Catherine Spence of South Australia (1825–1910) was a "novelist, journalist, preacher, public campaigner for social and political reform, suffragist and feminist." She was the first woman to write and publish a novel set in Australia—*Clara Morrison*, 1854—and she wrote the first social studies textbook used in Australian schools. Spence became active in the women's suffrage movement later in life, along with working for other changes. From age seventy-six until her death "she chaired the management board of the Co-operative Clothing Company, a shirt-making factory owned and run exclusively by women, in which the workers as well as the owners held shares."[58]

Australia was an innovator in women's suffrage. South Australia gave women the vote in 1895 after a six-year campaign had been waged. One of its leaders, Mary Lee (1821–1909), was a widowed mother of seven who emigrated from Ireland when she was fifty-eight and "worked single-mindedly for political and social reform" for the rest of her life. As secretary of the Women's Suffrage League, she organized a petition that obtained 11,600 signatures in favor of suffrage and presented it to the legislature: "Women 'deluged' members with telegrams and thronged the galleries during debates." Later Lee helped found the Working Women's Trade Union in South Australia and "visited clothing factories and workshops, persuading employers to adopt the union's rates."[59]

Women in other colonies also campaigned for suffrage, notably Rose Scott in Sydney and Vida Goldstein in Melbourne. In 1902, a year after Federation, women got the vote nationwide. "Australia thus became, at the federal level, the first nation in the world where women, with the exception of Aboriginal women in some states, had the right to vote and the right to sit in the Federal Parliament."[60]

After that victory, some Australian women turned to helping their counterparts in Britain get the vote. Goldstein spent time in England working as an organizer for the Women's Social and Political Union and writing suffrage articles. A contingent of Australian women marched in British suffrage parades in 1908 and 1911, under a banner designed and painted by Australian artist Dora Meeson. The banner showed Britannia (mother) aided by her daughter Australia who urged, "Trust the women Mother as I have done."[61]

Books such as those by Dixon and Summers, as well as the growth of a worldwide women's movement, helped bring significant changes in the position of Australian women. Anne Summers recounts that, as a member of an OECD Working Party on women in the early 1990s, she "learned that Australia had become an inadvertent pioneer on the status of women policies. The Working Party included women from Japan, Germany, Canada, France, and the United States and they were astonished, and envious, to learn about Australia's achievements."[62]

Australian women, finding themselves in second place, mobilized to get a fair go. Another marginalized group in Australia did the same. They were descendents of the country's earliest inhabitants, the indigenous Aborigines.

Five

Dispossessed:
The Indigenous People

Nothing in the past experience of the indigenous people of Australia prepared them for the arrival of the British in 1788 (or for what followed). "If blacks often did not react to the initial invasion of their country it was because they were not aware that it had taken place," says historian Henry Reynolds. "They certainly did not believe that the land had suddenly ceased to belong to them and they to their land."[1]

European ships had visited their shores in the seventeenth and eighteenth centuries, but not for long. The Asians who came did not stay either: Macassans from the Celebes (now Sulawesi) arrived each year on the north coast to fish for trepang — also called sea cucumbers or bêche-de-mer — which they dried and sold to the Chinese, who used the delicacy in soups. The indigenous people accepted the Macassans because as soon as they caught enough fish and prepared them for market, they sailed home. There was some interchange of goods but neither group tried to change the other's way of life.

The British were something new. "It was not the coming of the Europeans that provoked resistance, but their unrelenting seizure of all rights and uses of the land," Robert Hughes says of the period after the first convict ships arrived.[2] As it gradually became clear that these strangers intended to stay — and to take over the land — the indigenous people did fight back. Reynolds estimates that up to 20,000 indigenous people and 2500 Europeans died in nineteenth-century combat over the land.[3] Far more indigenous people would die of other causes. The indigenous people did not have a national leader who could summon reinforcements from afar when they were outnumbered, nor did they possess weapons with the firepower of guns.

In time Aboriginal leaders must have realized that they would have to fight these invaders in other ways than on the battlefield. By the 1920s they developed new methods to fight for their people's rights. This chapter and the next tell what happened.

How the Indigenous People Arrived in Australia

The first human beings in Australia are thought to have come from China and islands of Indonesia during the last Ice Age. More land was exposed at that time, because much water was frozen in large ice caps. This meant that sea journeys were shorter: a day or two on a canoe or raft brought people to dry land, enabling them to travel in stages. Scientists now believe that over a period of time, this is how the indigenous Aborigines came to Australia.

Until recently the first people were thought to have arrived 40,000 years ago or later. But in the 1990s, when the new technology of thermoluminescence, more accurate than carbon dating, was used on artifacts found at Kakadu National Park, the artifacts turned out to be 50,000 to 60,000 years old.[4] Tests by geneticists studying DNA samples from peoples around the world for the Human Genome Diversity Project likewise showed that the indigenous people had reached the Australian continent around 60,000 years ago.[5]

The land was greener than today when they first arrived. In time they spread across the continent, dividing into numerous groups of people with linguistic and cultural ties. Each group inhabited a distinct territory, and "owned" it in Western concepts. The size of the territory depended on the food and water supply: in arid central Australia, a people's territory might be quite large while in wetter coastal areas it was smaller.

Within groups people separated into smaller bands of fifteen to thirty people or less who traveled together each year to established sites where they knew that certain food would be available at various seasons. The women gathered the mainstay of their diet: fruits, vegetables, roots, and seeds, as well as small animals such as lizards. The men supplemented this food by hunting larger animals and by fishing if they lived near the ocean. Thus they ate a varied, healthy diet.

Bands came together periodically for festivals and ceremonies where they passed down their culture through dances, songs and plays. The links between bands in a tribe "were based on kinship and marriage ties, common ceremonial affiliation and shared ownership of, or responsibility for, sacred sites and objects."[6]

Nature and a close relationship with the land were embedded in traditions of indigenous people. For example, the Anangu people of Central

Australia, part of the language group that speaks Pitjantjatjara, use the word "Tjukurpa" to describe their beliefs and way of life. "Tjukurpa is the foundation of Anangu life and society ... [it] refers to the creation period when ancestral beings, Tjukarita, created the world as we know it as well as the present, the future, religion, law and moral systems.... None of the places existed until our Tjukurpa ancestors, in the forms of people, plants and animals, traveled widely across the land. Then, in a process of creation and destruction, they formed the world as we know it today."[7] Indigenous groups in all parts of Australia have their own creation beliefs but there are some similarities indicating contact among them.

Larger inter-tribal groups also came together periodically, so people became multilingual. Although there were differences in languages, kinship systems, art forms, and ceremonial practices, "these differences were probably less important than the underlying similarities which brought groups together for ceremonies, for trade, to intermarry, and which allowed the maintenance of myths, and of song lines and exchange cycles that extended over hundreds of kilometers."[8]

To trade, they went even further afield. "Through the Centre, people marched on the great trading journeys from gulf to gulf, pituri coming south and ochre going north for thousands of years."[9] Indigenous people traveled long distances to obtain materials needed for their way of life. But as Captain Cook found to his consternation, they showed no interest in objects of European origin. Cook recorded his impressions of the people at Botany Bay during his brief visit in 1770. One journal entry throws light on European as well as Aboriginal culture: "The lives of the natives might appear to be wretched," Cook wrote, "but in reality they are far more happier than we Europeans; being wholly unacquainted with not only the superfluous but the necessary Conveniences so much sought after in Europe, they are happy in not knowing the use of them. They live in a Tranquility which is not disturbed by the Inequality of Condition."[10]

These lines reflected the popular European concept of the "Noble Savage," made famous two decades earlier by French philosopher Jean-Jacques Rousseau. In 1749 Rousseau had entered a contest on the question: "Has the progress of the sciences and the arts contributed to the corruption or to the improvement of human conduct?" He won the contest with his argument that people's inherent good nature had been corrupted by "civilization," and that "savages" living close to nature retained their goodness.[11]

Rousseau had never been to the lands of "Noble Savages" but that did not matter. He was writing about Europeans' longings for less complicated lives, projecting a utopian vision of a simpler, more satisfying life onto unknown peoples far away. But Captain Cook was no romantic. He saw that the indigenous people had developed a life that worked for them. They had been following it for a long time.

After the last Ice Age ended about 30,000 years ago, the melted ice caps increased sea levels and water covered much land, making the Australian continent more difficult to reach. The people already there, estimated from 300,000 to a million, were cut off from those on other continents for tens of thousands of years. Their nomadic life prevented serious overpopulation, because a woman could only carry one baby at a time and small children and the elderly who could not keep up died along the way.

Hostilities and wars between groups did occur and some groups likely moved into the dry center to find a place where they could live undisturbed. But the protracted wars that occurred elsewhere, when two or more peoples wanted the same turf or some adventurer set out to conquer the world, seem not to have happened there. On a continent roughly the size of the United States, even a population of a million people left plenty of room for everybody. If one region was taken, there were plenty of other unoccupied places to claim. And basic subsistence took up a large part of their time and energy.

Cook described the coastal people he met as not warlike but "a timorous and inoffensive race, no ways inclinable to cruelty."[12] Their behavior may have reflected the security of a people who had not faced occupations by foreign invaders, or slavery or forced religious conversions—and never dreamt that such events could happen.

After the British arrived and built a penal colony, the gulf between their cultures soon became apparent. Because the indigenous people planted no fields and built no permanent structures or cities, the newcomers regarded them as backward and uncivilized. The indigenous people, in turn, felt the same about some European practices, as a contemporary journal reveals.

Watkin Tench, a Marine captain with the First Fleet who kept a journal, recorded an event that took place a few years after their fleet landed. When a convict was caught stealing fishing tackle from an Aborigine, Captain Phillip ordered the man flogged. He assembled as many indigenous people as possible to watch it, to show them that the British administered justice fairly. They saw something else: "There was not one of them that did not testify strong abhorrence of the punishment, and equal sympathy with the sufferer," Tench wrote. "The women began to cry and one man became so angry that he grabbed a stick and threatened the flogger with it."[13]

Despite their different perceptions, the presence of a governor and soldiers in Sydney gave the indigenous people some protection there; an authority was on hand to enforce laws prohibiting not only theft but also the murder of indigenous people. But once settlers began moving into the outback to claim land, there were few restraints on their behavior. With one or two exceptions (described ahead) they could kill indigenous people with as little thought as they shot kangaroos and suffer no legal consequences.

Estimates of how many indigenous people died between 1788 and the late nineteenth century range as high as two-thirds of the population. Some deaths occurred in military-type battles, others when bands of indigenous people returned to one of their seasonal homelands and found it occupied by recently arrived white settlers who treated them as interlopers. Far more died of other causes, including communicable diseases, such as smallpox, which were brought in by the newcomers. With no immunity to these diseases, the indigenous people perished in great numbers during epidemics.

But the major causes of death were malnutrition and starvation, brought about by the gradual destruction of the indigenous people's food and water supply. After Europeans settled on the land, the sheep and cattle they imported ate the roots, grasses and seeds that were staples of the indigenous people's diet. Grazing animals trampled other plants to death and fouled streams and creeks that had provided safe drinking water. In addition, the dogs imported to herd these new animals drove away kangaroos and smaller creatures that the indigenous people hunted regularly to round out their diet. Thus even when Aboriginal bands kept moving a few miles beyond the white settlements, their food supply diminished steadily.

Laws designed to protect them could have the opposite effect in practice. In 1805 a judge ruled that indigenous people could neither be prosecuted in court nor serve as witnesses, because they were incapable of understanding English law. If they committed crimes, those in charge should "pursue and inflict such punishment as they may merit."[14] This meant that indigenous people were prohibited from having a trial if arrested, they could not take someone to court if they felt they had been wronged and they could not be called as witnesses. In short, they were denied all legal rights.

Those Anglo–Australians who were disturbed by the wanton killing of indigenous people found that the law itself was a major stumbling block in bringing murderers to justice. One such man wrote in frustration: "They may be destroyed by their fellows, and what is worse, may be shot wholesale by Europeans, and yet the arm of the law has no power to punish unless the evidence of a white person can be procured."[15]

In one famous case, the Myall Creek Massacre, murderers were eventually brought to justice in part because white men did testify. In 1838, while the owner of the Myall Creek Station was away, eleven white stockmen rode into a camp where a band of indigenous people were staying temporarily. They roped the twenty-eight men, women and children together, took them to a field and killed them all. Then they hacked up their bodies, decapitating some, and tried to burn them.[16]

The station manager reported the killings to the nearest magistrate, Edward Denny Day, who notified Governor Gipps. The governor called for an investigation and ordered the accused men arrested. Even with compelling evidence against them, however, the jury acquitted the men.

But a crusading journalist, Edward Smith Hall, editor of the *Sydney Herald*, kept the story alive. He declared that the acts had no parallel "for cold-blooded ferocity, even in the history of Cortez and the Mexicans, or of Pizarro and the Peruvians."[17] As public opinion turned against the murderers, the governor managed to bring seven of the men to trial again—those he had the most evidence against. This time they were convicted and hanged.

The hangings sent shock waves through pastoralists in the outback. Many felt a sense of outrage that whites could be hanged for killing blacks; they developed a virulent hatred of Governor Gipps. But Edward Denny Day, the local magistrate who had investigated the killings, became a folk hero in time because of his persistence in gathering evidence in the case. "This remarkable officer possessed such zeal and humanity that his name was later honored in folk tales and ballads as well as in official reports."[18] There were two schools of thought about the indigenous people and how the law should work. But those who championed Aboriginal rights were few in number.

If the earliest pastoralists had no use for the indigenous people, the first explorers found their services indispensable. Men such as Charles Sturt, John McDouall Stuart, and Edward Eyre, who led parties into the unknown interior, soon realized that the indigenous people's knowledge of the land, and of sources of food and water, could make the difference between life and death so they were hired as guides.

One party of explorers, however, disdained the services of the Aborigines. Near the end of the Burke and Wills expedition, when a few Aboriginal men from a local group came into their camp bearing gifts of fish, Burke fired shots in the air to drive them away, regarding them as a nuisance. He and another man later died of starvation. John King, the one man left, realized that his only chance of survival was to find the indigenous people's camp and stay with them until a rescue party reached him. For two months the indigenous people fed King, nursed him back to health, and sent out scouts to search for white rescuers. In time they found the rescuers and led them to King, who lived to tell the tale.[19]

In her book *Kings in Grass Castles*, Mary Durack tells how her pioneer grandfather and his party were befriended by indigenous people in Queensland. Traveling in search of gold during a drought year, the men were desperate for water when a band of blacks appeared. "Astonishingly one spoke a few words of garbled English and was later found to have been in contact with King, the sole survivor of Burke's party of two years before.... They led the whitemen to a low, rocky outcrop and there, removing a cover of brushwood and stones, disclosed a well of stagnant water."[20] Afterwards they fed the hungry party. But when the Duracks asked them about the country beyond, their leader shook his head, scowled, and said, "Go! Go!" pointing in the direction they had just come from.[21]

In European settlements, when someone got lost in the bush and couldn't be found, it was customary to call in the local indigenous people; with their knowledge of the land they could usually locate a stray child or wandering adult. In his memoir, *A Fortunate Life*, Albert Facey recounted his own experience. In 1909, at age fourteen, Facey found a job with a group of drovers taking cattle to market in Western Australia. During a turbulent rainstorm he got separated from the group. For almost a week he wandered around on his horse, subsisting on roots and some meat he cut from part of a kangaroo carcass he found on the ground. Early on he saw "a black man, very wild-looking, with a long bushy beard," wearing only a loincloth; he was bent over, skinning a dead kangaroo.[22] Facey was petrified. His grandmother had read him accounts of a black man who went on a murderous rampage, killing every white in sight. He hid until the man left.

Several days later two indigenous people grabbed Facey and led him away. When they stopped at the top of a hill and started building a fire, Facey was sure his time was up, until he realized they were sending a smoke signal. After they reached the indigenous people's camp, he was astonished to find one of the drovers there. The man, who spoke the group's language, told Facey that the drovers had asked them for help in finding him. The man Facey hid from earlier had been searching for him and left the kangaroo meat for him to eat.[23]

G. A. Robinson, who camped with Tasmanian hunters in the 1830s, became aware of other specialized skills they possessed. He "respected their knack of reading the clouds and moon and stars and thereby forecasting the weather of one of the most changeable climates in Australia. 'I have seldom found them to err,'" he wrote.[24]

After Europeans began spreading across the Australian continent, the high court in London declared the land to be "Terra Nullis"—unoccupied territory. Because the indigenous people had built no permanent settlements, they had not "occupied" the land, the judges reasoned; therefore it did not belong to them. Europeans were free to claim it.

The British never negotiated land treaties with the Aborigines as they had with the indigenous Indians of Canada and the Maoris of New Zealand, and as the United States did with Native American tribes. Although such treaties were frequently broken, they at least gave indigenous peoples a legal foot to stand on.

Why were the indigenous people never offered peace treaties that dealt with land rights? This may have seemed unnecessary because the indigenous people could not raise a military force large enough to wage an effective war. They also lacked a leader with jurisdiction over groups to negotiate with, although the indigenous people might have appointed one if they had been given the chance. Perhaps the longevity of Aboriginal culture and the people's isolation from contact with other lands is another reason. They appeared so different from Europeans that it led many settlers to view them as inferior creatures who were barely human.

A landmark book inadvertently added weight to this outlook. In 1859 English biologist Charles Darwin published *On the Origin of Species*, which gave a new explanation for how animals, including humans, evolved. Chance variations occurred, he reported: if the change made a species better able to survive, it reproduced itself in great numbers and became a new sub-species; if it hampered a species, those with the new characteristic died off. Darwin called this process "natural selection."

In a book published a few years later philosopher and evolutionist Herbert Spencer coined the term "survival of the fittest." The two authors acknowledged each other and said their concepts were similar because both talked about evolving species.[25] But Spencer used the word "fittest" to mean superior; in time he developed a system "in which morality and survival are linked."[26] When Darwin's book received widespread attention, in part because of attacks on it by Christian theologians, the term "survival of the fittest" was attributed to him. It still is.

Darwin, a scientist, had no interest in racial theories but authors have scant control over readers' interpretations of their work. His book was used by others to suit their own purposes. In the *London Review*, for example, a reviewer of *On the Origin of Species* celebrated his own countrymen's superiority and denigrated the indigenous people: "Look at the educated Englishman and the Australian Indigenous people; the one gaining more and more mastery over the laws of the world; the other almost as helpless a victim of those laws as the brutes around him. Never in nature's kingdom do we see this immense gulf between individuals of the same species; we see it in man alone, because he alone in creation was free to rise or fall."[27]

As the Australian indigenous people continued dying out in large numbers, settlers invoked the "survival of the fittest" concept to justify their demise. These Stone Age people could not withstand the impact of a superior modern civilization, the popular argument went; naturally they were bound to perish. This reasoning led to the belief that the indigenous people were a doomed race, destined to soon become extinct. As this notion spread, even those who worked with the indigenous people and were sympathetic to them often accepted their collective death sentence as inevitable.

The indigenous people flouted the conventional wisdom by surviving. They were supported by a few Anglo–Australian groups and individuals and by one or two religious sects in England, who likewise refused to accept their evolutionary death sentence. The indigenous people could hold on, they insisted, if they could be shielded from the forces that were killing them off.

Around 1880 some white Australians who were appalled by the widespread killing of indigenous people formed the Aboriginal Protection Association (APA). Its goals were to stop the killings and give indigenous people a better life. "For its time, the APA was highly progressive. It rejected the popular notion that the Aboriginal people were doomed to extinction ... [and] it believed they should be compensated for the dispossession of their land."[28]

The best hope for Aboriginal survival, APA members believed, was to put them in reserves where they would be safe. Each colony should set up a Protection Board that would look after the welfare of the indigenous people living there. Filled with goodwill, the APA unleashed a system of Protection which in time became a mockery of its intent.

The move into reserves had started decades earlier. As in the United States, once settlers claimed land the indigenous population lived on and indigenous people attacked the settlements to get their land back, white settlers pressured the government to come to their aid. Eventually troops would come in to round up the indigenous people and force them to settle in some other area, usually on less desirable land.

Schools were set up on the reserves. Often they were run by religious missions, Protestant or Catholic, by people who came from Britain, Ireland, or in a few cases, Germany. What these teachers had in common was the desire to "civilize" their charges; that is, to stamp out their "heathen" practices, convert them to Christianity, and teach them European ways. But to their consternation, indigenous people showed little interest in being converted. Instead they persisted in following their traditional customs and were likely to scoff at white people's ways. Aboriginal children, under parental influence, reacted similarly. Their teachers soon concluded that the only way to civilize them was to separate children from their parents permanently at an early age.

The rationale for this policy was explained by a long-time Board member at the Australasian Catholic Congress in 1909: "Amongst all those who have had large experience with the indigenous people, and who take a deep interest in their welfare, there is no difference of opinion as to the only solution of this great problem — the removal of the children and their complete isolation from the influences of the camps.... In the course of a few years there will be no need for the camps and stations: the old people will have passed away, and their progeny will be absorbed in the industrial classes of the country."[29]

Two years later the Annual Report of the Aborigines Protection Board stated: "The Board recognizes that the only chance these children have is to be taken away from their present environment and properly trained by earnest workers before being apprenticed out, and after having once left the indigenous people's reserves they should never be allowed to return to them permanently."[30]

Long before Protection laws upheld this procedure, the practice of forcibly taking children from their parents had been followed informally. In 1838 at the town of Wellington in New South Wales, for example, "a missionary and two constables chased a woman, screaming and clutching her baby, into another missionary's house, then seized the child and took her off to the infants' dormitory. Next day the whole Aboriginal camp left and the work of the Wellington missionaries was never the same again."[31]

By the 1890s not only did Protection laws make it difficult for indigenous people to leave, but there were fewer places to go where the authorities could not track them down. If they went to the far north they encroached on the territory of other indigenous groups who might not want them there. The Aborigines found themselves in a no-win situation.

The children most often taken away were those of mixed parentage, usually having a black mother and white father. They had been half-civilized by birth, authorities believed, and would be easier to educate and place in the workforce. The old telegraph station above Alice Springs was one of many schools established during the second half of the nineteenth century to educate children of mixed parentage. But another practice contradicted this thinking: couples of mixed race were frequently expelled from the reserves. A different kind of prejudice seems to have contributed to this policy. White fathers were assumed to be lower-class types, former convicts from the criminal classes, and therefore potential troublemakers who might teach the natives bad habits or incite them to revolt.

Aboriginal children trained in mission schools read English and recited Christian prayers by age six or seven. This might have led their teachers to suspect that they came from the same species as Europeans, and that some might be taught to perform skilled or professional jobs. But so ingrained was their teachers' belief in the inherent inferiority of the indigenous people that their highest ambition was to turn their charges into reliable workers who would perform unskilled tasks satisfactorily for low wages.

Not all indigenous people lived in reserves. Some settled on the fringes of cities and towns, while large numbers continued to follow their traditional nomadic way of life in western and northern regions that the Europeans had not reached yet. By the 1860s, however, Europeans and some Asians began settling on the northwest coast. Most arrived by ship but a few ranchers from Queensland moved their livestock across the country and established stations in what is now Western Australia and the Northern Territory.[32] They raised cattle because it was too hot there for sheep. The ranchers took over vast tracts of land, in most cases leased from the federal government at low rates.

If indigenous people still lived on these lands—and they usually did at some time during the year—the pastoralists, with encouragement from the government, often let them stay on as employees. In time many indigenous people settled in one place and went to work for the newcomers. The men became stockmen looking after the cattle; the women became domestic servants. The larger stations had permanent Aboriginal settlements called camps. For both sides, there were plusses and minuses.

This arrangement enabled indigenous people to remain on their land and often to continue many of their religious and cultural practices. Unlike missionaries in the southeast, the pastoralists generally had little interest in converting the indigenous people; it was their labor they wanted. If following the old ways kept the natives happy and on the job, so be it. Working on a station also kept the indigenous people from starving because they were given food, typically flour, tea, and sugar, but sometimes also other commodities such as meat, jam, tobacco and liquor. In time this diet contributed to health problems.

The downside was that a shack and food were virtually all they got. Even when they were paid wages much later, it was only a pittance. In spite of working long hours, often seven days a week, they remained in poverty and dependence. Over time, as stockmen learned about the wages white workers received, they became increasingly dissatisfied with their situation.

Pastoralists' wives got domestic servants, a commodity otherwise impossible to obtain in those remote regions. Most important, the pastoralists got first-class stockmen: the intimate knowledge of animals and the terrain that Aboriginal stockmen brought to their work made them invaluable, while the cost of retaining them was minimal.

But there were frustrations as well. Stockmen might abruptly leave the station for a while to go "walkabout"—to make pilgrimages to sacred sites or to attend funerals whose ceremonies could go on for weeks. In time some went off on drinking sprees, following a new custom they learned from the Europeans. Pastoralists generally put up with such inconveniences in those days, because they had come to rely on the skills of their Aboriginal stockmen. They could not afford to lose them.

Keeping the indigenous people on the job became easier after Protection laws were passed. Disgruntled employees could no longer pack up and leave because their employers were designated as their protectors. It was illegal to quit or even to marry without their permission.

The story of one indigenous woman who grew up on a station in Western Australia early in the twentieth century brings out her untenable situation. Daisy Corunna's life is revealed gradually in *My Place*, a book by her granddaughter, Sally Morgan. In it, Corunna plays a pivotal role in Morgan's search for her Aboriginal roots.

Sally Morgan is a painter and writer whose work depicts Aboriginal themes. But as a schoolgirl in Perth in the 1950s, she had no idea that she was part Aboriginal. Her mother Gladys and grandmother Daisy never mentioned their past and her father, who was white, had no interest in it. When schoolmates asked about her ethnic background—was she Italian or Greek or Indian or what?—Morgan went home and asked. "Tell them you're Indian," her mother said.[33]

Morgan was also puzzled by her grandmother's behavior when officials from the local housing authority inspected their rented house each year. Daisy would clean the house for days before they came. After the inspection she would serve the men an elaborate tea and talk in a brittle, forced way that bore no resemblance to her usual manner. Only years later did Sally Morgan realize that her grandmother had been terrified that the inspectors would declare the family unfit and snatch her grandchildren, and she and Gladys might never see them again.

Daisy Corunna was born on Corunna Downs Station in 1900 of an Aboriginal mother and white father. At age seven she was taken from her mother to the big house of the owners, where she lived and worked as a servant. Her brother Arthur was sent away to a mission school as a young child. When her employers moved to a Perth suburb years later, they decided to take 14-year-old Daisy with them. They told her mother that in Perth she could go to school and learn to read.

That promise was forgotten. Daisy served as a full-time nursemaid to the family's children in Perth and also did the housework. While still a teenager, she gave birth to a daughter, Gladys. When she was three, Gladys was sent away to a mission school by the mistress of the house. Who was the child's father? Gladys didn't know and Daisy refused to talk about it. Gladys left the mission school as a teenager and got a job. After she married and had children, her mother, Daisy Corunna, joined the family.

Once Sally Morgan learned of her heritage she did detective work to make contact with her Aboriginal relatives, and began to learn about her culture. Uncovering her family's past also became important to her, including the identity of her grandfather and great-grandfather. She interviewed everyone she could track down who might have information about them. This included the 93-year-old widow of the late owner of Corunna Downs Station. The woman, who was living in a nursing home in Sydney, told Morgan that her great-grandfather had been the Maltese cook on Corunna Downs Station. But when Morgan relayed this opinion to a few former Aboriginal stockmen from the old station, they laughed.

The identity of Gladys's father was also a mystery. Perhaps he was the English engineer who had lived with the family in Perth for a time, the station owner's daughter suggested. Further clues, however, gave weight to the probability that Morgan's great-grandfather was the owner of Corunna Downs Station. And that he was her grandfather as well.

Daisy Corunna had grown up feeling helpless, unable to defend herself from the demands of her employers and others who had power over her life. As an adult she coped by hiding her past and avoiding white people as much as possible. But indigenous people born a generation or two later, including her granddaughter, often had a different outlook. Instead of hiding their past, they wanted to uncover it fully. Instead of accommodating themselves to having an inferior status, they set out to change their place in Australian society.

Six

A Place in Two Cultures

In 1988 Australia celebrated its Bicentennial — "200 years of European Settlement." Festivities abounded. The highlight came on Australia Day when Britain's Prince Charles made a congratulatory speech to an appreciative audience in the Sydney Opera House. But while the prince was speaking, a different kind of gathering was also taking place.

Citizens of Aboriginal descent staged a massive Day of Protest. They came in on convoys of buses or by car from all over Australia. Their numbers, including white supporters, were estimated at forty thousand, making it the largest protest in Australia since the days of the Vietnam War.[1] The indigenous people considered January 26, 1788, Invasion Day. They saw nothing to celebrate. With traditional Aboriginal dancers leading the way, their "March for Freedom, Justice and Hope" arrived in central Sydney in time to be on display for the television cameras. And they did make the evening news

The scale of the protest may have surprised many Australians of European ancestry. By 1988 Australia had made extensive changes in its earlier policies towards the indigenous people, moving from protection to assimilation to self-determination. As in affirmative action programs for ethnic minorities in the United States, the Australian government started a variety of programs in education and job training, aimed at helping indigenous people get out of poverty. These programs, as in the United States, caused resentment among low-income white people who were not offered such benefits. When Australians watched the indigenous people's protest on the evening news some may have thought: What do these people have to complain about?

Most Australians could not answer that question. "What you've got to remember is that before the late '60s, people weren't studying Australian history, never mind Aboriginal history," historian Henry Reynolds points out. "For the most part you studied British history."[2] Australian history was seen in the context of the British Empire and its colonial administrators. If the indigenous people were mentioned at all, it was as a stone-age people whom the British had civilized.

Starting in the 1970s schools did begin teaching more about the indigenous people with an emphasis on their cultures, to show that their way of life, although different, was also valid. This was a worthwhile endeavor; but without an accompanying history of what happened to them before and after 1788, it was difficult for non–Aboriginal Australians to understand the protests.

If Anglo–Australians learned little Aboriginal history, however, the reverse was not true. Aboriginal children were taught European history with emphasis on the British Empire. Some may have learned more than their teachers realized. Most Aboriginal schoolchildren likely paid scant attention to descriptions of the exemplary government on the other side of the world, but for those who followed their lessons closely, a contradiction became apparent. They were taught that the British government gave people fundamental rights and had a legal system that dispensed justice for all, and that Australia followed this system. But as indigenous people they were denied these rights.

In the twentieth century Aboriginal leaders turned to self-help and political action to fight for their peoples' rights. Few records of the earliest organizations remain but one group formed in 1924 "managed to hold three annual conferences before being harassed out of existence by police acting on behalf of the NSW Aborigines Protection Board."[3] Such activity was a threat to the status quo.

The indigenous people who founded political groups in the 1930s became more sophisticated about ways of keeping their organizations from meeting a similar fate. Seeking as much publicity as possible was one tactic. In 1932, William Cooper and Ebenezer Lovett in Victoria started the Australian Aborigines League. It sent a much-publicized petition to King George V in England, calling for "special electorates for Aborigines to be established in the federal parliament."[4] The petition never reached the king. That same year they proposed "a national department of native affairs."[5]

In 1937 Aboriginal leaders in New South Wales formed the Aborigines Progressive Association. Some of the reforms they sought were changes in the Protection Board: better living conditions on the Board's reserves and "the reconstruction of the board so that Aboriginal people comprised half the membership."[6] The next year, when Australia celebrated its sesquicentenary (150 years since European settlement) these two organizations came together to sponsor a "Day of Mourning." Their press conference outside Australia Hall in Sydney brought them widespread newspaper coverage.[7]

Six • A Place in Two Cultures

Leaflets advertising a meeting to follow stipulated that "Aborigines and persons of Aboriginal blood only are invited to attend the conference to be held inside." At that gathering leader John Patten read a resolution: "We, representing the Aborigines of Australia ... on the 150th anniversary of the whitemen's seizure of our country, hereby make protest against the callous treatment of our people ... and we appeal to the Australian nation of today ... for full citizen status and equality within the community."[8] A few months later Patten and fellow activists William Ferguson and Pearl Gibbs were part of a delegation that met with the prime minister. They presented him with a list of ten objectives, including full citizenship and civil rights for indigenous people, and control of Aboriginal affairs by the federal government.[9]

But the federal government lacked the authority to govern Aboriginal affairs. The 1901 Constitution had not given the federal government a mandate to make laws for indigenous people; by default that power remained with the former colonies, which were now states. To extend this right to the federal government would require a constitutional amendment, with more than half the nation's voters and at least four out of six states approving it. There was no movement for this amendment in the 1930s. Even if there had been, it is doubtful that it would have passed at that time.

Aboriginal advancement groups played an important historical role in building a consensus of support for such an amendment — as did later groups where blacks and whites worked together. But changes came slowly. Legislators had scant reason to listen to people who could not vote. Several decades would elapse before the basic rights that indigenous people asked for in 1938 became the law of the land.

After the second world war, the old protection policy was replaced by one stressing assimilation: the indigenous people should discard their traditional ways and live like white Australians did. But new ideas would soon enter the country and help usher in a different policy.

Except during wars and invasions people often view what happens in their own country as determined entirely by events within their borders. But similar changes may take place in several countries in roughly the same time period, not only in economic matters such as depressions and booms, but also in main currents of thought. New ideas may emerge as relevant for an age and begin spreading from border to border, in time altering the conventional wisdom of many countries.

The concept of basic universal human rights was one such idea. "All human beings are born free and equal in dignity and rights ... endowed with reason and conscience," the United Nations' "Universal Declaration on Human Rights" said in 1948. Another document said, "Everyone has the right to recognition everywhere as a person before the law."[10] The indigenous people would use this concept to their advantage in 1966.

Australia's policies towards the indigenous people started changing in the 1960s. An umbrella organization, The Federal Council for the Advancement of Indigenous People and Torres Strait Islanders (FCAATSI), played an important role for more than a decade. Founded in Brisbane in 1958, its first delegates represented churches, trade unions and Aboriginal advancement groups whose members were white; but gradually it was able to draw in several Aboriginal groups as well.[11] In retrospect, FCAATSI's most significant project was promoting a petition drafted earlier by an all–Aboriginal group — the Aboriginal Australian Fellowship of New South Wales. The petition proposed a constitutional amendment to give the federal government, as well as states, the right to pass laws and develop policies for programs that related to the indigenous people.[12]

In some regions people strongly opposed the amendment, seeing it as a personal threat. This included Western Australia, the Northern Territory, and the outback regions of Queensland and New South Wales, which all had huge cattle or sheep stations that were owned — or more often, leased from the government — by white pastoralists. These regions also had sizable rural indigenous populations who were clamoring for land. As station operators saw Aboriginal Land Rights groups springing up, they worried that their land might be taken away from them and given to indigenous people.

Meanwhile other important changes were taking place. In 1960 the old Protection legislation was dismantled in every state and indigenous people became citizens, making them eligible for the same social service benefits as other Australians. In 1962 they were given the vote. But despite these victories, indigenous people felt frustrated at how little their lives improved. They believed that without land reform and better economic opportunities, little would change. Feeling stalemated in Australia, indigenous people looked outside for support. They forged ties with other indigenous peoples and got practical advice from activist Native Americans and New Zealand Maoris on strategies for obtaining land rights. But their trump card then was the United Nations and its Declaration of Human Rights.

In September, 1966, the Northern Territory Aboriginal Rights Council sent a petition to the Secretary General of the United Nations claiming that their human rights were being denied. "After years of degradation and inferiority, we have been granted citizenship and the right to vote," the petition said in part. "But this equality is only on paper until we have equal pay for equal work, proper housing, education and training and some control at least over our sacred tribal areas."[13]

Unlike the earlier petition to King George V, this one did reach the Secretary General. When the United Nations sent investigators and found validity in some complaints, the petition became an embarrassment to the Australian government. The following year in May, 1967, the government placed on the ballot a referendum for a constitutional amendment that would enable the federal government to make laws for indigenous people. It also proposed that indigenous people be counted in the national census. The measure passed overwhelmingly with more than 90 percent of the electorate voting for it.[14] The outcome of the referendum gave a boost to another movement that had been growing for years—the indigenous people's claim to their ancestral lands.

By the 1940s Aboriginal stockmen on cattle stations were paid wages, but they were about a fifth of what white workers received for similar work.[15] Their main pay was still a shack to live in and basic food rations in return for full-time work. During the second world war many indigenous people worked for the military in Darwin or served in the army, an experience that showed them how other people lived and were treated. After the war they chafed under the old system.

In 1946 stockmen from 25 stations went on strike in the Pilbarra region of Western Australia; they demanded higher wages and better living conditions. When a policeman told one of their leaders: "Your boss is a good man; you should go back to work," he replied, "If he's so good, then you work for him."[16] The organizer was an Aboriginal, Dooley Bin Bin, but because a white man, Don McLeod, was also involved, newspapers in the region portrayed the strike as led by a militant communist agitator who was inciting the otherwise contented natives to revolt. The Pilbarra strike continued in one form or another for twenty years. A few indigenous people returned to the stations but most did not. In time some formed Aboriginal communities in the region and looked for other ways to earn a living.

In the Northern Territory during the 1960s, the legislature passed an equal pay for equal work ordinance, which meant that Aboriginal stockmen must receive the same wages as white workers. Station owners appealed and got a three-year delay to help them make the transition. When that period was up many pastoralists fired their indigenous workers. The cattle industry had been built on the cheap labor of indigenous people. At a time when Australian beef was facing competition from other countries, few ranchers were ready to pay standard wages to their Aboriginal stockmen. If the law made such pay increases mandatory, they would do without them. Station owners did what we now call downsizing, revamping their operations and bringing in labor-saving devices that would enable them to run their operations with fewer workers.

Little information about this situation seems to have reached people in the populous southeast. A friend in Sydney who had emigrated from Europe felt empathy for the indigenous people, but he had one reservation: "It's too bad that many Aboriginal stockmen quit their jobs because it was so easy to get on welfare" he said. "They were excellent stockmen; they should have stayed on the job." His information apparently came from his neighbors.

In fact there were widespread evictions of indigenous people whose families had lived and worked on stations for generations. As one cattle drover in the area recalled: "Those station managers just came out and said, 'We can't afford to pay you the basic wage, and we can't afford to keep feeding you. The Welfare mob have a lot of money for you to live on in the town. So pack up your camp and start walking.'"[17]

In the small towns they moved into, there were few jobs and when openings did occur, employers typically favored whites over blacks. Large numbers of displaced indigenous people lived permanently on welfare. The rash of problems seen among the poorest indigenous people with no way to make a living and time on their hands—alcoholism, domestic violence, brushes with the law, and poor health—increased after the evictions. Many became despondent, seeing no way out. But some others were determined to change the situation for themselves and their people. They became political activists.

The failure of the equal pay law that would have increased the wages of Aboriginal stockmen had an unforeseen side effect. It gave a new burst of life to the land reform movement. In 1966 workers from the Gurindji people went on strike at Wave Hill Station, a large cattle station owned by an English lord.[18] Initially these Aboriginal workers in the Northern Territory were protesting the three-year delay in pay raises. But as the strike continued for years, their leaders realized that their chances of receiving the same wages as white workers were nil. They began calling instead for the return of their traditional lands so they could operate their own cattle stations.

The strike attracted widespread publicity and helped build support for Aboriginal land rights. When the Labor Party came to power in late 1972 the new prime minister, Gough Whitlam, appointed a commission to study the feasibility of land grants for indigenous people. After their investigation the commission recommended grants in the form of land trusts to specific indigenous groups who would manage their lands collectively. It also suggested that two Land Councils with strong Aboriginal representation be set up in the Northern Territory to help evaluate and administer the grants. Out of these recommendations came a proposal for an Aboriginal Land Rights Act for the Northern Territory.[19]

Before the Whitlam government could pass this act, however, the governor general suddenly fired the prime minister and dissolved Parliament

Six • A Place in Two Cultures

in November, 1975 (for details about the firing and dissolution, see the early pages of Chapter Eleven). When new elections were held, a Liberal-Country Party coalition came to power and Malcolm Fraser, a moderate Liberal, became prime minister. Many expected the Land Rights Act to be scrapped, but it was not. Although some provisions were watered down, the law passed at the end of 1976, incorporating many of the commission's recommendations.[20] After the law passed, land claim settlements in the Northern Territory became more frequent. In 1978 the Walbiri and Kartanangaruru-Kurintji were granted land south of the Wave Hill area. In 1983 the Gurindji were given title to a substantial part of their tribal lands; they set up their own cattle business as a communal enterprise.[21]

For the Anangu of Central Australia, the large monolithic rock structures of Uluru and Kata Tjuta were their most sacred religious sites. (During the colonial period they were called Ayres Rock and the Olgas.) But the

The 1985 Handover/Leaseback ceremony of Uluru and Kata Tjuta (once called Ayres Rock and the Olgas) National Park in the Northern Territory. The government gave title deeds to the park to the Anangu, who accepted on behalf of all indigenous peoples of the region, then leased it back to the National Parks and Wildlife Service for 99 years (by permission of the National Library of Australia).

Anangu were denied claim to these sites because they were in a national park. Then a practical solution was worked out. The Anangu and other indigenous peoples of the region were given title to the area in 1985; they in turn leased it back to the National Parks Service for 99 years, with some restrictions on its use to protect their religious sites. The old tourist town near Uluru was given to the Anangu as a community settlement, while a new tourist enclave, Yulara, was built some 18 miles away, complete with luxury hotels and a visitors' center. This has enabled the tourist industry to thrive, providing a living for many black and white Australians in the region.

Much activity for Aboriginal land rights centered in the northwest. But the case that overturned two hundred years of legal precedents came from an obscure island off the mainland that few Australians had ever heard of.

Eddie Mabo of the Meriam people came from one of a group of small islands in the Torres Strait, located between the northeastern tip of Australia and Papua New Guinea. These islands, annexed by Queensland in 1879, are now part of that state. The indigenous people there are called Torres Strait Islanders because they come from a different ethnic stock than mainland indigenous people.

In 1982 Mabo and four other Torres Strait Islanders applied to the courts for confirmation of their traditional land rights. Murray Island where they lived "had been continuously inhabited and exclusively possessed by the Meriam people who lived in permanent communities within their own social and political organization," their suit argued; therefore they claimed jurisdiction over the land. The High Court agreed. In June, 1992, it ruled in their favor, six to one: "the lands of this continent were not *terra nullius* or 'practically unoccupied' in 1788," the justices concluded. The Meriam people were entitled to "possession, use, and enjoyment of the lands of Murray Island."[22]

This landmark decision caused celebration in some quarters and panic in others. At first people phoned talk-show hosts to voice their fears that now any Aborigine could appear on their doorstep and claim their backyard. Wild rumors spread, such as a story that the indigenous people planned to reclaim downtown Brisbane, the capital of Queensland.

The government published a pamphlet to counteract some of the most egregious falsehoods. It explained that Mabo applied only to peoples who had continuously occupied their traditional lands for hundreds or thousands of years. Land already purchased or occupied by non-indigenous people — whether pastoralists, businesses, governments, or individuals—could not be claimed under Mabo.[23] The decision would affect so few indigenous people, in fact, that the 1993 Native Title Act (passed to implement Mabo) had a Land Fund provision to help Aboriginal peoples that did not qualify under Mabo to buy land for their communities.

In Western Australia, where desert outback regions were found to contain vast mineral wealth, the Mabo decision led to fierce legal battles over ownership of such land. In Perth in 1994, for example, Western Australia sued the federal government over the validity of the Native Title Act, while the feds sued the state over legislation it had recently passed interpreting and modifying the Act's intent. The High Court later rejected the state's suit, 7–0.[24]

Land reform became the major issue for indigenous people in the final decades of the century. But it was not the only one. The effects of another former policy still rankled its victims and called out for restitution — the practice of kidnapping indigenous children to remove them from parental influence. These children have been called the Stolen Generations.

For their own good, Protection authorities had believed, Aboriginal children must be separated from their parents and their "primitive" society. This was their only chance to have a decent life and become productive Australian citizens. As we saw in Chapter Five, the practice was most common for children of mixed parentage, but any indigenous children could be taken if the authorities deemed their parents unfit. The term Protection was changed to Welfare in the 1940s. By then instead of taking children to mission schools or orphanages, usually they were placed in white foster homes or adopted by white families.

Archie Roach was one of those taken. In the late 1950s, when Archie was three, welfare officials and a policeman arrived at the small house where he lived with his parents and older siblings. The officials put him and two sisters into their car, told them they were going on a picnic, and drove away. He never saw his parents again. Roach was placed with a series of white foster parents but didn't find a compatible one until he was nine and went to live with a Scottish immigrant couple, the Coxes, and their children. They became his family.

Then a schoolmate asked, "How come your parents are white?" It set him thinking. A few years later his sister Myrtle, who had managed to trace his whereabouts, wrote to say that their mother had died. As journalist Wayne Cooley recounts: "He vaguely remembered Myrtle but who was his mother? ... In the space of a year or so, Archie Roach changed from being a suburban North Strathmore teenager to a young man fighting for survival on the streets of Melbourne." There he met and married Ruby, who had also been taken from her parents. For a while they were alcoholics but after they started a family and Ruby saw how their drinking affected the children, she insisted that they stop. They went through a recovery program and stopped drinking.

Over the years Roach wrote songs and sang in cafés; he built up a following in Melbourne. His song "Took the Children Away" hit a chord of recognition. When he was interviewed on a local radio station about the song and its origin, "the station switchboard lit up." Today Archie Roach is a well-known songwriter and performer in Australia. He is close to his Aboriginal relatives, whom he first met as an adult, but also is in touch with the daughter of the white foster family that he lived with as a child.[25]

The abduction of indigenous children ended in the late 1960s. But the quest to stamp out all vestiges of Aboriginal culture continued in many places. Deana Vlam, who had emigrated to Australia from the Netherlands with her parents as a child, saw this policy first hand when she was 19 years old and worked on an Aboriginal reserve as a hospital aide. "We were all trying to make white people out of them," Vlam told researcher Maryon Allbrook. "You know — the tablecloth and the vase of flowers and three meals a day while sitting around a table. If they did that, then they were 'good people.' I thought the reserves were a terrible disgrace and I felt embarrassed as a white person working there."[26] A 1975 newspaper cartoon expressed a similar sentiment: it showed a white man slathering white paint over an Aboriginal man. The caption read: "Old White Man Ceremony called Assimilation."[27]

The child-snatchings stopped but tens of thousands of indigenous people who had been kidnapped did not know who their people were. In 1980 two indigenous people who themselves had been taken away, Coral Edwards and Peter Read, formed Link-up, an organization "to reunite Aboriginal adults who had been fostered, adopted, or institutionalized as children." All staff members at Link-up had been taken from their parents.

In their book *The Lost Children*, Edwards and Read told the stories of thirteen kidnapped Aboriginal children who made contact with their biological families as adults through help from Link-up. Some of the oldest ones had been placed in orphanages at birth even though their parents were living. The youngest had been abducted and turned over to white families. They all felt the need to learn about their Aboriginal roots.[28]

Over the past few decades the indigenous population has increased steadily. In 1911 it was estimated at 93,000, but by 2001 there were 406,180 indigenous people and they made up a little more than two percent of the nation's people. The increase was partly due to better living conditions and health care, but it also reflected growing numbers of people of mixed parentage who chose to identify as indigenous people.

Peter Smith was one of them. The son of an Aboriginal mother and white father, Smith never thought about his ethnic identity while growing up in a country town in Queensland. His mother didn't talk about her childhood and she died when he was in his twenties. Decades later, Smith related, while on a field trip for his work he met an elderly Aboriginal woman who looked vaguely familiar. She began questioning him about his mother.

The woman turned out to be Smith's aunt, his mother's youngest sister. She told him that the Protection authorities had taken his mother away when she was a teenager. The family never saw her again. Piecing together his mother's history, Smith learned that she had been taken to another town and placed with a family as a maid. In that town she met and married a sailor from Liverpool who had jumped ship in Australia — Smith's father.

Meeting his aunt gave Smith an entree into his lost Aboriginal family and culture. He felt at home among them. And learning what had been done to his mother made him angry. He started identifying as an indigenous person and became interested in his people's history and culture. During the 1988 Bicentennial he marched in an Aboriginal protest in Brisbane, carrying a sign that said, "White Australia has a Black History."

Smith seemed to feel at home in both cultures. His wife was white and they had nine children. He lived in a small mining town and worked for the Electoral Commission, visiting indigenous communities in the region to inform residents of current issues and the voting process.[29]

Children of mixed parentage are obviously of two cultures. But in another sense so are all Australian indigenous people today. For the most part they identify with their heritage and want to preserve their culture. But they are also Australians of the twenty-first century who want the same fair go as other citizens. And they want a role in their country's political process.

John "Sandy" Atkinson, of Yorta Yorta descent, is an Aborigine who has found a place in the two cultures. From his office at the state library in Melbourne, he heads the Koorie Oral History project. Much of his time these days is spent in the field with a video camera, recording the stories and memories of elderly indigenous people in Victoria. But his interests and experience are not confined to oral history. After working as a sheep shearer and truck driver in his youth, Atkinson became active in promoting community services for his people: legal aid, housing, health care, and childcare. In 1975 he designed and set up Sheppardton Keeping Place, "the first major Aboriginal-owned and managed museum." This interest led him on a new career path that has included membership on Aboriginal Arts Boards, the Australia Council, and a UNESCO subcommittee advising the state government on archaeology and Aboriginal relics.[30]

Atkinson emphasized the need for all Australians to learn more about Aboriginal history. He recounted the years when he set up museum displays and conducted tours; if he started telling about a massacre, "people would walk away and you'd end up talking to yourself. They couldn't handle it. In the US you've faced up to your past, you've made films about massacres of Indians and blacks. The truth can't hurt you."

He was equally outspoken in his views on the larger society. "They're scared of change," he said of Australians who favor retaining the British monarch as head of state. "They still want to be the kids of the Poms [slang for the English] instead of growing up and being themselves."

Atkinson saw the Mabo land decision as a watershed: "Mabo has brought a sense of responsibility to us. It means we've all got to play some role even if it's only to stand up and be counted as indigenous people."[31]

Extending a fair go to indigenous people has not been easy. As Aboriginal leader Lowitja O'Donoghue explained the situation: "Our people are imprisoned by poverty, poor education, and appalling health conditions. Their infant mortality rate is three times higher and their life expectancy 15 to 20 years less than other Australians. Their unemployment rate is four times the national average, their income level is about half, and they are 27 times more likely to be arrested than other citizens."[32]

Indigenous people remain the most disadvantaged group in the country. But from 1973 through 1995, the country and the indigenous people took some giant steps forward to improve this bleak picture.

When the federal government set up the Department of Aboriginal Affairs in 1972, it hired indigenous people as part of the staff and named indigenous people to boards and commissions. This reflected the new policy of self-determination, that is, indigenous people should be involved in the decisions that affected their people's lives. In 1980 the government set up the Aboriginal Development Commission "to acquire land for Aboriginal communities and to make loans and grants available for housing, and for business enterprises."[33] These two agencies merged in 1990 to become the Aboriginal and Torres Strait Islander Commission, or ATSIC, as it is popularly known.[34]

ATSIC functions at community, regional, and national levels. With the country divided into 36 regions, indigenous people elect a chairperson for their region every three years and a councilor for their local community. They help "draw up and carry out regional plans for improving the social, economic, and cultural life" of indigenous people in their region.[35] At the national level an ATSIC Commission with representatives elected from seventeen zones meets in Canberra a few times a year to help administer federal programs for indigenous people in areas such as employment, community services, health and community development, commercial (land acquisition and business enterprises) issues, and social justice, including legal aid.

Lowitja O'Donoghue was the Commission's first chair. She became politicized as a young woman "after being refused entry, as an Aboriginal, to the Royal Adelaide Hospital to complete her nursing studies." O'Donoghue later became that hospital's first Aboriginal nurse trainee in 1954.[36] She went on to work in health care, welfare, and Aboriginal administration. A low-key, effective leader, she helped guide ATSIC through its first six years and has represented the Aborigines at international meetings of indigenous peoples.

Like the American anti-poverty programs of the 1960s, the scope of ATSIC has made it controversial. Some say it was long overdue; others see it as a huge bureaucracy that has not solved basic problems of poverty. "ATSIC is not perfect," a booklet explaining its operations pointed out. "It cannot be expected to redress two centuries of neglect in a few short years."[37] But during the 1990s ATSIC helped bring health clinics, education, employment opportunities, and other services to indigenous people across Australia.

Racial prejudice has been one barrier standing in the way of change. In an effort to heal the historic rift between blacks and whites,

Indigenous Leader Lowitja O'Donoghue in 1984 when she was named Australian of the Year. A nurse, she had worked in health care, welfare and administration. In 1990 O'Donoghue became the first Chair of the Aboriginal and Torres Strait Islander Commission, or ATSIC, a new federal program that gave indigenous people a direct role in setting up and administering programs in education, health and jobs for their people (by permission of the National Library of Australia).

Australia formed the Council for Aboriginal Reconciliation (CAR), bringing representatives from the two groups together to better understand each other and try to resolve their differences. Established by a unanimous act of Parliament in 1991, the Council had fourteen Aboriginal members and eleven "representing the wider community," that is, non-indigenous people. On both sides they included high-level leaders who have worked for better conditions for indigenous people and also representatives from relevant groups such as ATSIC and Aboriginal Land Councils, along with the Council for Trade Unions, the Farmers' Federation, and the Mining Industry Council.[38]

After the Mabo land decision, the Council's Mining Committee became one of its most active sections. Its 1993 publication *Exploring for Common Ground* set out strategies for reaching mining settlements on Aboriginal lands that were agreeable to both sides.[39] These strategies have been used in several successful agreements worked out between Aboriginal communities and mining companies. Galarrwuy Yunupingi, who headed the Aboriginal Land Council of the Northern Territory in the 1990s, said the Mining Committee's meetings were "a chance for Aboriginal people like us to go inside the boardrooms of the big companies and to hear what they are thinking and what they are understanding. If we don't sit down and talk these issues through in confidence, we will never come to a proper relationship."[40]

The Council saw education as one way to lessen prejudice. In partnership with ATSIC it published booklets suitable for classroom use that described the culture and history of the indigenous people in every state and in the Northern Territory. ATSIC also helped fund the two volume *Encyclopaedia of Aboriginal Australia,* published in 1994. This work contains myriad facts, history, and information about the indigenous people, a lot of it hard to track down elsewhere, that most Australians (including indigenous people) don't know. For example, it is commonly believed in Australia that the 1967 referendum made indigenous people citizens and gave them the vote; in fact, as this chapter described earlier, they became citizens in 1960 and got the vote in 1962. Passage of the 1967 referendum meant that the indigenous people were counted in the national census for the first time. More important the measure empowered the federal government, as well as the states, to pass legislation pertaining to the indigenous people.

At the ATSIC library in Canberra, the librarian was using an online version of the encyclopedia as she helped an Aboriginal couple. They were urban indigenous people who had come there to learn more about their heritage. Where do most indigenous people live? The general perception, in Australia and abroad, is that they live mainly in the bush in small, remote enclaves in the northwest. This belief is wrong on all counts. Less than a third of indigenous people live in rural areas anymore. Forty-one percent live in medium-size cities or in towns, and twenty-seven percent live in large urban areas.[41] Nor do most indigenous people live in the western half of the country.

Part of this misconception may come from looking at state and territory percentages instead of at the numbers themselves. For example, 27 percent of the Northern Territory population are indigenous Aborigines and 70 percent of them do live in small remote communities, especially in Arnhem Land, a large reserve for indigenous people. But the entire Northern Territory had only 188,078 people in 2001. Of these, 50,845 were indigenous

Six • A Place in Two Cultures

Aboriginal boys who live in a public housing estate in Melbourne. The general perception is that most indigenous people live in remote outback regions. In fact, two-thirds of Australia's indigenous people live in towns or cities (*Centre for Immigration and Multicultural Studies*, photograph by Elizabeth Gilliam).

Aborigines.[42] By contrast, New South Wales, the most populous state, had 6,326,569 people that year. Indigenous people made up only 1.9 percent of the state's population but they numbered 120,047. More than half of all indigenous people in Australia live in two states: Queensland and New South Wales.[43]

Perhaps another reason why people think the indigenous people still live mainly in remote bush areas relates to a fascination with their ancient culture. The indigenous people of Australia have the oldest continuous culture on earth so the intense interest in their past is not surprising.[44] But taken to extremes this leads to a view of indigenous people as museum relics that should be preserved in their original state for anthropologists and others to study. Of the many dozens of photographs of indigenous people seen while researching this book, most were taken in remote outback areas, often in the Northern Territory, and showed scantly clad indigenous people sitting on the ground holding spears or gathering food the way their ancestors did. The word "mysterious" was sometimes used to describe them.

Fascination with Aboriginal culture alone, however, cannot explain the extent to which many people dwell on their past. It may also reflect a modern version of Rousseau's "Noble Savage" theory. As in Rousseau's day, people in urban areas throughout the world who yearn for simpler, more satisfying lives and greater spirituality may project their dreams of such an existence onto the Australian Aborigines.

In the Aborigine section of bookstores in Australia, books describing aspects of their traditional cultures predominated, so one about the careers of living indigenous people stood out. The author was himself an indigenous person. *My Kind of People: Achievement, Identity and Aboriginality*, by journalist Wayne Coolwell, profiled a school principal, professional football player, educator, doctor, land rights advocate, two television broadcaster-journalists, and five indigenous people in the arts: painter, actor, opera singer, dancer, and singer-songwriter.[45]

The land rights activist Noel Pearson grew up in the small Aboriginal community of Hopevale on Cape York Peninsula in northern Queensland. After graduating from the University of Sydney, Pearson returned to Hopevale; his familiarity with both indigenous and mainstream Australian culture helped make him an effective land rights negotiator, says Coolwell.[46]

Pearson earned a law degree in the 1990s and switched his focus to finding ways for young indigenous people in rural communities to avoid substance abuse and support themselves without welfare. He helped set up partnerships with a few corporations to start a furniture factory, an art center and a tourism venture that would create jobs locally. This brought him kudos from the state and federal governments. But in time Pearson clashed with some indigenous leaders in other parts of the country because he presented his programs as the only way to go and criticized other approaches.

One issue of contention was the treatment of "dysfunctional" indigenous families who spent their money on drink and didn't send their children to school. If parents refused to change, the government in the early 2000s believed, their welfare money should be cut off—and Pearson accepted the policy for a time. But Aboriginal elder Lowitja O'Donoghue and several others thought this was unfair to children. If parents did not send their children to school, she suggested, "the approach should be one of individual case management by education departments, as it would be if the family was white."[47]

Many Aboriginal leaders see education as a way to improve their people's lives. Every state has special programs for indigenous students but they differ in what they offer. A few programs on the west coast give a sampling. At Curtin University in Perth, the Centre for Aboriginal and Torres Strait Islander Studies offers degrees in two fields: community management and health services. The Centre concentrates on training students from traditional (rural) communities to be more effective back home. A student must have a job in the community, either paid or voluntary, and a year or two of work experience to be accepted. Some classes are held on the Curtin campus, but students' main training is on the job, supervised by their employers and by Centre faculty who visit them regularly. [48]

In Darwin, the Centre for Aboriginal and Islander Studies at Northern Territory University offers a diverse program, from teaching English to students who speak only Aboriginal languages to preparing others for professional training. Director Isaac Brown sees the Centre as an enabling program: "Say a student who dropped out of high school now wants to become a lawyer. He can take the courses here he needs to catch up and then enter law school."[49] The Centre also has several branches in smaller towns, he said, teaching everything from the basics to courses in eco-tourism.

Sixty miles south of Darwin, Batchelor College, a small college for indigenous students, attracts Aborigines from rural areas who may feel uncomfortable at universities. Students on the Batchelor campus can, if they like, bring their children and spouse with them. This option gradually developed, said the college's information officer Eric van Dissel, after the staff found that some students from traditional communities did better if they were not separated from their families.[50] But most course work is done close to home at branches in Alice Springs, Darwin, Nhulunbuy, Katherine, and Tennant Creek as well as several one-room operations in Arnhem Land. The college offers certificates and degrees in education, health, community work, languages and linguistics, community management and office practices, technical studies, women's issues, broadcasting and journalism, alcohol and drug studies, environmental sciences, arts and crafts, and recreation and youth work.

As a result of educational programs across the country, more indigenous people are earning degrees in their field of interest. They have become teachers, professors, librarians, doctors, nurses, social workers, engineers, lawyers, ministers, administrators, businesspeople and more. They work in law enforcement, health care, technology, the media, the arts, and numerous other areas. The numbers in the professions are still small but they are growing.

Sandra Eades is one such professional. After graduating from high school in Perth, Eades won a scholarship to Newcastle University on the east coast and went through medical school there.[51] When Coolwell interviewed her she was a staff doctor at Perth Aboriginal Medical Service. She told him she was chagrined when people assumed that because she succeeded she must be part white. "But my parents and grandparents are all Aboriginal."[52]

Indigenous people have a different history from all others in the country. But they share some experiences with another group of Australians. These are the immigrants who were neither British nor Irish. Like the indigenous Aborigines, they once were urged to behave as if they had been born and bred in England. They too resisted and ultimately put their mark on the country. Their story takes us back more than 170 years, when they started coming.

Seven

Immigrants and "White Australia"

News of an unfilled continent spread fast. By the 1830s people from Continental Europe were starting to arrive. So were a scattering of Asians. As long as their numbers remained small all were absorbed quietly into the vast land. But that scenario ended with the discovery of gold in 1851. A man named Hargraves set off the rush that followed.

Edward Hargraves had lived on three continents by the time he was 33 but fortune eluded him. The move from his native England to Australia failed to make him rich, so on hearing the words "gold" and "California" in 1849 he boarded a ship to San Francisco and spent two years panning for gold.[1] He never found any. But what he saw there would change the dynamics of Australian history.

Hargraves noticed that the hills of California's gold fields looked a lot like land he remembered outside of Bathurst in the Blue Mountain region. Returning to Australia in 1851, he went there and found gold.[2] His discovery set off an epidemic of gold fever. Eight months later larger gold deposits were discovered in Ballarat and Bendigo, towns within 80 miles of Melbourne. By the middle of 1852 these two fields were shipping out half a ton of gold a week, unearthed by some fifty thousand fortune-seekers.

People poured in from around the globe, including China, nearly tripling Australia's population in ten years. The colony of Victoria, where Melbourne, Bendigo and Ballarat were located, grew by more than 600 percent in that period.[3] With so many people at work, the surface gold was gone in less than a decade. Miners moved on to the cities in search of jobs. At first there was plenty of work, but by the 1880s the gold boom had subsided and Australia also felt the effects of a worldwide recession. The unemployed looked for someone to blame. In Australia as in California, they fastened on the same culprit—the Chinese.

A newspaper article of the 1880s shows the fears that beset the populace: "The Chinese question never fails," the Melbourne *Argus* reported. "At every meeting somebody in the hall has a word to say about it, and visions of countless millions of the barbarians sweeping upon the colony in a solid body rises on the mental horizons of every man present."[4]

Such fears helped fuel the restrictions on immigration that became known as the "White Australia" policy. This chapter looks at the development and practice of that policy and its effects on the Chinese. But it tells of other immigrants as well. Some sought religious freedom. The colony of South Australia took them in.

South Australia differed from the other five colonies in two respects: its 1834 charter prohibited convict labor and it specified religious freedom. In Prussia, after the king decreed that only the prayer book he favored could be used in services, dissenters there began to flee. By 1836 entire congregations of German Lutherans were arriving at Adelaide with their pastors. Most initially settled in surrounding rural areas such as the Barossa Valley; in time they built several towns and a wine industry.[5] Polish dissenters also came as did many Britons who belonged to Methodist, Unitarian, Congregationalist, Baptist or other non–Anglican sects.[6] By 1869 there were 568 churches and chapels in the colony. Adelaide, its capital, became known as "the city of churches." It also had a Jewish synagogue by then.[7]

By mid-century, Germans and other Europeans were emigrating for political reasons as well. But the largest numbers of immigrants were poor people in search of a better life. Groups that came to South Australia during the nineteenth century included Cornish, Welsh, Lebanese, Afghans, Polish, Irish, Germans, Wends (Sorbs from northeast Germany), Scots, South Americans, Italians, Scandinavians, Chinese, Jews and Quakers.[8]

The discovery of copper in South Australia in the late 1830s and early 1840s caused a "major influx" of Cornish miners to emigrate there.[9] Likewise the copper mines attracted many miners and smelter men from Wales.[10] In Ireland a devastating potato famine in the mid–1840s caused the poor there to emigrate in increased numbers. In the Scottish highlands, subsistence weavers and farmers, called "crofters," whose families had lived on the same land for generations, found themselves displaced by effects of the Industrial Revolution. As the growth of new textile mills increased the demand for wool, their landlords, finding that sheep were now more profitable than people, carried out large-scale evictions of their tenants and replaced them with flocks of sheep. Some crofters displaced by these "Highland Clearances" obtained assisted passage to Australia. These immigrants from rural areas of Scotland, Ireland, Wales and Cornwall had little in common with the English, not even language; often they spoke only a Gaelic tongue.

Seven • Immigrants and "White Australia"   99

Small numbers of immigrants from countries in Asia and the Middle East came out during the nineteenth century. Men from the Philippines and from what are now Indonesia and Malaysia dove for pearls in the northwestern coastal towns of Broome and Port Hedland. Chinese settlers in the east coast settlements of Port Douglas and Cairns fished for *trepang* (sea cucumbers), the delicacy prized, when dried, by the Chinese. Lebanese men came to Port Pirie in South Australia in the 1880s to work in the iron smelters. Many saved up money and went into business for themselves as peddlers (hawkers) or proprietors of small stores. As they prospered they sent for their families. Most of these early Lebanese were Christians such as Orthodox or Maronite.

Camels were initially brought to Australia in 1860 for use in the Burke and Wills expedition into the unknown interior. Six years later Thomas Elder, a wealthy sheep-raiser from Scotland, saw the potential of camels for commercial cartage. He imported 124 camels, and 46 "cameleers" to look after them, for Beltana, his sheep station in South Australia. These workers, who came from Afghanistan, India, and present Pakistan — and became known as "Afghans"— were predominantly Muslim.[11] They built the first mosque, a small building of mud and twigs, in the country at Beltana. When Elder's

Afghans loading camels in Western Australia in 1900. Starting in the 1860s some sheep station owners began bringing out camels, along with "cameleers" from Afghanistan, India and present Pakistan to take care of the animals. Camel caravans transported loads through outback regions with no roads for four decades. The cameleers, called "Afghans," were some of the first Muslims in Australia. Their descendants live there (courtesy Battye Library, image No. 005632D [7586B]).

camel caravans proved a convenient method for transporting goods through dry regions, other station owners began importing camels and cameleers.

For fifty years, or until good roads and eventually trucks made camels obsolete, these caravans carried wool and other products to railheads and ports in western and central Australia. In time some cameleers became merchants who "established a commercial cartage industry.... Camels were bred in Australia and merchants periodically sailed to Karachi to recruit men and purchase more camels."[12] The Afghans, who for some years lived in small enclaves near freight depots called "Ghan" towns, practiced their traditional culture and religion, building small mosques along their trade routes. Coming without wives in the early days, many married local women — often widows or women whose husbands had deserted them. The wives usually converted to Islam so their children were raised as Muslims.[13]

Successful cameleers helped finance the large mosques that were built in Adelaide in the early 1890s and in Perth in 1905. After the camel caravans ended, most Afghans moved to cities or towns. The train that still runs from Adelaide to Alice Springs initially went along old camel routes in parts of the outback; known as "The Ghan," the train's cars have a camel logo on them, commemorating the earlier era.

These were some of the immigrants who came out in the nineteenth century, and whose descendants remained in Australia. But their numbers pale in comparison with those who came in search of gold. Melbourne was the key city.

"Gold made Melbourne," said Anthony Trollope and history bears him out.[14] As the port city for the gold rush towns of Bendigo and Ballarat, it soon burgeoned with wealth and population. For several decades "Marvelous Melbourne" as it was known in its heyday was larger and more important than Sydney. To this day the two cities are keen rivals. Sydney's population is a little larger, but people in Melbourne believe their city is ahead culturally.

Melbourne has much in common with another city that was made by gold — San Francisco. Although poles apart in their physical attributes, both developed an ethnic mix in the 1850s which produced a lasting diversity. The two cities shared another characteristic as well — a layer of educated, affluent immigrants from Europe who came out in part for political reasons.

Revolutionary movements had erupted across Western Europe in the 1840s, culminating in the revolts of 1848. These revolts were brutally suppressed but the iron regimes that clamped down, and the disaffected who seethed at their treatment, caused political and economic uncertainty. There was also persecution of minority groups including Jews. These circumstances caused people who ordinarily would have stayed home to leave their native lands. New York was the most popular destination, but publicity about San

Francisco and Melbourne during their gold rushes led some to settle in those cities.

In both gold rush cities, these immigrants increased the small core of upper-echelon citizens who were already there. Thus by the mid–1850s Melbourne and San Francisco both had a number of residents who arrived with capital instead of in search of it. Or, if not wealthy, they had enough know-how and self-confidence to make money swiftly in a booming economy.

For the most part these immigrants did not spend much time panning for gold. Instead they supplied miners with provisions and services, built businesses in the city, or practiced their professions. When they prospered they helped establish the cultural and recreational amenities they had enjoyed at home: theaters, opera houses, museums, libraries, parks, botanical gardens, zoos, and swimming pools. Melbourne residents gave large sections of city land for its Botanic Gardens, while San Franciscans turned its sand dunes into Golden Gate Park. Melbourne had the first zoo and opera house in Australia; San Francisco was the first city in the western United States with these facilities.

In Australia effects of the gold rush swelled Sydney, Adelaide, and Brisbane as well. Reports of booming cities and good jobs brought emigrants to all of them. A letter in the Caernarfon *Herald* in 1856 is typical: William Jones, a young Welshman who had gone out to digs and then settled in Melbourne assured his countrymen that "there is no fear of overdoing this country for hundreds of years to come, the place is so vast and extensive, and the wealth so proverbial, exceeding that of every other known part of the universe. I would recommend every labouring man to emigrate here, as he will find abundance of employment. No person who will work need be afraid to come."[15]

Jones knew nothing of the recession of the early 1840s when working men in Australian cities became destitute for lack of jobs; nor could he anticipate the severe recession that would engulf the country a few decades later. He looked around during the best of times, assumed this was the norm, and expected it to continue forever. Descriptions like his helped fill up ships bound for Australia. But not all growth was a spinoff of the gold rush.

Queensland became the center of a thriving sugar industry after cane fields were planted near its coast in the 1850s. The Colonial Sugar Refining Company emerged as the giant, but there were smaller growers as well. They soon experienced that familiar bugaboo, a labor shortage. Convict labor was gone, the Aborigines would not submit to the rigors of the plantation system, Europeans demanded high wages—if one could get them at all—and the British Parliament had outlawed slavery in its colonies in 1833.

Growers found a solution by importing Melanesian and Polynesian workers from islands of the South Pacific, a group of people who came to be known as the "Kanakas." At first the Kanakas were brought in by "blackbirding":

plantation owners sent boats to these islands, and the crew invited young men to come aboard and see the wonders of their ship. Once several Kanakas had been lured below deck, the hatches were fastened and the ship took off for Queensland. In other words, these men were kidnapped.[16]

Arriving in Queensland, the young men learned that they were indentured on a sugar cane plantation for three years, meaning they could not quit during that period, regardless of conditions there. After word of such practices reached the islands they came from, recruiters changed their tactics. They came to the islands with glowing pictures of high wages and ideal working conditions. Once the Kanakas signed up for a stint, they had no recourse when they arrived in Queensland and found low wages and grueling working conditions under overseers who sometimes carried guns. As historian Clive Moore points out, "coming from more than seventy different islands of the southwest Pacific, speaking numerous languages, and having no sense of unity other than that imposed upon them by the regime under which they worked," it was difficult for the Kanakas to organize and demand better treatment.[17]

As stories of mistreatment leaked out, Australian officials became concerned. Sugar growers began to realize that if they did not modify their practices, their supply of cheap labor might be cut off. In 1868 the Queensland legislature passed a law stipulating a minimum wage and basic standards of health, clothing and food for indentured Kanakas. In Britain, which was also receiving complaints, Parliament passed the Pacific Islanders Protection Act in 1872, which made it illegal to kidnap workers.

By the 1880s, Kanaka immigration was regulated, says historian Brij V. Lal of Australian National University.[18] Many Kanakas in Queensland renewed their indenture contracts and settled there. Some brought out wives from home, others married local women. The earliest immigrants, who were given concessions by law, started their own farms or businesses such as market gardening and boarding houses. But while Queensland was integrating the Kanakas, opposition to "colored" immigrants was growing in other colonies, with fear and animus concentrated against the Chinese.

By the 1830s, small numbers of Chinese were already in Australia, working for squatters as shepherds. In the next decade some Chinese men settled on both coasts to fish or work as pearl divers. Feelings against them began to mount during the gold rush years of the 1850s when they arrived in groups and became keen competitors of Australian diggers, and of men who came out from European countries to make their fortunes. They resented the way the Chinese worked together as a team, lived frugally, and rarely took time out to relax. From the white men's perspective the Chinese seemed determined to carry off most of the gold. These miners did not realize that the Chinese miners usually arrived laden with debt. Typically passage money for a group of clan members was advanced by a wealthy merchant at home, with the clan's holdings used as equity. Thus Chinese gold miners had their entire clan's land and honor riding on their ability to send money home regularly.[19] They could not afford to relax.

To men of European descent, the Chinese miners seemed like alien creatures with their conical hats, hair braided in long queues, loose-fitting garments and incomprehensible language. And there were so many of them. The large numbers of Chinese who came out during the gold rush years heightened fears and increased prejudice against them. There were several riots against Chinese miners at various digs. In Australia, as in California, nearly 50,000 Chinese arrived during the first years of their gold rushes. Although the majority in both places returned home, sizeable numbers remained. In the colony of Victoria, where Bendigo and Ballarat were located, the Chinese soon made up 15 percent of the male population.

Many who stayed carved out niches for themselves despite the prejudice against them. Some prospered and made contributions to their new country, as the histories of two very different Chinese immigrants illustrate. Chen Ah Kew arrived in Australia in 1853 with a group of his countrymen.[20] He was seventeen. By then the Chinese were charged a high entry tax if they docked at Melbourne, so the ship's captain followed the custom of landing at Robe, South Australia, near the border. From there the men walked a few hundred miles to their destination. The group Chen came with never went to the gold fields. Instead they walked across Victoria to Wagunyah, a small town near the border of New South Wales, where the government was building roads.

Chen's granddaughter, Elizabeth Chong, thinks they may have been indentured to the road builders. Whatever the arrangement, they arrived knowing that jobs awaited them. Gold had brought in enough money to build roads connecting major cities of the southeast; but with most men at the digs and convict labor no longer available, it was difficult to find workers, especially for the arduous job of clearing the bush. In those years road contractors were eager to hire the hardworking Chinese.

Chen soon stood out as an efficient organizer. He became a supervisor and rode long distances on horseback from one project to another. By age 23 he had a few hundred men working under him. He also arranged to bring out more workers from China. In time he anglicized his name to Jimmy Kew.

Kew made friends with John Foard, an Anglo-Australian resident of Wagunyah who owned the town's general store. Kew worked for Foard and eventually took over the store after Foard retired. In middle age the successful merchant arranged to have a Chinese bride sent out. She was 18, he was 58; they had six children in a decade. In 1901 Kew returned to China with his family and built a large house in his native village.

Another immigrant, Mei Quong Tart, became the best-known Chinese Australian of the century.[21] Son of a prosperous Chinese merchant, Tart was nine years old when he arrived in the small town of Braidwood with an uncle in 1859. At first he worked in the general store there and lived with its Scottish immigrant owners, the Forsythes. But a woman from a prominent Anglo-Australian family was so taken with the little Chinese boy that she insisted on carrying him home to live with her and be educated British style. As a young man Tart went home for a visit but thwarted his mother's efforts to arrange a Chinese marriage for him. Returning alone he settled in Sydney and became an importer of tea and other Chinese products. Later he married Margaret Scarlett, a school teacher from Lancashire, England. In 1889 Tart opened the Loong Shan Tea House in King Street which, along with tea, provided "moderately-priced meals and light refreshments."

Quong Tart kept a foot in western and eastern cultures. A formal photograph showed him in Mandarin robes, his wife Margaret likewise dressed in Chinese gown and cap. But he was equally comfortable in Western suits.

Quong Tart and his family in Sydney around 1900. Arriving in Australia with an uncle at age nine, Tart grew up to become an importer of Chinese tea and owner of a popular restaurant. He married Martha Scarlett, a schoolteacher from Lancashire, England. A genial, well-liked person, he was the best-known Chinese Australian of his time (Mitchell Library, State Library of New South Wales).

He had the Australian passion for sports—his activities included horseback riding, sailing, cycling, cricket, and swimming—and served as president of the Bondi Swimming Club. An enthusiast of Scottish culture, developed during his time with the Forsythes, Tart attended meetings of the Caledonian Club wearing a kilt and was said to speak English with a Scottish accent.[22] As relations between Australia and China grew strained, he was often called in to help. For the local Chinese community he wrote a petition warning that if the Chinese were barred from Australia, "the Chinese Emperor might well decide to reciprocate and withdraw the right of British residents in Canton, Shanghai, and other ports to own and operate along the coast of China." But after shipping lines in Hong Kong refused to sell Chinese people tickets to Australia, and China protested, the Australian government asked Quong Tart to explain their situation to the government of China. He obliged, causing the *North China Herald* to comment sardonically: "It would rather appear that Mr. Quong Tart has come up to present the Australian side of the question."

The good-natured Tart apparently responded to all requests but his heart seems to have been with his family and community. "He gave a charitable feast for the pensioners of the Parramatta Asylum," says his biographer Robert Travers, "but he also invited the last remnants of the once flourishing Aboriginal tribes to dine at his expense and to enjoy an outing to the Zoological gardens." In 1902 a robber attacked Quong Tart in his business office, hitting him over the head with an iron bar. He seemed to recover but his health went downhill; the next year, soon after the birth of his sixth child, George, he died at age 53. People of Chinese and Anglo-Celtic ancestry came to his funeral in large numbers to mourn this man who had done so much for Sydney.[23]

When the Australian colonies became a federation of states in 1901, one of the new government's first acts was to pass a law aimed at keeping out people of color. Working people and their unions were strong supporters of the policy then, fearing that an open immigration policy would cause a flood of cheap labor from Asian countries and threaten their jobs. The exclusionary policy also enjoyed wide support among middle- and upper-class Australians. Convinced of their own superiority, they wanted to reserve the country for people like themselves. Half a century before, a colonial secretary had set forth this view.

In 1843 a group of squatters wanted to solve their labor problem by importing Indians as indentured workers. But when they wrote to London for permission, Sir James Stephen, undersecretary of state for the colonies, vetoed the plan: "introducing the black race there," he wrote, "would, in my mind, be one of the most unreasonable preferences of the present to the future.... There is not in the globe a social interest more momentous—if we look forward for five or six generations—than that of reserving the Continent of New Holland as a place where the English race shall be spread from sea to sea unmixed by any lower caste."[24] (Well into the nineteenth century many people in England still called Australia "New Holland," the name the Dutch had once given the continent.)

But if Indian indentured servants were not brought out in large numbers to do heavy labor in the outback, smaller numbers came from British India to work in the homes of wealthy Australians. An 1883 advertisement for "East Indian Servants" pictured a well-dressed, dignified Indian man holding a small tray, the kind that might have held the calling cards of visitors to a stately home. The ad gave the name and address of a company in Flinders Lane, Melbourne, "from whom full particulars can be obtained."[25] Many Asian servants were imported during the nineteenth century.

As the debate over immigration policy heated up at the turn of the century, several people from the upper echelons proclaimed their approval of a White Australia policy. "We are guarding the last part of the world in which the higher races can live and increase freely for the higher civilization," wrote Professor Pearson.[26] Alfred Deakin, who served three times as prime minister of the new Federation, campaigned in 1901 for "a White Australia, in which the absolute mastering and dominating element shall be British."[27]

Such sentiments were not universal, however. One member of Parliament protested the unfairness of the act to the Chinese: "No race on the face of the earth has been treated in a more shameful manner than have the Chinese," he said. "They are about the most conservative race in the world and up to late years they had no desire whatsoever for any intercourse with what they called the outer barbarians, but they were forced at the point of a bayonet to admit English and other Europeans into China. Now if we can compel them to admit people into their land, why in the name of justice should we refuse to admit them?"[28]

In the decade before federation, every colony except Queensland, which wanted to keep its Kanakas, had already passed some kind of restrictive racial legislation. This proved an embarrassment for the British government, which in time disallowed these laws. Half a century had passed since the days of Sir James Stephen's tenure. The world was a different place and British foreign policy had changed with the times. Japan showed signs of becoming a world power; China was a colossus that could not be ignored; Indian leaders must be reassured that its British occupiers harbored no racist feelings and were only there to help them modernize. And now that the United States had become an industrial rival, the need for strong export markets was more important than ever. The last thing England wanted to do in 1901 was alienate Asian nations.

When Australia proved determined to keep its country white, the British colonial secretary suggested that they achieve this indirectly by adopting the policy used in Natal.[29] This province in southeastern Africa on the Indian Ocean was then a British colony (and is now part of South Africa). In the 1860s, sugar cane growers there imported indentured laborers from India to work in the fields. Many stayed on and their relatives kept joining them. By the mid–1890s more Indians than Europeans lived in Natal.

This situation must be reversed, the British felt, but how could they risk offending India, the "Jewel in the Crown" of their empire? Someone came up with a solution. They would give immigrants a dictation test in a language they didn't know and reject them on grounds of literacy rather than race. It was this test that the colonial secretary suggested and Australia copied. The dictation test became the basis of the country's White Australia policy.[30]

The 1901 Immigration Restriction Act specified that immigrants must past a 50-word dictation test in "a European language" to be admitted.[31] The word "European" was replaced in 1905 by the phrase "a prescribed language"—to avoid offending Japan and India, historian Manning Clark believed—and in 1912 the word "restriction" was removed from the law's title; but the dictation test remained on the law books until 1958.

Confidential instructions sent to immigration officials in 1901 by Atlee Hunt, secretary of the Department of External Affairs, stated the law's intent baldly: "It is not desirable that persons should be allowed to pass the test, and before putting it to anyone the Officer should be satisfied that he will fail. If he is considered likely to pass the test in English, it should be applied in some other language of which he is ignorant."[32]

The vague wording of the law gave immigration officials the power to reject anyone they didn't like. In 1914 a young Irish woman was given the dictation test in Swedish and sent back to Ireland when she failed it.[33]

The policy was hidden from nations whose people had dark skins but could be spelled out for others. When a letter arrived in 1911 asking if anarchist Emma Goldman would be admitted to give a series of lectures, Hunt replied affirmatively: "the Immigration Restriction Laws of Australia are designed for the purpose of excluding coloured persons, persons of bad moral character, and persons likely for reasons of health to become a burden on the State or to spread contagious disease. It is not the practice to exclude any other classes of persons."[34]

Some sections of the 1901 law applied to people already living in Australia, such as the Kanakas. The law said they must be deported by 1906. When sugar growers objected, they were given compensations: stiff tariffs on sugar coming in from other nations, and a bounty on every ton of sugar processed by white labor.[35]

At least 6500 Kanakas were living in Queensland in 1906. A viable community by then, they formed the Pacific Islanders Association to fight the deportation order, and managed to get a few concessions. In the end up to 2500 Kanakas stayed on, including those who were born in Australia or had lived there for decades, as well as some who hid and remained illegally. But the majority of Kanakas were deported.[36]

Over the years the Act occasionally was used to reject people for political reasons. In 1934 the government used it against Egon Kisch, a Czechoslovakian journalist on the political far left, who had been invited to speak at the Australian Congress Against War and Fascism. When immigration officials refused to let him disembark at Melbourne, Kisch jumped off the ship onto the wharf and broke his leg. Officials gave him a dictation test in the hospital. Kisch spoke several European languages so they tested him in Gaelic. He flunked. But after publicity about his shoddy treatment made Kisch into a sympathetic figure and a celebrity, the embarrassed government agreed to pay his court costs if he left, which he did in 1935.[37]

Kisch's story lives on because it was outlandish, but it is an exception to the usual rejection based on race. The Chinese were a major target even after they entered legally. Another provision of the 1901 Act said that for up to five years after entry, immigrants could be given a dictation test at any time and deported if they failed to pass it.

A relative of Jimmy Kew became a victim of this loophole. One of Kew's sons, William Wing Young, returned to Australia at the age of 14 — he had this right because he had been born there. Wing Young built a thriving produce business in Melbourne, brought out a bride from China, and started a family. A few years later, his wife suddenly was summoned to take a dictation test in English. Her daughter Elizabeth Chong does not know why the authorities decided to invoke the Act at that time. Whatever the reason her mother, who only spoke Chinese, failed the test. She was deported. The whole family went to China with her and Chong was born there. But Wing Young's business brought him back to Australia frequently. Eventually he managed to get his family readmitted.[38]

In the first decades of the twentieth century, immigrants were largely British or Irish. This reflected not only the White Australia policy but also a reinvigorated policy of the British Empire. At an Imperial Conference in London in 1907, delegates passed a resolution that "it is desirable to encourage British emigrants to proceed to British colonies rather than to foreign countries."[39]

Farms to train immigrant teenagers as agricultural workers were set up in many countries including Australia. But the country needed miners and industrial workers more than farm hands. British immigrants usually shunned such jobs, looking instead for well-paying city jobs. They had no desire to settle in forlorn places like Broken Hill and coax minerals out of the earth.

Broken Hill was settled in 1885 after silver and then lead and zinc, was discovered there. This isolated town near the border of New South Wales and South Australia became a mining center. Its workers came from many countries including Ireland, Italy, Germany, Malta, Yugoslavia, and Albania. The mine owners soon diversified, and Broken Hill Proprietary, Ltd. (known as BHP), in time became the nation's largest industrial conglomerate. In 1915 BHP opened a steel plant at Newcastle in New South Wales, shipping ore from its South Australian mines to this coal-producing region near the coast. And in 1935 it opened an even larger steel mill at Wollongong, south of Sydney.[40]

Once World War I started and ships carrying British-made goods could no longer get through, industrial production increased nationwide. The Australians discovered that they were capable of manufacturing much of what they needed. This in turn created more factory jobs. After the war they were often filled by the rural poor of southern and eastern Europe.

When America clamped down on immigration in the 1920s, the change affected Australia. After nearly a century of open immigration for Europeans, the United States passed a law in 1921 setting up national quotas: it would accept 3 percent of the number of people from a country—for example, Greece—who had been living in the United States at the time of the 1910 census. In 1924 Congress restricted immigration even further: now the United States would accept annually 2 percent of those from each country who had been living in the United States at the time of the 1890 census. "The changed formula ... had the effect of allocating the greater part of the total quota to the nations of older immigration, the nations of northern and western Europe, and of giving small quotas to the nations of newer immigration that were predominantly from southern and eastern Europe," wrote immigration specialist E. P. Hutchinson. "Quite clearly the 1890 base was chosen for precisely that effect."[41] (More restrictive law for Asians were already on the books or would be passed later, for example, the Chinese Exclusion Act of 1882.)

Under the quota system, people wanting to emigrate from southern and eastern Europe might have to wait years, or even decades, before they were admitted to the United States. Many of the excluded looked for other countries that would accept them. Australia was one of them. Immigrants came there from several countries during the 1920s but especially from Italy and Greece, which already had thriving communities in Australia.

Italians had first arrived during the gold rush of the 1850s. Later emigrants settled in cities such as Melbourne and Sydney as well as in rural areas that offered job or business possibilities. For example, Giacamo Lucini built a pasta factory at Hepburn Springs, Victoria, in 1853, offering "Macaroni,

Vermicelli and Spaghetti. Made with celebrated Hepburn Mineral Waters," said his ad.⁴² A Swiss-Italian family, the Borsa, who came out for the gold rush, also settled in Hepburn Springs, forming the partnership of Borsa and Crippa, butchers, in 1864.⁴³ In Northern Queensland, Italian immigrants often worked in the sugar cane fields and later largely replaced the deported Kanakas. Gradually many bought land and planted their own sugar cane fields; today Italian families in Queensland own several plantations and sugar refineries. Another growth spurt occurred between 1922 to 1928, when thousands of Italian immigrants opted for Australia after the Americans restricted their entrance. Italians settled throughout Australia in time, including Perth and Darwin.⁴⁴

Greeks, like the Italians, started coming to Australia during the gold rush years and came steadily in the years that followed, with a large upsurge in the 1920s after the U.S. quota system barred most of them from America.⁴⁵ So

A Greek wedding in Toowoomba, Queensland, in 1932. Angela C. Kalokerinos married Michael J. Londy. Guests included the bride and groom's families and members of the Andronicos, Conomos and Kentrotis families. People of Greek ancestry live throughout Australia, with the largest concentration in Melbourne (State Library of Queensland, image No. 41532).

many Greek immigrants settled in Melbourne that it was said to have the third-largest Greek population of any city, after Athens and Thessaloniki (the former Salonica). Large numbers of Greeks also settled in Queensland; some worked in the sugar cane fields, but more opened cafés or food businesses.

The increased numbers of poor people from southern and eastern Europe set off the panic button among Australians who still wanted a "pure" Anglo-Saxon country. Back in 1901 Alfred Deakin had said: "our Antipodean suspicion is directed at immigrants of the lower Latin type and ... decidedly antagonistic towards newcomers from South-Eastern Europe."[46] When Parliament debated the immigration issue in 1925, it provided an outlet for those with pent-up fears and prejudices. One MP told of Greeks doing shift work in a South Australian town: "The beds they occupy never get cold. As soon as one man leaves it is occupied by another of his fellows.... How can we expect such people to adjust themselves to our standard of living?"[47] Another described the typical immigrant from Southern Europe as "a cheap foreign immigrant who can live on the smell of an oil rag."[48] The legislators concluded that such people were "quite unsuited ... ever to become worthy citizens" of Australia.[49]

The cover of a 1929 pamphlet designed to entice young working-class women in Britain to emigrate to Australia. Immigrants from several southern and eastern European countries were filling job slots by then, but the government wanted to keep the country predominantly British so it paid ship fare for British women who agreed to come. A similar pamphlet to attract young British men also offered assisted passage (by permission of the National Library of Australia).

The Australian government continued trying to attract young immigrants from Britain by offering assisted passage to girls who would work as domestic servants and boys as farm hands or laborers. The cover illustration of a 1929 pamphlet that circulated in England, "Australia Invites the British Domestic Girl," showed a smartly uniformed young maid outside a large country estate picking a bouquet of roses. The estate might have been in Sussex or Somerset. On the cover of a companion pamphlet, "Australia for the

British Boy," a young man on horseback waved his hat exuberantly at a cow, haystack and silo. Eucalyptus trees alone identified the rural landscape as Australian. Neither illustration gave a clue that most Australians lived in cities.[50]

But impoverished peasants from southern and eastern Europe needed no enticing pamphlet to persuade them to emigrate. Despite the rhetoric against them, they continued coming. They were admitted because their labor was needed. What finally decreased immigration was the Great Depression of the 1930s, followed by World War II, when immigrant ships could not get through.

After the war Australia inaugurated a massive immigration program centered at first on war-torn Europe. That action set in motion a change in the country that earlier generations could not have imagined.

Eight

A Multiethnic Nation

Joe DeLuca was pleased. "Two Vietnamese woman have agreed to serve on our Board in Alice Springs," he said.[1] From his office in Darwin, DeLuca ran the Northern Territory branch of the Ethnic Communities Council, a national organization that helps immigrants. In the mid–1990s DeLuca was setting up its first chapter in Alice Springs, the desert town in the center of the country that epitomizes the Australian outback. Italian families had been growing vegetables in outlying areas for decades, he said. Now Filipino, Cambodian, Vietnamese and other peoples were moving there. Two families had arrived recently from war-torn Croatia.[2]

Over the past century peoples from some 240 countries and places have come to Australia. The majority settled in large cities, predominantly Sydney and Melbourne, but immigrants live in every state — in cities, towns, and hamlets of all sizes. Six million of the country's current twenty million people have arrived since 1947, or are children or grandchildren of immigrants.

One striking fact about this change in the nation's makeup is that it happened peacefully. There was no rioting in the streets. A few minor incidents occurred at most. Considering that Australia once tried to restrict immigration to people of British or Western European stock, how did this turnaround happen? And how was it achieved without turmoil? No day can be singled out as the decisive moment when past policies were rejected and new ones heralded as the nation's future course. To the contrary, these changes evolved gradually.

When the Second World War ended, Australia had seven and a half million people, not nearly enough to meet its future military and industrial needs. Vigorous recruiting campaigns in Britain brought out many people but the country needed more, so it turned to war-torn Europe. Australia set up a large-scale immigration program centered on the Continent. Between 1947 and 1969, more than two million Europeans settled in Australia under the program's aegis.[3] At first refugees came directly from Displaced Persons camps: predominantly Eastern Europeans, they came from countries such as Poland, the Baltic States, Hungary, Croatia, and Czechoslovakia.

The country's need was not the only reason for expanding immigration: "Human decency also played some part in making people want to help displaced persons and other victims of the war in Europe," historian Russel Ward has pointed out.[4] In the first years after the war Australia took in 25 percent of all emigrants who left Europe. "Unlike the United States and Canada," wrote James Jupp, "Australia offered resettlement to all refugees who agreed to work wherever they were directed by the government for two years."[5] He also noted that "southern Europeans ... were effectively barred from United States until 1965," when the last vestiges of the quota system set up in the 1920s were rescinded.[6]

Once all those in Displaced Persons camps had been relocated in various countries, Australia continued its large intake of immigrants by signing treaties with a number of European nations. In 1948 it signed an immigration treaty with Malta; in 1951 and 1952 with the Netherlands, Italy, Austria, Belgium, West Germany, Greece and Spain; and in 1954 with the United States, Switzerland, Denmark, Norway, Sweden and Finland. By the end of that decade, two-thirds of the immigrants coming in were non–British.[7]

Large-scale immigration continued through the next decade. By 1966 Australia had "a greater proportion of migrants in its population than any other country in the world apart from Israel."[8] That year 10,000 Lebanese Christians arrived and "in 1967 a migration treaty with Turkey brought substantial numbers of Muslims to Australia for the first time. In 1971, 10,000 Turks had arrived in Australia."[9]

In addition, Australia had signed the United Nations Convention on Refugees treaty in 1954, agreeing to take in people whose lives were in danger because of oppressive regimes in their country. After the Soviet invasion of Czechoslovakia in 1968, for example, Australia took in 5500 refugees who fled the country.[10] The numbers of refugees it accepted under the Convention expanded significantly from 1970 onwards when the country opened its door to Asians and other non–Europeans. Over the next 35 years, in addition to its regular immigration programs the country consistently took in its fair share of people displaced by civil wars and other strife, absorbing refugees from Korea, Vietnam, Cambodia, China, Lebanon, Argentina, Chile, Afghanistan, Congo, East Timor, El Salvador, Eritrea, Ethiopia, Iran, Iraq, Myanmar (Burma), Somalia, Sudan, and several countries of the former USSR and Yugoslavia.

In a memoir, journalist Geraldine Brooks recalled some of her neighbors in Sydney during the 1960s: "The Serbs next door were survivors of the fascist Ustasha.... The Turk over the back fence had lived through two coups. Mrs. Papas's Greek family had felt the heavy hand of the military junta." They all found a new life in Australia.[11]

Back in 1947, immigration minister Arthur Calwell had worried that Anglo–Australians might not accept Europeans with "foreign" ways. "It is my hope," he said, "that for every foreign migrant there will be ten people from the United Kingdom."[12] This was wishful thinking because, as we have seen, the people who responded in greatest numbers were the rural poor from southern and eastern Europe along with those from troubled countries in regions such as the Balkans, who jumped at the chance to go to a land that offered jobs and democracy.

These "New Australians," as they were called, turned out to be just what the country's businesses and industries needed. They took any job that provided them with a living and went to any region that wanted them. They worked in the mines of Broken Hill and Mt. Isa; they dug coal in the Hunter Valley; they formed the backbone of the workforce at the great steel mills in Newcastle and Wollongong; they provided labor for the massive Snowy Mountains hydroelectric scheme, which substantially increased the nation's supply of electrical power. (That project also brought irrigation to parts of the dry Riverina, whose problems Anthony Trollope had written about—see Chapter Four—making it possible for the region to grow a variety of fruit and vegetable crops including wine grapes.) In cities immigrants worked in factories such as the huge General Motors/Holden auto plant outside Adelaide. Many women immigrants sewed clothes for garment companies or worked on the assembly lines of light industries.[13]

Postwar European immigrants worked long hours in difficult jobs, sometimes under arduous conditions. They had no choice because in return for assisted passage out and the opportunity to become Australian citizens, they had agreed to take whatever jobs the government gave them for the first two years. But that was not the only constraint they faced in those years.

Immigrants were also urged to assimilate and become "Australian," which then meant embracing British-type customs and traditions. A 1948 government pamphlet, "The Australians and You," cautioned: "Australians are not used to hearing foreign languages.... Speaking in your own language in public will make you conspicuous, and make Australians regard you as a stranger.... Also try to avoid using your hands when speaking."[14] Immigrants who spoke their native language on the street might be called "Reffos" (refugees), "Balts" (from the Baltic counties), or "Wogs," and told to go back where they came from. (The term "wog" originated in England and in postwar Australia became an epithet for immigrants from countries such as Greece and Italy.)

But hostility toward immigrants rarely went beyond verbal taunts. For the most part the old Australians simply ignored the new ones and got on with their own lives. An unemployment rate that hovered around two percent during the post-war growth years surely helped as did the country's vast spaces where suburb after suburb was built at the edges of cities.

In time old and new residents influenced each other in ways they hardly noticed. Immigrants learned to eat barbecued meats and spread Vegemite on their bread while old guard Australians developed an appetite for spaghetti and rice. Sophisticates no longer had to go to Rome for cappuccinos—they could sip them at home in sidewalk cafés opened by Italians and Greeks. And if first-generation immigrants had noticeable accents, their children spoke English like the native Aussies they were. When they grew up, more than a few married people of Anglo-Celtic stock. "It's quite funny now," recalled a daughter of Italian immigrants, "because some of the people who were anti–Catholic and anti–Italian have married into Italian families."[15]

In retrospect we can see that Calwell's fears that people would not accept "foreigners" underestimated the resiliency of the Australians. That said, it seems unlikely that in 1947 people would have accepted large numbers of Asian migrants without protest. For nearly a century Australians had been warned that Asian immigrants would mean loss of jobs and a possible takeover of the country. They had been schooled to fear "the Yellow Peril." The twenty years of heavy European intake served as an introduction to people from other backgrounds. Europeans paved the way for the Asians and Africans who came later.

But small numbers of Asians did come in legally during the first post-war decades. Japanese wives of Australian servicemen were admitted in 1949 as were some 800 non–European refugees.[16] The Colombo Plan for foreign students, started in 1951, enabled Asians from several neighboring countries to study at Australian universities. Some of them stayed on. Soon after Prime Minister Robert Menzies, a strong supporter of the White Australia policy, retired in 1966, his successor Harold Holt extended the "distinguished persons" category to Asians and began admitting skilled technicians and other educated people from Asian nations. Over the next four years, 4800 immigrants, including their dependents, came from Burma, Hong Kong, India, Indonesia, Malaysia, the Philippines, Singapore and Sri Lanka, to name the countries supplying the largest numbers.[17]

A new way of thinking about immigrants was circulating in several countries in the late 1960s and some Australians embraced it. Called "cultural pluralism," it challenged the "assimilation" theory of the late nineteenth and early twentieth centuries that still reigned as the conventional wisdom about immigrants. In that earlier period cities such as New York and London had large numbers of immigrants living in slums; most came from small rural villages of many countries, had little or no education and often were desperately poor. These immigrants and their customs appeared backward to the middle-class people who set out to help them assimilate; that is, to make them discard their "foreign" ways and embrace the dominant "advanced" culture of their new land. Through the melting pot of assimilation, everyone would come out alike. The melting pot imagery came from a play of that title, written by British author Israel Zangwill but initially produced in the United States in 1914. Virtually everyone in the pot was European.

Country after country found, however, that peoples did not in fact shed their cultures (which might also be related to their religions) so easily. Although the first generation born to immigrant parents usually wanted to be just like their classmates and were often embarrassed because their parents were different, the second, third, or fourth generations might find merit and richness in the culture of their ancestors. By the late 1960s the numbers of young people wanting to connect with their ethnic roots as a way of giving meaning to their lives became palpable.

The proponents of cultural pluralism believed that countries were enriched by the cultures of new immigrants—by their music, dance and food, for instance. (American jazz, which grew out of the music of African Americans, is one famous example.) Cultural pluralists argued that immigrants could retain their traditional customs while also becoming loyal and productive citizens of their new country.

Professor Jerzy Zubrzycki, an immigration specialist at Australian National University in Canberra who favored the new approach, introduced it at a national citizenship convention in 1968. Instead of the usual talk about helping foreigners assimilate, he presented a model for cultural pluralism which, he told them, "stands for the retention of ethnic identity and continued participation of individual settlers in minority group activities. It implies, therefore, a rejection ... of any assumptions of Anglo-Saxon superiority and the necessary conformity to English-oriented cultural patterns." His talk "fell like a lead balloon," Zubrzycki recalled in a 1995 speech. "But a beginning had been made."[18]

In 1977 Zubrzycki and Professor Jean Martin wrote a report, "Australia as a Multicultural Society," which concluded: "What we believe Australia should be working towards is not a oneness but a unity, not a similarity but a composite, not a melting pot but a voluntary bond of dissimilar people sharing a common political and institutional structure."[19]

In Melbourne, some community groups that gave direct help to immigrants also became supporters of cultural diversity. Among them were Walter Lippmann (the late Australian Walter Lippmann and American journalist Walter Lippmann were different people) of the Australian Jewish

Welfare and Relief Association, George Papadopoulos and Spiro Moraitis of the Australian Greek Welfare Society, and David Cox and Alan Matheson of European Australian Christian Fellowship, which later became the Ecumenical Migration Centre.[20] Professor James Jupp, who came to Australia from England in 1956 to teach at the University of Melbourne, soon became interested in immigrant settlement and in what came to be called multiculturalism. He did research on these community groups' services, as well as on those provided by assimilationist groups, and used the results in *Arrivals and Departures* (1966), which looked in part at why some immigrants were leaving.[21]

Gough Whitlam, leader of the Opposition Labor Party, campaigned in 1972 on a platform that "renounced discrimination between prospective migrants on any ground of race or colour of skin or nationality."[22] When the Labor Party won national elections that December after 23 years out of office and Whitlam became prime minister, he made good on his campaign pledge. His administration imported the term "multiculturalism" from Canada, where it was being used to promote a bilingual policy of English and French. In Australia the word took on the broader meaning of replacing assimilation with a policy that validated diversity.

As his immigration minister, Whitlam appointed Al Grassby, who came from the Riverina area of New South Wales where he had developed "a particular affection for the region's sizeable Sicilian and Calabrian minorities."[23] Grassby was fervently committed to making Australia a truly multiethnic society. But he was also "passionately opposed to the Anglo-conformism of hard-line assimilationism," says Mark Lopez in his book, *The Origins of Multiculturalism in Australian Politics, 1945–1975*. Grassby could "charm one category of voters while inducing antagonism and resentment in another section of the audience."[24] The picture that comes across in Lopez's book suggests that Grassby made substantive changes but may have hardened the views of assimilationists instead of winning converts.

The immigration reforms of the Whitlam administration were firmly in place in late 1975 when the Labor government suddenly fell and a Liberal Country Party coalition returned to power. Malcolm Fraser, leader of the Liberal Party, became prime minister. Many assumed that the old White Australia policy would be reinstated in some form, and that immigrants would again be urged to assimilate. Instead the Fraser government continued the reforms of the Whitlam government in these areas.

Why did the policy of cultural pluralism receive bipartisan support? It was not a need for migrant labor because by the mid–1970s the country was already beginning to experience labor surpluses. Both major parties rejected race-based immigration in part because the old White Australia policy had become a political embarrassment and an economic liability for a country at the edge of Southeast Asia. And Malcolm Fraser, like Gough Whitlam, believed in cultural pluralism.

The country could have simply expanded its admissions policy to include non-whites but done little to help immigrants after they arrived. The fact that Australia went further and did so much for its immigrants cannot be attributed solely to politics and economics. What occurred reflects the good will of the Australians. It also shows the role that government leaders can play in fostering cooperation and an acceptance of change.

Between 1965 and 2000 numerous papers, reports and documents appeared on multiculturalism; this study focuses on two key reports that played significant roles in shaping Australia's policies. The first, published in 1978, was *Review of Post-arrival Programs and Services to Migrants.* It became known as the Galbally Report, named for its chair, Melbourne barrister Frank Galbally. One committee member whose input influenced the report was 30-year-old Petro Georgiou, who had emigrated from Greece with his family as an infant.[25]

The Galbally Report established multiculturalism as a guiding principle in Australia, saying "every person should be able to maintain his or her culture without prejudice or disadvantage and should be encouraged to understand and embrace other cultures."[26] But its major emphasis was on providing useful services to newly arrived immigrants. "Essentially multiculturalism at the federal level has had very little to do with culture, and a great deal to do with immigrant settlement," Jupp wrote in *From White Australia to Woomera: The Story of Australian Immigration.*[27]

Migrants should use general community services whenever possible, the Galbally Report said, but "special services and programs" were also necessary. These "should be designed and operated in full consultation with clients, and self-help should be encouraged as much as possible with a view to helping migrants to become self-reliant quickly."[28] In practice this meant that more funds were given to ethnic associations whose staff came from the same background as its clients and spoke their language.

After the report was accepted by both major parties, the Department of Immigration significantly increased grant-in-aid money to community organizations that worked directly with migrants (it was already giving them some money). The Department also opened Migrant Resources Centres in sections of cities where immigrants clustered; these helped newcomers connect with the services they needed. Free English-language instruction for immigrants, another recommendation, was also expanded.

When results of services put into place as a result of the report were evaluated in 1982, the committee found they had been "of substantial benefit" to migrants as well as the community as a whole and that Australia had "perhaps the most comprehensive system of migrant and multicultural services in the world."[29] The particulars were new, relating to the change in the country's ethnic makeup, but the tradition they followed was not. As we saw in Chapter Three, when English novelist Anthony Trollope visited Australia in 1871 he was struck by "all that has been done for the welfare of the people generally." And the country's 1901 Constitution specified several areas where the government might make laws to meet its citizens' needs.

The services Australia provided early in the twentieth century made it an innovator among nations in this regard, although such help then was for whites only. But after the country replaced assimilation with cultural pluralism, its policies, now for everyone, were again innovative compared with other nations. For example, it helped fund the "Saturday schools" run by various ethnic groups where children learned the language and customs of their people.

A second seminal document underpinned this change in outlook. After Bob Hawke, leader of the Labor Party, became prime minister in 1983, he formed an Office of Multicultural Affairs (OMA) within the Department of the Prime Minister, making this a priority of the government. When the OMA decided to formulate national policy on multiculturalism, it made a special effort to build a consensus for it among people with divergent views. Its committee, chaired by barrister Sir James Gobbo, spent two years getting input from a wide range of citizens. Along with "public forums in each capital city and major rural centres," the committee met with "key government and non-government bodies" including the Australian Council of Trade Unions, the Business Council of Australia, the

An Iraqi girl learning Arabic at a "Saturday school" in Shepparton, Victoria, in 2004. Australia's multicultural policy encourages people from other cultures to maintain their traditions and language as well as to become loyal Australians. The class, run by the Iraqi Cultural Association, is held at the local high school (by permission of the National Library of Australia, photograph by John Immig).

Returned Services League (war veterans), organizations of social services providers and consumer groups, and the Ethnic Communities Councils. In addition, "in order to reach the public at large, advertisements were placed in the major newspapers and ethnic presses in November, 1987 inviting submissions from interested individuals and groups," and letters were sent to union, business and community organizations asking for their comments. "Altogether over 150 written submissions were received from a wide range of organisations as well as many individuals." Some suggestions from groups and individuals were incorporated into the final document.[30]

Such input paid off. When the government published *National Agenda for a Multicultural Australia — Sharing Our Future* (NAMA) in July, 1989, its recommendations became the cornerstone of public policy in this area. There was no public outcry against them. The opening page asked: "What is multiculturalism?" and defined it as "simply a term which describes the cultural and ethnic diversity of contemporary Australia." NAMA identified three dimensions of this policy: cultural identity, social justice and economic efficiency (utilizing the skills and talents of all). These policies, it made clear, "apply equally to all Australians, whether Aboriginal, Anglo-Celtic, or non–English speaking background."[31]

NAMA stressed the need for a cohesive policy: "The fact is that the challenges of a multicultural society do not simply resolve themselves. Government action — in the form of multicultural policies — is needed in certain areas to promote social harmony, to ensure a fair go and to harness our human resources in the most productive way for Australia's future."[32]

The report also showed the diversity of the population: "Today well over 20% of Australians were born in another country, of whom more than half came to Australia from non–English speaking countries in Europe, the Middle East, Asia and South America. Combined with their Australian-born children, they constitute 40% of the population."[33]

Multiculturalism had limits, the report stressed. All the country's people "should have an overriding and unifying commitment to Australia, to its interests and future first and foremost"; the policies "impose obligations as well as conferring rights."[34]

Many of the programs it recommended were already in existence: the report validated their merit by saying they were good for the country. The success of multiculturalism in those decades was grounded in services for immigrants, with small community groups forming the backbone. Some started early.

In 1949 churches and civic groups formed Good Neighbour Councils in an effort to help newly arrived immigrants. In the early 1950s the federal government published *A Handbook of the Good Neighbour Movement*, which gave 101 suggestions on how to start new branches and give help to immigrants.[35] These groups gave practical assistance but their framework was firmly in the old assimilation mode. Staff members only spoke English. Dedicated to helping newcomers from other cultures shed their old ways and embrace "Australian" culture, they were "reluctant to encourage ethnic organizations ... [thus] The southern Europeans were not effectively incorporated into the Good Neighbourhood movement."[36]

Another avenue of help gradually overshadowed these early efforts. Immigrants to any country typically develop their own cultural and social institutions, often through their religious organizations, to preserve their traditions and identity. In Australia, too, "most minorities soon set about establishing choirs, folk-dancing groups, theaters, Saturday schools, and Scout groups."[37] Ethnic groups started their own social services as well; but the incomes of recent immigrants were usually low, so it was hard to raise enough money to keep them going.

These grassroots immigrant groups were strengthened by the government, which as we have seen applauded their efforts in time and provided funds. What sets Australia's programs for immigrants apart is the degree to which the government gave approval and financial help to small ethnic projects while at the same time letting these groups retain considerable autonomy.

The Federation of Ethnic Communities' Councils of Australia (FECCA) is the nation's largest multicultural network. This nongovernmental umbrella organization was set up in 1974 to consult with government and make it aware of immigrants' needs. FECCA has branches in every state, which in turn have several hundred member groups from various ethnic communities as well as individual members. The state branches are called Ethnic Communities Councils (ECC). The offices the author visited in the 1990s were either in low-income suburbs where recent immigrants clustered or in buildings that offered space to many community organizations. Their facilities were barebones and their staffs skeletal but their work made a difference to countless immigrants.

A ten-minute walk from the Redfern train station led to Waterloo, a low-income inner Sydney suburb where the Ethnic Communities Council had its New South Wales office. The state had 320 member groups, Chairperson Edna McGill said. The majority were in Sydney but the industrial cities of Newcastle and Wollongong also had several member groups from various ethnic communities, as did some other towns in the state.[38]

Instead of providing direct services to individual immigrants, she said, the ECC usually worked with member groups to help them set up services for their own people. "What we're good at is working with individual ethnic communities and giving them support." Staff would meet with leaders of a new group member and ask: "What's the most important thing your

Eight • A Multiethnic Nation   123

community needs now?" Whatever that was—jobs, child care, English-language instruction, help for the elderly or for women at home who felt isolated—the ECC tried to assist them in getting it, she said. "But we can't do everything."[39] In specialized areas such as help for the disabled, they formed liaisons with organizations doing this work.

If ethnic communities were too small or fragmented to start their own services, the ECC tried to provide direct help. McGill said her office obtained a small grant to work with communities from Thailand, Myanmar, Ghana, Indonesia, and Bangladesh; they used the money to hire five social workers who came from these countries, for ten hours a week apiece. She also mentioned that more refugees had come in from African countries in recent years because of civil wars there; for example both Ethiopians and Eritreans had fled the conflict between them.

The nearby suburb of Redfern has a large indigenous Aboriginal population, so the question of whether the EEC had Aboriginal member groups came up. "The Aborigines don't want to be identified with immigrants," McGill explained. "They were the first Australians."[40] Indigenous people had their own organizations, she said, but the two networks came together on issues that affected both, such as their Anti-Racism subcommittee.

In Melbourne, Hakan Akyol, executive officer of the Victoria ECC, said he spent much time representing ethnic communities at forums and government advisory committees. He told them of immigrants' needs in areas such as employment and social security, and offered to work with government agencies to help meet them. One joint venture, for example, produced pamphlets explaining government services. Several dozen languages are spoken in Melbourne so they could only afford translations into a few languages of the largest immigrant communities, Akyol said.[41] But the committee rewrote the English-language pamphlets using the most simplified wording possible, a service that the general population must also have found useful.

Richmond, the Melbourne suburb where the ECC's offices were located, had long been a Greek district. But as Greek Australians prospered and moved to outer suburbs, more recent immigrant groups took their place. The Vietnamese now have the largest enclave in Richmond: the shopping area along Victoria Street, lined with Vietnamese shops and restaurants, is called "Little Saigon."

Melbourne has had a heady mixture of ethnic groups since its gold rush days in the 1850s as we saw in the last chapter. Nowhere is this continuing pattern more apparent than in the city's restaurants. Like the gold rush city of San Francisco, Melbourne is one of the world's ethnic gourmet capitals. A book of restaurant reviews reprinted from Melbourne's *The Age* gave the picture. Its index of cuisines included Afghan, Argentinean, Australian,

Austrian, Balinese, Brazilian, Burmese, Cajun/Creole, Chinese, Dutch, Filipino, French, German, Goan, Greek, Hungarian, Indian, Indonesian, Italian, Jamaican, Japanese, Koori (Aboriginal), Korean, Laotian, Lebanese, Malaysian, Mauritian, Mexican, Mongolian, Nepalese, Polish, Portuguese, Russian, Serbian, Spanish, Sri Lankan, Swedish, Thai, Tibetan, Turkish, and Vietnamese.[42]

Sydney is not far behind in its variety of ethnic fare. And throughout the country, restaurants in cities and small country towns serve the traditional dishes of their immigrant owners. Although most Australians live in the concentrated southeastern arc of settlement, some other areas of the country are growing rapidly, thanks in part to the immigrants who settle there.

Darwin, the capital city of the Northern Territory, had a mixture of European and Asian residents from the beginning. Men from China, the Philippines and parts of present Indonesia and Malaysia were settling on the northwest coast by the 1860s, diving for pearls or fishing. Anglo–Australians from the east coast were also beginning to move there. Darwin was established as the Northern Territory's port city by 1869. Two years later the discovery of gold in the Territory attracted a rush of settlers, especially from China. The gold proved to be scant, but many Chinese stayed on and some became merchants in Darwin. By 1881 the Territory had 4108 Chinese and 660 European residents, mainly British.[43] Not until 1911, after the White Australia policy was in full force, did ethnic Europeans outnumber Chinese there.

Indigenous women in Darwin often married or formed lasting relationships with Asian or European men who had come out alone. In time, Greek and Italian communities developed there. By the 1990s Darwin had 85,000 residents with people from several dozen cultures. Immigrants from the Philippines, Malaysia, Vietnam, Indonesia, East Timor, Cambodia, Thailand, China, India, Sri Lanka, and Papua New Guinea are some of the peoples who have built communities there over the past half century. The city has had two Chinese Australian mayors.

Many ethnic groups in Darwin are not large or organized enough to set up their own service networks, so the Ethnic Communities' Council there tries to provide direct help for them. ECC chair Joe DeLuca was able to get federal funds to hire three community welfare workers. One worked with Portuguese-Timorese immigrants, a second with Filipinos and Thais, while a third served the general community. Collectively the three workers spoke Tagalog, Tetum, Portuguese, French, Greek, Italian and Arabic. DeLuca knew the Territory well because he grew up there: his family emigrated from Sicily when he was seven and he attended local schools in Darwin.[44] He was committed to helping today's immigrants and put in long hours, although his post as chair was voluntary, so he received no salary.

Along with the ECC, numerous organizations, institutes and programs have facilitated the growth of multiethnic Australia. The Prologue of this book opened with a description of a parade and concert of children in Adelaide, South Australia, who attended Saturday schools to learn the language and culture of their people. The more than fifty schools that participated were set up and run by people from their ethnic communities. But these communities all belonged to the Ethnic Schools Association of South Australia, the umbrella group that sponsored the parade, and gets government funds. Other states have similar organizations.

Another ethnic umbrella network is the Multilingual Broadcasting Council, which promotes radio broadcasts in the languages spoken by people in various areas. In the Northern Territory, for example, 23 groups broadcast in 26 languages including programs in both Mandarin and Cantonese. Judith Ventic, a Filipino Australian who worked as a secretary at the university, was a volunteer broadcaster who hosted a weekly program in Tagalog. She said the local Irish Club did a Celtic hour in Gaelic.[45]

In 1988 immigration specialist James Jupp established the Centre for Immigration and Multicultural Studies at Australian National University in Canberra. The Centre collects materials about the numerous ethnic groups and nationalities in Australia. Dr. Jupp also edits the Centre's premier publication, *The Australian People: An Encyclopedia of the Nation, Its People and Their Origins*. Drawing on contributions from hundreds of scholars, the large volume's essays cover all Australians: indigenous Aborigines, British and Irish settlers, and other immigrants. For peoples with sizable communities—Chinese, Dutch, Germans, Greeks, Italians, Lebanese, Maltese and Vietnamese, to name but a few—there may be long essays on various aspects of their lives in Australia; but even groups with 500 members or less, such as Icelanders, Mongolians, Tatars, and Welsh Patagonians, have a single entry. Essays usually also include a brief history of the country emigrants came from and tell why they left.[46]

With 240 languages other than English spoken at home in Australia—nearly fifty of them Aboriginal—teaching languages is a major concern.[47] The government set up The National Languages and Literary Institute in Canberra, under language specialist Joseph LoBianco, to assess the situation, devise policies and coordinate programs. Its four-pronged recommendations, which became government policy in 1979, said every Australian should become proficient in spoken and written English; the teaching of languages other than English must be expanded and improved; Aboriginal languages should be maintained and developed where its peoples desired this; and last, translation and interpreter services should grow and libraries should expand their foreign-language collections.[48]

Along with government-funded programs that enable immigrants to learn English, Australia has made an effort to teach other languages as well. Starting in the primary grades, Australian teachers are encouraged, though not required, to teach one foreign language, usually combining language instruction with the history and customs of the people who speak it. In the Northern Territory in the 1990s all primary school students were learning Indonesian, the language of their neighbor, while some other states left the choice to the school districts. At a visit to the Museum of Chinese Australian History in Melbourne, a class of primary school children came through. These were "country children" from a nearby mountain region, the Dandenongs, their teacher said. The museum guide asked the children if they were studying Chinese. "No, we're learning Japanese," one replied.[49]

Libraries make an effort to carry books in the languages their users read. The state public library system in Queensland, for example, collects books in 45 languages and has a computer system that enables libraries throughout the state to borrow them for their patrons. A lot of these books go to small towns where immigrants have settled: "Laotians live around Tully, and Hmong, also from Laos, live around Ingham."[50] In coastal sugar-growing areas, recent Filipino, Vietnamese, and Chinese immigrants work in the cane fields. Queensland also has Finnish, German, and Dutch enclaves as well as Spanish, Croatian, and Sikh communities.[51]

Interpreter and translation services are another link in Australia's languages network. Since 1973 the government has run a free Telephone Interpreter Service (TIS) to help new immigrants arrange for basics such as jobs, housing, and school. A page in the local telephone directory describes the service, giving a paragraph about it in each language for which help is available. The TIS is funded by the Immigration Department but also relies on volunteer translators from various ethnic communities. In Sydney the Ethnic Affairs Commission of New South Wales, a state-run agency, provides interpreters and translators in 89 languages. Some services are free, such as interpreters who appear in court with immigrant defendants who do not understand English. But the Commission charges for most of its translation and interpreting work, and uses the money earned to help fund its many projects.[52]

Some critics are concerned that all the services given to immigrants, along with encouragement to maintain their traditions, will result in a polarized nation; they worry that ethnic groups will remain apart in ghettos instead of mixing and becoming "Australian." But statistics give a different picture, one that has led some ethnic groups to believe that too much mixing has occurred.

Multiethnic Australia is also intermarried Australia. "The most rapidly growing group in Australian society are those of combined Anglo-Celtic and non Anglo-Celtic ancestry" said NAMA. "Over 60% of Australians have at least two different ethnic origins, and 20% have four or more."[53] The family of Hakan Akyol of Melbourne's ECC, fell between these figures. Himself a Turkish Kurd who emigrated in 1969, he said his Australian wife had an Irish mother and a German father.[54] Journalist Manika Naidoo is a sixth-generation Indian South African who came to Australia as a child: "Both my parents have remarried — Mum to an Englishman and Dad to a Burmese woman," he wrote. "My niece is South African–Indian–Greek-Australian, and I have a half-sister who is South African–Indian-Burmese-Australian. Where else in the world would such mixed couplings occur across three generations, within 10 years?"

It seemed remarkable that a country which once tried to keep out people of color had turned itself around in this regard in less than forty years and did so without serious upheavals. How did they do it? Its network of services and its multicultural policy were likely factors, but was more involved than programs and policies? Some Australians gave other reasons.

Journalist Ilsa Sharp mentioned "mateship" to help explain the paradox of Australians who criticize immigrants in the abstract yet get along with those they know personally. As she put it in *Culture Shock! Australia*: "The same Australian who has just made disparaging remarks about Asians to white friends over the dinner table, will the next minute deck any white who insults the Asian friend and neighbor with whom he has been enjoying a pint of beer at the pub for the past few years—'Cause mates are mates, see?'"[55]

Rita Erlich, a writer in Melbourne, compared Australia and the United States. "Australians are not as romantic as Americans, not as rhetorical," she said. "They are a practical people. They have a willingness to give things a try." Erlich thought the country had coped "astonishingly well" with the continual waves of immigrants over the past few decades, perhaps more for practical reasons than from a natural sympathy for the newcomers.[56]

"Australians don't like to give up their weekends," said Sandra Theseira, who emigrated from Malaysia.[57] She meant that Australians would choose to spend Saturday at the beach instead of attending a protest rally against immigrants. The "laid-back" attitudes for which Australians are known and sometimes criticized may have contributed to the success of multiculturalism in the postwar period. As long as jobs and benefits enabled them to live comfortably and they felt secure about the future, people were likely to uphold the national tradition that everyone deserved a fair go, even if they thought some of the newcomers had strange ways.

NINE

Diversity and Dissent

Most Australians likely paid scant attention to changes in the nation's immigration and settlement policies in the 1970s and 1980s. Small numbers who adamantly opposed these policies would in time make them into a national issue, aided by a recession and the arrival of refugees in small boats. But overall the country became increasingly diverse, quietly absorbing immigrants from many lands and backgrounds.

The populous states on the southeast coast attracted the most immigrants but other regions became centers of migration as well. Western Australia, considerably closer to Asia than east coast states, was one of them. The arid west coast of Australia that early Dutch explorers declined to colonize turned out to be packed with mineral wealth. As mines were developed to unearth these minerals and roads built to take them to waiting ships, the state's economy flourished. Perth, capital of Western Australia, had 1,400,000 people by the early 2000s and continues to grow.

Descendants of earlier British and Irish settlers still make up a good part of the city's population and there is also a stream of white immigrants from countries such as England, New Zealand, and the United States, who are attracted by its thriving economy. But Perth has numerous other ethnic communities as well. Europeans who arrived during the massive postwar immigration program and their children and grandchildren are one swath of the population.

When migrants came out by ship after World War II, Perth was their first stop. Many who had planned to go on decided to stay. In her book *Journeys of Hope: Six Stories of Family Migration to Western Australia, 1937–1968*, Professor Maryon Allbrook of Edith Cowan University used oral history to let families from Macedonia, Greece, Italy, Holland, Spain, and Burma, speak about their lives there. By also interviewing the children and grandchildren of the original settlers, her book gave a rounded picture of how these families lived and fared.[1]

Anthony Mylonas, whose grandparents came from Greece, had felt accepted at his local high school: "There were about three Greeks, a lot of Italians and Yugoslavs, quite a few Aboriginals, and a lot of Asians," he told Allbrook. "Occasionally someone might call me names but it wasn't a hassle; they were still my friends." In his early twenties when Allbrook spoke with him, he said: "I like the friends I have at the moment. I mix with a lot of different people, ranging from Greeks who wear business suits and drive BMWs, to freaks who have green dread-lock hair and ripped jeans. The friends I see most regularly aren't Greek although I know virtually hundreds of Greeks my age." But his Greek heritage was important to him. Mylonas was glad he had attended Saturday school and learned Greek; he had already made two trips to Greece. He prized "the strong family bond which we have.... If I don't go and see my grandfather for three days, he wonders where I have been."[2]

Mary Della Vedova, whose grandfather came from Tirano in the Italian Alps, said, "Even though we live in a suburb that has a high percentage

Mick and Lucy Catalano in front of their sugar cane farm in Babinda, Queensland, in the 1980s. His father, Mariano Catalano, emigrated from Sicily in 1921 to work in the canefields. Gradually he saved enough to buy his own farm and passed it on to his son. At present, after the British and Irish, Italians are the next largest ethnic group, followed by Germans (courtesy Ethel Ruymaker).

of Italian people, we tend to have multi-cultural neighbours and friends. The majority of my school friends of Italian background have married into Australian or other European families."[3]

On the other side of the country in Queensland, Mick and Lucy Catalano have a sugar cane farm in Babinda, a small town south of Cairns. Mick Catalano's father emigrated to Australia from Sicily in 1921 when he was 26. He worked as a cutter in sugar cane fields in Ayr and Innisfail, bought property in 1930 and sold it in 1952 to buy the farm in Babinda that his son now runs. Lucy Catalano's father came out from a different town in Sicily in 1921, was in the sugar cane business with his brother-in-law for several years, then bought a grocery shop in Innisfail in 1947.

The Catalanos are both Australian born as are their daughters Anne-Marie and Teresa. Anne-Marie wrote that her parents "along with their siblings have realised the dreams of their parents and passed on important morals, values, beliefs and customs of our family to the next generation."[4] She cannot look to the family farm for a living, however; with so much sugar for sale on the world market, the industry has declined in Australia. But Anne-Marie has other options: at school she studied Japanese, her parents hosted a Japanese student who came to Australia for a year to attend high school and learn English, and in 2004 Anne-Marie lived in Japan and taught English there. With fluency in Japanese, Italian and English, along with university training, she has already worked in the tourist industry.[5]

In the 2001 Census, after the British and Irish descended (including New Zealanders), Italians were the next-largest ethnic group. But the numbers of Italians emigrating to Australia have dropped in recent years, as have the numbers from most Western European countries. Higher living standards there have reduced the motivation to leave, and if European Union members do want to move, they can go to a member country closer to home. People from countries on other continents are taking their place.

If you add up the people who come to Australia from Asian countries each year, collectively they now provide the most immigrants. Perth attracts many of them. Some Asian immigrants still fit the old mold of the poor seeking economic advancement; others come for different reasons.

Edmund and Janet Seagh Teo, journalists from Singapore, left well-paying jobs with good benefits to emigrate. At home they worried about the pressure their son, then four, would face once he started school. Children in Singapore must pass a stringent examination at age ten, they explained, which determined their future education and career path.[6]

Language compounded the problem. The Teos are "Straits Chinese" from Malaysia and speak a kind of pidgin Malay. To them Mandarin is a difficult foreign language. But in Singapore all ethnic Chinese children must also pass an examination in Mandarin. The Teos had friends there whose young children went to school all day and then were tutored in several subjects in the evenings and on weekends; they worked ten to twelve hours a day and were under tremendous pressure. "I want my son to have a childhood," said Seagh Teo.[7] In Perth, where the Teos were writing about Australia for papers in Singapore, they had more time for their son and each other. "We gave up a lot to come here," said Edmund Teo, "but it was mainly money."[8] His wife said Western Australia seemed close to Asia: friends in Singapore thought nothing of flying to Perth for the weekend to play golf.

Ramdas Sankaran had not intended to settle in Australia. The son of an affluent family in southern India, he came through as a tourist in the late 1970s as a young man. He planned to go on to the United States and Canada as part of a world tour, but he liked Australia and stayed. Many years later his elderly parents wanted him to return to India and help manage their property. He considered going back. His wife was willing; of Indian ancestry, she grew up in Malaysia where her family had lived for three generations, but she had studied in India and liked it. Their eight-year-old son, however, resisted the move. "I'm an Australian," he insisted and wanted to stay there. In the end they stayed; Sankaran made periodic trips to India to help his parents, juggling the two pulls on his life.

In Perth Sankaran went into social work and eventually became director of the state Ethnic Communities Council. He praised Australia's multicultural policy and was proud of what the country had achieved: "If you look at the scale of world migration over the past 25 or 30 years and think of countries like Germany, Britain, the United States and Canada," he said in the 1990s, "you see that Australia hasn't had the kinds of problems they did. It shows that it's possible to live together."[9] But his work as an advocate for ethnic communities made him aware of the struggles many immigrants faced, especially poor people with scant education. Language was a considerable barrier to getting ahead. People who spoke little or no English had difficulty finding even low-paying jobs, he said.

A Perth newspaper told of Mrs. Nguyen, a Vietnamese widow who had spent twenty months looking for a job as a cleaning woman. The director of Perth's Catholic Migrant Centre spoke of "a subtle discrimination that puts them last on the list."[10] Mrs. Nguyen, still looking for work, was supporting two teen-aged children and a niece on government benefits until they graduated from high school and found jobs. This younger generation, who were becoming fluent in English and developing marketable skills, should have an easier time making it than their parents.

Tjut Najak Hadisah Banta, from Aceh Province in Indonesia, came to Australia as a student in the late 1960s. After completing her secondary education she studied pharmacy at the University of Sydney. In May, 1972, she was married in Sydney at the home of the Counsel-General for Indonesia. The groom was Adam Colin Freestone, a young Anglo-Australian who lectured at a college in a northern city of the state. The traditional Indonesian ceremony was televised.

The press release describing the wedding was put out by the News and Information Bureau of the Australian government. The groom, it said, had converted to Islam, spoke Indonesian and had led a group of 19 Australians on a study tour of Indonesia a few months earlier. After the ceremony the groom's parents, when congratulated, "replied that they were delighted to welcome a beautiful and loving daughter into their family."[11]

Another student, Vannary Imam from Cambodia, arrived in 1971, a few years before chaos engulfed her country. But growing up in Phnom Penh she was aware of the tensions there, partly due to her mixed ancestry. Her

A traditional Indonesian wedding ceremony in Sydney in 1972. Tjut Najak Hadisah Banta, a pharmacy student from Aceh Province, Indonesia, married Adam Colin Freestone, a college lecturer. The groom had converted to Islam and spoke Indonesian. The wedding ceremony was televised (by permission of the National Library of Australia).

father was a Cambodian Buddhist, her mother a Vietnamese Christian. Because of the historic enmity between the two countries, she experienced prejudice as a child. When she took an exam to qualify for a university scholarship and the man in charge made derogatory remarks about her Vietnamese background, she walked out and did not finish the exam. But without a scholarship she could not attend a university.[12]

France, Cambodia's former colonizer, said it might give her a scholarship after she got to Paris but would not provide the airfare out as it once had. Lacking the money to get there, Imam tried the embassies of Britain, Canada, Japan and the United States in turn without luck. Almost as an afterthought she tried Australia. The country gave her a nine-month scholarship under the Colombo Plan to study English in Sydney and then return home. But she was able to get another scholarship and earned a degree from Monash University in Melbourne.

Her memoir, *When Elephants Fight,* tells what happened. (The title is from a Cambodian proverb: When elephants fight ants get killed.) In Melbourne she met and married a Lebanese refugee who was a Muslim. They became Australian citizens and raised three children. She chose the new last name of "Imam" from his religion but remained a Theravada Buddhist. Looking back in 2000 Imam said: "Australia gave me more than a scholarship. It adopted me and saved me.... This country has educated me, shaped my maturity, and provided me with security."[13] But had she arrived twenty years later as a refugee on a small boat, Imam's experience would have been quite different, as we will see in Chapter Twelve.

Events in other parts of the world contributed to the conflict over ethnicity that Australia experienced by the end of the century. When formerly colonized nations became independent after World War II, civil wars broke out in several of them, as rival factions tried to seize control of their governments. And people in some countries with contiguous borders and a long history as enemies fought each other over turf. This caused large numbers of people to flee turmoil or persecution at home and seek asylum as refugees. Some set their sights on Australia. The majority of refugees who arrived from 1975 through the end of the century came from the same region — the Indochinese countries of Vietnam, Cambodia, and Laos. But the largest numbers by far were Vietnamese. Their increasing presence would have an impact on Australia and its future policies toward refugees.

They came as a result of war — what the Vietnamese call the American War and the Americans call the Vietnam War. After Communist forces in North Vietnam invaded South Vietnam, the United States sent troops to help the latter resist. The conflict escalated into a major war and several other countries, including Australia, also sent troops. After a decade of fighting, however, the Communists captured Saigon in 1975 and American and other foreign troops withdrew.

Thousands and in time tens of thousands of South Vietnamese fled after the Communist takeover. Most who managed to get out went to a few refugee camps that were hastily set up by the United Nations High Commissioner on Refugees (UNHCR) in nearby Southeast Asian nations. There, living under primitive conditions, they waited for countries such as the United States, Australia, Canada and France to offer them asylum.

Australia was initially slow to react to the crisis, Professor Nancy Viviani says in her book *The Indochinese in Australia, 1975–1995*, because the government feared that the public might respond negatively to a large Asian influx.[14] Meanwhile the Vietnamese sitting in these camps worried that no country would offer them asylum. In 1976 some took matters into their own hands, obtained boats and sailed to Darwin. Others followed. The alarm this raised helped push the government into negotiating a "generous resettlement policy" from the camps, says Viviani. It agreed to take in "around 15,000 Vietnamese refugees a year, at a time when the total migration program was around 70,000 people per annum."[15] In later years it negotiated with the Vietnamese government.

The Vietnamese refugees who came in under the agreement "lived in special government hostels where they were taught English, learned about government services and were generally introduced to Australian life."[16] Viviani found that "the reception and settlement of these early groups was quite successful."[17] One reason was the way services were delivered, she believes. "The Galbally migrant settlement policies of 1978 changed the whole context for settlement of migrants and refugees ... [and] shifted the responsibility for settlement services to ethnic associations and line government departments."[18]

The Vietnamese, like other ethnic groups before them, soon set up their own community organizations. The Department of Immigration remained in charge of immigrant settlement, but following the Galbally directives it gave organizations run by Vietnamese a large role in the process. This "permitted the delivery of services to clients in their own languages.... It meant that ethnic associations like the Vietnamese Community Association were funded to employ a Grant-in-Aid or welfare worker in their local community and to channel new arrivals to the relevant government departments."[19] In addition, the government set up Migrant Resource Centers in major cities and Vietnamese refugees could use these services as well.[20] In time, the Vietnamese settled in many parts of Australia, with the largest settlement in Cabrametta, an outer suburb of Sydney.

These refugees faced many handicaps: prior to the war there had been no established Vietnamese presence in Australia so initially they stood out

An English lesson. A Vietnamese mother at home with her small children in Melbourne learns English with the help of a volunteer tutor. Only a handful of Vietnamese lived in Australia until the mid-1970s but 156,000 people from that country had settled there by 2001 (Adult Migrant Education Service, State Library of Victoria).

as different — and felt the same about the people in their new country. If they spoke a European language it was likely French rather than English; and they were quite fragmented ethnically. But gradually the Vietnamese built communities and became Australians like other immigrants before them. The services they received in the first years provided a needed boost that enabled them to make the transition.

Once the government worked out an arrangement with the UNHCR for Vietnamese refugees to enter legally, the boatloads of refugees stopped coming. From 1981 until late 1989, no unauthorized boats with refugees arrived on Australia's northern shores. Of the Vietnam refugees who came to Australia between 1976 and 1982, only 2050 were boat people while 55,711 entered legally. By 1995 the Vietnamese in Australia, counting the children born there, had reached 195,000.[21] In proportion to its population, Australia took in more refugees after the war in Vietnam than any other country.[22]

Although this massive intake caused no major protests or violence, the increased presence of the Vietnamese, coupled with the many immigrants and refugees who came from other Asian countries during those same years, did upset many Australians. The historical fear of being taken over by Asians resurfaced. Rising unemployment rates in the early 1980s also contributed to this reaction although there is no evidence that Asian immigrants exacerbated the job scarcity. To the contrary, some immigrants created jobs. For example, many affluent businessmen in Hong Kong, unsure what would happen after their city reverted to mainland China in 1997, hedged their bets by emigrating to Australia, setting up businesses there — and hiring workers. But their contribution to the job pool was not apparent to people laid off or who worried that they might be.

The man who emerged in the 1980s as spokesman for the discontent over rising Asian immigration seemed an unlikely choice. Historian Geoffrey Blainey, a professor at the University of Melbourne, had published several well-regarded books, including *Triumph of the Nomads*, a book favorable to the indigenous Aborigines. He surprised many when he started saying that too many Asian immigrants were coming in. After he gave a speech in this vein at a conference in a small country town in March, 1984, and the Melbourne *Age* reported it on page one, a controversy erupted. Some people denounced Blainey as a racist; others saw him as a hero who dared to say publicly what they had long felt.

Later that year Blainey published a book, *All for Australia*, to explain his position on Asians and criticize the country's multicultural policy: "The old Australians see the newcomers everywhere: they hear a strange language in the supermarket. They wonder what their own familiar world is coming to." Recalling his childhood he wrote: "I cannot remember seeing a Jew until I was thirteen.... The dairying town where I first went to school had, to my incomplete knowledge, not one foreigner."[23]

In his book, Blainey devoted several pages to a letter he received after his controversial speech. The writer came from the outer Sydney suburb of Campsie, where many immigrants from Vietnam, China and Arabic countries were living. She had a litany of complaints. Her Vietnamese neighbors were noisy and parked their cars in inconsiderate places, she told Blainey; at one point they even dried their noodles on the clotheslines in the backyards. "She dislikes the strange smells from the cooking and the smells of the garbage, and she names the nationalities who in her view produce the worst garbage.... This is her land but now she feels dispossessed.... She also knows that hundreds of unemployed Australians in her suburb are worse off than they have ever been while immigrants pour in and take jobs and social services." His correspondent predicted race riots, Blainey reported: "There will be bloodshed in this country," she warned in 1984.[24]

Four years later another well-publicized critic of multiculturalism surfaced. John Howard, leader of the Opposition Liberal Party, told the National

Press Club in June, 1988, "There are profound weaknesses in the policy of multiculturalism. I think it is a rather aimless, divisive policy and I think it ought to be changed."[25] A week later, at a state Liberal Party conference in Esperance, Western Australia, Howard put forth the idea of "One Australia" as a counterweight to multiculturalism, resuscitating the old belief that immigrants should assimilate to the country's dominant culture. In the months that followed he said that Asian immigration should probably be slowed down; if elected, he would look into this.[26] As a result of such speeches and interviews, Howard was criticized by some of his colleagues as well as by ethnic community groups. His poll ratings dropped. At the end of the year he was replaced as leader of the Liberal Party. But he would regain that position in 1995 as we will see in later chapters.

Geoffrey Blainey, who was not running for political office, expressed his views candidly. In his weekly column in the *Australian*, he wrote in 1988, "multiculturalism, as espoused by both parties, is utterly shoddy. Morally, intellectually and economically it is a sham."[27] And earlier in *All for Australia* he declared that "multiculturalism itself is quietly anti–British, and the department of immigration and ethnic affairs could well be called the department of immigration and anti–British affairs."[28] Such a statement may have pleased his supporters but it was contrary to fact. In 1984 more immigrants were still coming to Australia from Britain every year than from any other place; this would be the case until 1996 when New Zealand edged out Britain slightly as number one. The Department of Immigration's point system — with points given for such factors as age, education, work skills and fluency in English — gave the British a built-in advantage since English was their native language.

In popular usage the word "immigrant" came to mean newcomers with dark skins who couldn't speak English or spoke it with a "foreign" accent. Even if English immigrants had arrived only the day before they could walk the streets of any city and not stand out as newcomers. Their presence was unnoticed.

Blainey and his supporters seemed to yearn for life the way it used to be, for the time when everyone, including Irish Catholics and British Protestants, lived in harmony, they remembered, because of their shared values and culture. The world they cherished fondly was one of British traditions, transplanted to Australia along with rose bushes and photographs of Queen Victoria. It was a monocultural world that does not exist in Australia — or in Britain.

Countries change continually but immigrants remember their homeland as it was on the day they left. Toula Somas Mylonas (who is Anthony Mylonas's mother) came from a small Greek village with her family when she was five. She found her life as a teenager constrained because of her parents' memories. When she joined the school basketball team, they refused to let her go to Adelaide with the state team: "No. You know good Greek girls don't go," her mother told her.[29] Thirty years later, Mylonas recounted in *Journeys of Hope*, her mother visited Greece and "was shocked that Greek girls are now exactly like Australian girls. They go out with boys, they even live together."[30]

For many of British ancestry in Australia, clinging to old ways could go even further. Their beliefs, honed over two centuries, fed on long-held assumptions: that "civilization" was synonymous with Western Europe, that Britain represented the pinnacle of human achievement there and that Australia must compensate for its convict origin and "distant" location by being more British than the British. By the end of the twentieth century such views were fading rapidly. But fragments of these embedded legacies remained.

Ten

Embedded Legacies

"Waves of uncertainty sweep over us. Is this continent really our home, or are we just migrants from another civilization, growing wool and piercing the ground for metals, doomed to be dependent for our intellectual and aesthetic nourishment ... on what is brought to us by every mail from overseas?"[1] Writer Nettie Palmer posed these questions in 1930 and answered the latter with a resounding "no." She and her husband Vance Palmer "passionately championed a distinctive Australian national culture, one that was no longer passively responsive to British and European influences."[2]

They faced an uphill battle. In 1930 the idea that Australia had a distinctive literature worth teaching was considered laughable in most circles. This outlook was expressed by the popular phrase, the "cultural cringe," which meant that any art or literature developed in Australia was categorically inferior to works imported from England. Other former British colonies showed symptoms of this malaise, but Australia had the most advanced case. Coupled with the perceived shame of the "convict stain," another popular phrase, it caused self-effacement among a wide swath of the populace.

At the same time, as we have seen, Australia became a vigorous country that offered people freedom and the opportunity to work and have a good life. This led many Australians to see their country in a highly positive light. Two views of Australia existed side by side; their divergent outlooks exerted a two-way pull on the populace. One side saw a distinctive nation with its own culture and traditions. The other thought of Australia as a spinoff of England; for them the country had merit only insofar as it copied British ways. This divide, exacerbated by class and religious differences, has continued to the present day.

When Jill Ker Conway attended an Anglican girls' school in Sydney in the 1950s, she found herself steeped in the pull towards England: "Our curriculum was inherited from Great Britain ... and ignored our presence in Australia,"[3] she recalled in her memoir *The Road from Coorain*. "We might have been in Sussex for all the attention we paid to Australian poetry and prose. It did not count."[4] Her schooling had been "training me to imitate the ways and manners of the English upper class ... the people I and my brothers had known in school were working not on Australia's social and political problems, but on gaining recognition from an external British world."[5] When Conway later visited London she found that the downgrading of Australia was reinforced from Britain. After a weekend at a country house, the "ultimate compliment" her host could bestow was the assurance, "You know, my dear, one would hardly know you were not English."[6]

English journalist Malcolm Muggeridge, who visited Australia for a short time in 1958, gently ridiculed the idea that Australia had substance. "Australians do have a past, or are busily engaged in inventing one," he said in a radio speech in Sydney, "and would be most incensed by any suggestion that they have no future ... [their] writers and artists strive to demonstrate the existence of an indigenous culture [his use of the word "indigenous" here meant Australian rather than British or European] and try, not always convincingly, to avert their eyes from Europe and America, and fix them on their native land."[7] There were moments when a brief visitor like himself "sees Australia as a remote and rather forlorn European outpost.... Won't they, he asks himself, get ever lonelier here?"[8]

Such views have declined in recent decades but not entirely. When asked how the British viewed Australians, a Scot from Glasgow replied without hesitation: "The British see Australia as a land of beer-drinking macho men, a place of little value whose people have no depth." A columnist for the London *Sunday Telegraph* wrote in 1992: "There is a kernel of truth in the view of Australians as somewhat simple minded folk. Originally settled by the detritus of 18th and 19th century Britain, Australia has the distinction of being the world's only entirely proletarian country.... Their architecture, sense of humor, and culture are almost entirely lower class."[9]

A novel by a famous English author contributed to the image of Australians as working-class yahoos. In 1922, D. H. Lawrence and his wife spent three months in Australia, mostly in the country town of Thirroul south of Sydney where he wrote the novel *Kangaroo*.[10] Its main character, Robert Lovat Somers, was a British writer who spent a few months in Australia, mostly in a country town. The book's meat was a series of monologues and dialogues on political systems that expressed Somers's disdain for Australia, working people and democracy.

A thin plot line ran through the book. The Somerses met Benjamin Cooley, leader of a right-wing movement to overthrow democracy in Australia. His followers called him "Kangaroo." Somers had political discussions with Kangaroo and some of his supporters. Later he attended a raucous protest rally in Sydney where the leader was shot and then visited him in the hospital. Kangaroo died and the Somerses left Australia.

The novel's opening paragraph introduced its theme, showing workers in Sydney eating lunch on the grass, men who "had that air of owning the city which belongs to a good Australian."[11] The Somerses tried to negotiate with a taxi driver but he quoted a price they thought was outrageous. When they protested the driver said take it or leave it. His mates supported him. "Aren't they *vile!*"[12] Somers's wife said afterwards. Near the end of the chapter Lawrence set down his first monologue: "Now Somers was English by blood and education, and though he had no antecedents whatsoever, yet he felt himself one of the *responsible* members of society, as contrasted with the innumerable *irresponsible* members. In old, cultured, ethical England," the responsible people became the rulers.[13]

"But in Australia," said Somers, "nobody is supposed to rule, and nobody does, so the distinction falls to the ground. The proletariat appoints men to administer the law, not to rule. These ministers are not really responsible, any more than the housemaid is responsible ... it was a granted condition of Australia, that Demos was his own master.... And this was what Richard Lovat Somers could not stand."[14] More attacks in this vein occurred in several parts of the book.

When *Kangaroo* was published in 1923, many Australians found the book hard to stomach. The country's government was, after all, based on Britain's parliamentary system although it did incorporate features from other democracies such as an elected upper house and a written constitution. At first Australian writers thought the book too ridiculous to dignify with a response. But as critics abroad kept quoting from *Kangaroo* as if Lawrence was an expert on their country, they hit back. A. D. Hope, one of the country's leading poets and a professor in Canberra, described *Kangaroo* as "ignorant, slapdash, shoddy, carelessly written and a travesty.... [Lawrence] took not the slightest trouble to find out about Australia."[15] Writer Miles Franklin praised Lawrence's descriptions of the landscape but otherwise found nothing else to like: "Extraordinary mess as a novel, No novel at all ... it is the poor pathological man's spiritual and intellectual gropings."[16] Novelist Katharine Susannah Prichard declared, "How fatuous and absurd are yards of Somers' drivel about Australia."[17]

Lawrence's letters make clear that he was impressed with Australia's landscape but detested its people. He wrote to his agent in the United States about "the hateful newness, the democratic conceit, every man a little pope of perfection.... Is America awful like this?"[18] As biographer Brenda Maddox put it: "Lawrence had decided within a day that he did not really like the egalitarian Australian personality."[19]

Kangaroo came back into the spotlight in 1981 when Sydney journalist Robert Darroch published a book that said the novel's Australian characters were based on people Lawrence met during his short stay. Benjamin Cooley, the man known as "Kangaroo," was modeled on Sir Charles Rosenthal, an Australian of German descent,[20] who served as a general during World War I, Darroch said. A few years after the war Rosenthal headed a short-lived group, the King and Empire Alliance, and was involved with a "secret army" of disgruntled veterans who planned to overthrow the government. Darroch described members of the Alliance as "the cream of Sydney and NSW."[21]

Some Australians are not convinced that Cooley was based on Rosenthal.[22] But Simon Leys, a Belgian Australian professor in Canberra, accepted Darroch's findings. In an article Leys published in the *New York Review of Books* in 1994, "Lawrence of Australia," he drew on Darroch's work and presented *Kangaroo* as the quintessential novel about Australia. Many in the country disparaged the book, he conceded, but "for any non–Australian reader," Leys insisted, "it is absolutely evident that *Kangaroo* is a lyrical hymn celebrating the land and people of Australia."[23]

American writer Paul Theroux had a different reaction. "It took him less time to write the book than I took to read it," Theroux said of Lawrence and *Kangaroo*, "because it is practically unreadable ... Lawrence is flat-footed in this book but never mind! You have to admire his speed. And now and then he surpasses himself, describing a plopping wave or a jellyfish."[24]

Unlike Lawrence, other British visitors before and after his stay noticed a strong bias there against the working classes. An English observer wrote in 1903: "It is sometimes said that in Australia there are no class distinctions.... It would probably be truer to say that in no country in the world are there such strong class-distinctions in proportion to the actual amount of difference between the 'classes' ... the 'classes' collectively distrust and fear the 'masses' far more than is the case at home."[25]

Several decades later Scottish journalist John Douglas Pringle wrote about class in Australia. "D. H. Lawrence thought there were no class distinctions in Australia" he began, and then spent several pages describing these distinctions.[26] Pringle, who served as editor of the *Sydney Morning Herald* from 1952 to 1957, found that "Australian society is much more complicated than Lawrence thought, and beneath the democratic surface a surprising number of class distinctions do exist.... The great difference between Australia and England, however, is that in Australia the pretensions of these classes [middle and upper] are simply not recognized by the great mass of the people. They are not so much resented as ignored."[27]

British journalist Michael Davie, who like Pringle got to know Australia when he edited a newspaper there (in his case the Melbourne *Age* from 1978 to 1981), also developed a positive view of the country. Davie excoriated both Brits and Aussies who persisted in portraying people there in glib stereotypes. "The British upper class and middle class still seem to feel the need ... to think of Australia as an uninteresting country inhabited by beer-swilling louts who talk in a comic accent," he wrote in 1984.[28] "Their misconceptions are fed by some of the best-known, and highly talented, Australian expatriates.... The comedian Barry Humphries [creator of Dame Edna Everage] ... presents a savage picture of Australian suburbia and culture that brilliantly fuels the prejudices of his audience."[29]

Welsh writer Jan Morris found many indications of class pretensions in Sydney in 1992: "There is plenty of snobbery too, still.... It is not entirely a desire for an excellent education, we may be sure, which ensures that the great Sydney private schools have waiting lists of thousands." And this world traveler commented: "Where one lives is also more socially important in Sydney than in most cities of my acquaintance."[30]

Historian Manning Clark believed that "from the beginning of squatterdom's domination until the present day class conflict has played a major role in our history."[31] Clark, who had a foot in two classes by birth, struggled to define himself and his country. His father, a minister, came from a working-class family in London that emigrated to Australia when he was two. His mother was descended from Australia's elite: the Reverend Samuel Marsden, who arrived in 1794, was an ancestor. "My mother's class had luxury, they had elegance," Clark recalled in a memoir published shortly before his death in 1991. "They behaved as though they were not only different but also superior to all other people. I remember during one visit to Sydney, hearing a Sydney patrician say to my grandfather, 'The mistake we made was giving workers the vote.'"[32]

Growing up in the 1920s and 1930s Clark accepted the prevailing belief that "there was only one culture in Australia — European culture; only one way of life — the transplanted European way of life."[33] As an adult Clark decided to pursue graduate studies at Oxford University and looked forward to meeting a superior breed of people there. This assumption had its first upset on the trip over when his ship stopped at Gibraltar and several English people boarded: "They made it plain by facial expressions of disdain and contempt that everything we Australians did — the way we spoke, the way we walked, the way we dressed — was all vulgar, crude, coarse, loud-mouthed, and lacking in both subtlety and refinement."[34]

Arriving at Oxford Clark visited one of his tutors: "He asked me whether Australians were quite as coarse as they were portrayed in D. H. Lawrence's *Kangaroo*. I said I hoped not."[35] But Oxford failed to meet Clark's expectations. The lectures "were not the eye-openers I had been led to believe were performed at Oxford each term.... England soon became one of my many lost illusions."[36] He returned home feeling more Australian than ever. Later when Max Crawford, his former professor at Melbourne University, asked him to put together a course on Australian history, Clark eagerly accepted. His course brought in Australian literature as well, including the work of poet Henry Lawson. Moving on to the university at Canberra, Clark spent the next thirty years writing his six-volume study *A History of Australia*. Its emphasis on Australia as a country in its own right would influence a new generation of historians. The work remains controversial among scholars there, however, as much for its personal idiosyncratic style as for its point of view.

Clark of course was not the first Australian to champion Australian history, literature and art. Vance and Nettie Palmer were two of the most dedicated and persistent early voices in the twentieth century. (This chapter opened with a quote from Nettie Palmer written in 1930.) Vance Palmer, born in 1885, published his first article in *Steele Rudd's Magazine* at the age of nineteen. He followed Rudd's advice to go abroad to further his career and went to London; but like Clark a generation later, the experience made him feel more Australian. Returning home in 1915, "he felt intensely the need for a living and distinctive Australian culture. He traveled the country speaking ... for the development of a national sentiment, a national culture which would silence those who felt 'nothing in art or life is important unless it comes out of England.'"[37] In 1917 he arranged for a reissue of Joseph Furphy's outback novel *Such Is Life* and wrote the preface. His wife Nettie Palmer published *Modern Australian Literature, 1900–1923* in 1924 to bring readers up to date on writing after the era of the bushman poets.

Australian writers found themselves in an untenable situation then. Not only did local critics ignore works published there, but it was even difficult to find a publisher in Australia. A group of writers in Sydney formed the Fellowship of Australian Writers (FAW) in 1928 "to foster wide and practical appreciation of Australian literature, and to create a congenial atmosphere for the production of literary work."[38] In 1934 the FAW took action after it found that in the official list of books that schoolchildren in NSW must study for a mandatory examination, "there was not one single text book written by an Australian or published by an Australian firm (one book alone being edited in this country)."[39] This meant that the viewpoints of these books were entirely British and that royalties went solely to authors in the U.K. After Fellowship members pointed this out to the Minister of Education he began considering their suggestions of works by Australian authors for use in the schools.

By the early 1940s professors at a few universities taught courses on Australian literature although at first they had to stand up to opposition and ridicule. When poet A. D. Hope set up such a class, one skeptic asked "What Australian literature?" while another said, "You wouldn't want your daughter to be a B.A. in Australian literature, would you?"[40]

Australian authors often went to Britain, or in some cases the United States, to further their careers. Christina Stead, for example, moved to London in 1928 after no Australian publisher would take her first book. She remained abroad for 47 years, in part because of a man she met there and eventually married. Her novels gradually brought her critical acclaim in Britain, Europe and the United States (her best-known book was *The Man Who Loved Children*) but in Australia it was hard to find copies of her work, even in libraries. The first Australian edition of one of Stead's books came out in 1966.[41]

Novelist Patrick White was sent to England for school and university by his mother, who had been brought to Australia as an infant but identified so strongly with her old homeland that she would only hire maids who had been born in Britain. (His father came from a family of wealthy graziers.) After White completed his education he remained in England to write and eventually found publishers in London and New York. After sixteen years abroad, including a stint in the military, he returned home. His widowed mother, who was about to move to England, assumed that her son would join her there. But he settled in Sydney, continued writing novels about Australia, and in 1973 became the country's first, and thus far only, Nobel Laureate in literature.

Earlier, Miles Franklin (whose real first name was Stella) went to the United States in 1906 after her first novel, *My Brilliant Career*, was published. She settled in Chicago where she lived at Jane Addams's Hull House for nine years and worked for the Women Workers' Trade Union League. After World War I broke out she moved to England to do war work and stayed there for 12 years. Then she returned home, gave up her political and social work, and devoted herself to writing novels about Australia.[42] Although living a reclusive life, she became a champion of Australian writing. At a literary dinner in 1951, after one speaker was patronizing on the subject, "Her passionate pleas for the inclusion of Australian literature in university courses brought down the house."[43]

The move to develop a distinctive Australian literature was one strand that influenced the country's development. Another potent strand was mentioned earlier — the strong class divide among the populace, especially in regard to the country's relationship with Britain. This conflict came to the fore in both world wars of the twentieth century.

During World War I Australians split over the issue of whether or not to draft young men into the army. The conflict brought out class differences with religious overtones as well. At first men from all classes volunteered for the army, eager for adventure but also wanting to show the world the mettle of Australian manhood. They served under British officers as part of the Empire's forces.

In 1915 thirty thousand Australian and New Zealand soldiers were sent to the Gallipoli peninsula on the western side of the Dardanelles. Their mission was to fend off the enemy so British ships could sail through to Constantinople. But their officers were unprepared and the plan was ill-conceived: "Its intelligence was out of date, its maps were inaccurate, it had insufficient shells."[44] Although the men fought bravely, their exposed position enabled the Turks to slaughter them in great numbers. The operation was a military disaster.

In Australia, however, Gallipoli was depicted as a moral victory. Prime Minister Billy Hughes "announced that the defeat at Gallipoli was a feat of arms almost unparalleled in human history," wrote historian F. G. Clarke. "When such bravery, nobility, and self-sacrifice could emerge, how could it be said that the war was wholly evil? Frequent allusions were also made to the belief that Gallipoli somehow raised Australia to nationhood and maturity in the eyes of the world."[45]

But as wounded soldiers returned home with details of the Gallipoli fiasco, and then casualty lists from French battlefields mounted, workers lost their enthusiasm for war. By 1916 voluntary enlistments no longer kept pace with British requests for more troops. Hughes, who had come to power through the Labor Party, favored conscription but with Labor MPs split over the war, he didn't have enough votes to get a draft bill through Parliament. Instead he put a conscription referendum on the ballot. Despite his government's strong campaign, the referendum failed.

The furious Hughes left the Labor Party and teamed up with some conservatives to form a new party. In 1917 he again put forth a conscription referendum. It lost by a wider margin than the first one. This time, says historian Ian Turner, "the consensus on the war had broken, very much along class lines. Middle-class Australia was still fervently behind the war effort, but working-class Australia had come to believe that the allied demand for unconditional surrender was a cloak for national aggrandisement"—and that they were being used as cannon fodder.[46]

Some historians believe that Britain's harsh response to a rebellion in Ireland a year earlier also played a role in defeating Australia's second conscription referendum. In Australia, "the ancient Irish hatred of Britain was fanned into new life by the suppression of the 1916 Easter Rebellion in

Dublin," wrote Ward.[47] Clarke recounted that in Melbourne, Catholic Archbishop Daniel Mannix "became a leading campaigner for a vote against conscription, compounding Irish hatred for English policies towards the country of his birth with the view that Australians ought not to be compelled to die in England's war."[48]

Twenty years later, the Second World War caused a conflict between Australians' allegiance to the British Empire and concern for their own safety. Japan had invaded China and was conquering Pacific nations, but British Prime Minister Winston Churchill decided to win the war against Hitler before turning to the conflict in Asia. Churchill requested so many Australian troops that not one trained division was left at home to defend the country in case it was attacked.

Australia's prime minister in the late 1930s was Robert Gordon Menzies, a man who identified more with Britain and its empire than his own country. (He was the grandson of Scottish immigrants.) Menzies swiftly filled all Churchill's requests for more troops, secure in the belief that if the Japanese dared to attack Australia, forces from Britain's impregnable naval base at Singapore would rush to their aid and repulse the enemy in short order. Many Australians agreed, certain that Britain would always take care of them. Others were less sanguine: they became nervous as they saw Japan making inroads in the region — and as Churchill transferred ships from the fleet at Singapore to the Mediterranean.[49]

Meanwhile Menzies spent much time in London where he hoped to forge a new political career, according to historian David Day in his book *The Great Betrayal*, a study of Australia and Britain during the early years of World War II. Returning from a trip in May, 1941, Menzies wrote in his diary of "the sick feeling of repugnance and apprehension [that] grows in me as I approach Australia."[50] Although now facing considerable criticism, he clung to his beliefs, urging Australians to be "true children of magnificent Britain from where we come."[51] But with opposition to his policies mounting within his own party, Menzies resigned as prime minister in August, 1941.

The leader of the Country Party led the nation for two months and then Labor Party leader John Curtin became prime minister in October. Curtin immediately began sending a stream of cables to Churchill apprising him of Australia's dangerous situation and urging him to send more troops, ships and planes to Singapore. Churchill, accustomed to unquestioned acquiescence by Britain's Dominions, was infuriated by such demands; he told his doctor, Lord Moran, that the Australians came from bad stock.[52] At the same time, although Churchill kept assuring Curtin that Britain would defend Singapore and Australia, he soon decided that securing Burma was more important than holding on to Singapore.[53]

Nor was Churchill the only British official badmouthing Australia in those years. In a letter to a colleague, Sir Ronald Cross, Britain's High Commissioner in Canberra, referred to the Australians as "an inferior people."[54] He later advised the War Cabinet in London that Australia was "so dependent on our good-will that we can use a big enough stick to get our way."[55]

On December 7, 1941, the Japanese bombed Pearl Harbor, an American naval base in Hawaii. A few weeks later Curtin made a major foreign policy decision: "We look for a solid and impregnable barrier of the Democracies against the three Axis powers, and we refuse to accept the dictum that the Pacific struggles must be treated as a subordinate segment of the general conflicts ... we know, too, that Australia can go and Britain can still hold on. We are, therefore, determined that Australia shall not go" he wrote in part.[56] The country would work with the United States to shape a plan and fight together against the Japanese incursion.

Churchill finally did send troops to Singapore but they arrived after the Japanese had invaded and were "marched off ships in Singapore harbour in time to join their comrades for the march to Changi prison."[57] On February 15, 1942, Britain's naval base in Singapore fell to the Japanese. Four days later more than 100 Japanese planes bombed the northwestern city of Darwin, Australia, killing 243 people and destroying 8 ships and 23 aircraft.[58]

The Australian General Staff then ordered three of its divisions, which had been fighting on the Middle Eastern front, to return home and fight the Japanese in the Pacific. Churchill balked. He wanted the Seventh Division to go to Burma instead and ordered the fleet already taking the men back to Australia to change course and head for Burma.

But Curtin insisted that the Seventh Division come home. His insistence "astonished" Churchill. "This was not the sort of deferential behavior British statesmen had become used to from Menzies and Churchill also had Roosevelt bring pressure to bear on Curtin but to no avail. Reluctantly the orders were sent to the fleet to change course again, for Australia."[59] Japanese troops were already in nearby New Guinea, which could serve as a launching pad for an invasion of Australia. The seasoned troops of the Seventh Division returned home in time to fight in New Guinea and helped defeat the Japanese there. During that same period American General Douglas MacArthur arrived in Australia and set up headquarters for the Allied forces in the region. In May, an American and Australian fleet defeated the Japanese at the Battle of the Coral Sea; a month later the Battle of Midway gave the Allies a decisive victory over the Japanese. Australia was not invaded.

After World War II the move toward a distinctive Australian consciousness grew slowly. Although the steady influx of immigrants from so many countries made the old distinctions between Anglo-Saxons and Celts, Protestants and Catholics, less important, embedded roots of the past proved hard to dislodge. For a time the country embraced Britain with renewed fervor, in a love fest led by their smitten prime minister. He was Robert Menzies, the same man who had resigned as head of government in 1941. This time he made his mark in Australian politics, serving as prime minister from December, 1949 through March, 1966.

The Menzies government was involved in some diplomatic activity with nearby Asian countries as former colonies of Britain, the Netherlands and France became independent nations. The aim of the former colonizers, as of Australia and the United States, was to ensure that none of these new nations embraced communism. But Menzies showed scant interest in building relationships with Asian countries. He continued making frequent trips to England and often visited the royal family. "His reluctance to visit Asia was always contrasted by critics with his willingness to visit England and to accept British imperial honors such as a Knighthood of the Thistle," said one such critic.[60]

Menzies is remembered for articulating the doctrine that Australia needed "great and powerful friends," because it was so "isolated" and insignificant. The powerful friends he meant were Britain and the United States. The further a country was from the Atlantic Rim, the closer to Australia geographically, the less it counted in his eyes.

Journalist Geraldine Brooks, who grew up in Sydney during the Menzies years, remembers that "his pro–British, pro-monarchy rhetoric infected us all with the sense that we were second-raters—inferior convict stock who should continue to look to the culture and history of our colonizer rather than trying to forge an identity of our own.... We decorated our walls with portraits of Queen Elizabeth and prints of landscapes by Constable and Turner."[61]

Such attitudes did not disappear as soon as the Menzies years ended. They were most persistent among people in the middle and upper echelons including, in the past, even some diplomats: "I have met Australian diplomats, ostensibly charged with the job of promoting their country," wrote Ilsa Sharp, "who were only too eager over a private dinner table to disassociate themselves from what they saw as the unspeakable yobbos of their homeland."[62] Sharp regarded this attitude as part of the lingering cultural cringe, reflecting the tendency of those who still identified with Britain to disparage everything Australian, including most of its people. Australian-born journalist Ross Terrill, who interviewed a number of his former countrymen for his book *The Australians* reported: "Australian intellectuals talk and drink and spend their leisure like other Australians, yet often their minds are in Europe and their concrete plans (a trip this year, a grant next year) focus on the United States. It is puzzling that at one moment they react as nationalists while the next they speak of Australia as if it were little more than a hotel in which they are for the moment staying."[63]

Foreigners visiting the country and seeing its many assets were sometimes puzzled by the attitudes they encountered. "One of the oddest things for an outsider to do is watch Australians assessing themselves," Bill Bryson commented in his travel book *In a Sunburned Country*. "They are an extraordinarily self-critical people. You encounter it constantly in newspapers and on television and radio—a nagging conviction that no matter how good things are in Australia, they are bound to be better elsewhere."[64] Another travel writer, Paul Theroux, concurred: "The Australian image abroad is one of swaggering confidence and contented good humor," he wrote, " but in Australia itself there is nagging self-criticism, a constant theme of *What's wrong with us?* ... no one is more mocking of Australia than the Australians themselves."[65] Ethel Ruymaker, an American educator who taught at two Australian universities during the 1980s, had some students who agonized over their country's identity. One asked plaintively: "Do you think we really have a national culture?" Ruymaker, an Australia enthusiast who maintains close friendships with several people she met during her years there, believes that "Australians do tend to undervalue themselves."[66]

So does Australian journalist Paul Kelly. In "The Paradox of Pessimism," he wrote: "The repeated impression left by senior overseas visitors to this country is their admiration for our achievements and astonishment at the complacent devaluation of this achievement by the host community. Australians are trapped in a contradiction — too reluctant to grasp their success outside sport, too willing to overlook genuine national progress as a role model."[67] In 2002, Katie Lahey, who heads the Business Council of Australia, wrote: "With the possible exception of sports— where it seems we have no peers— and possibly movies, we seem, as a country, unwilling or unable to celebrate our achievements, our successes."[68]

But such sentiments were not universal. The number of Australians with confidence in their country kept growing steadily. And along with the Britain-worshippers, Australia has consistently had another contingent of citizens who had little regard for England. "Poms," the Australian slang for the English, often had a negative connotation there.

For English immigrants who arrived after the Second World War, the reality of Australia must have been a shock. All they had heard at home led them to believe it was a rough frontier society, inferior to theirs in manners and culture, whose citizens would welcome them as emissaries from the superior motherland. And Australia's eagerness to recruit English migrants led it to print slick brochures extolling the country's economic opportunities and enchanting lifestyle in the sunshine. When English migrants arrived and were put in hostels that were sometimes in disrepair, and when they were not greeted with enthusiasm, many balked. Nearly a quarter went back to England within a few years. When researchers interviewed a sampling of those who left, they found some had assumed that Australia was no farther from England than Spain or France.[69]

As Jupp explained in *The English in Australia:* "Over several generations Australians had absorbed the idea that people came because it was better than their own country and stayed for the same reason. Consequently they should be grateful."[70] Australians scorned English immigrants who kept criticizing their country. They were called "whingeing poms" (a whinger is a complainer) or "pommy bastards." The literature reflected these feelings. In *Boomerang* George Mikes wrote: "It is always the Pommy Bastards who, instead of being grateful, keep on complaining,"[71] while a character in Thomas Keneally's novel *The Chant of Jimmy Blacksmith* says: "Pass a law to give every single wingeing bloody Pommie his fare home to England."[72]

Australians who visited Britain in turn often spoke out against the condescension they experienced there. When workers found their English relatives living in cramped quarters on wages lower than what they earned in Australia — and then heard their own country downgraded and themselves ridiculed because their accent and manners were different — they gave their hosts an earful about the glories of Australia.

Australians of Welsh origin, whose ancestors were Celts, might also balk at acceding to English cultural dominance. They welcomed Lewis Lloyd, a historian from Wales who has written about Welsh immigrants to Australia. When this author met Lloyd in Canberra, where he was doing research for an updated version of his book, *Australians from Wales,* he pointed out Welsh contributions to Australian culture. Eisteddfod, a popular annual music and dance festival in Australia, was Welsh in origin, he said, as were Cambrian choirs.[73] The introduction to Lloyd's book reflected the feelings of many there: "The Irish, the Scots, the Welsh, and the Cornish who were transported or who emigrated to Australia should not be written out of the story by the misuse of the term 'Anglo-Saxon'.... The foundations of modern Australia, warts and all, were laid by Celts as well as Saxons and some of the former were Welsh (*Cymry*)."[74]

In the last decades of the twentieth century there was a sea change in the numbers of Australians who expressed confidence about themselves and their country. Some of the people Ross Terrill interviewed reflected this growing pride. Barry Cohen, arts minister under the Hawke government, told Terrill: "People are no longer embarrassed about being Australian.

They're proud of their accent."[75] Bill Hayden, governor general under Keating, declared: "I think the chip on the shoulder, the cultural cringe, has gone. Now we're more confident."[76] Ilsa Sharp found that "there is an attractive sense of security, pride and identity in the ordinary Australian's conviction that he has got it right."[77]

The author saw this same confidence in most Australians she talked with or got to know and in one group observed from the sidelines. At an exhibit of Australia's responses to British royalty, which showed memorabilia such as a plate commemorating Queen Victoria's Golden Jubilee and a photograph of the young Queen Elizabeth, a class of teenagers came through with their teacher. "How many of you have a picture of Queen Elizabeth at home?" she asked them.[78] The students seemed amused by the funny question. When no one answered affirmatively, the flustered teacher said: "It's because your parents came from other places." But glancing at the students' faces it seemed likely that several had British ancestors. Times had changed.

Eleven

Turbulent Times

Journalist Paul Kelly found much to be proud of when he summed up his country's assets in 1999: "Australia has a highly educated workforce, a rapid take-up of new technology, a deep attachment to the rule of law, a diligence about democratic process, a sophisticated financial system, vast natural resources, a political tradition of adaptation and pragmatism, a balance between individual initiative and state support," he wrote. "It is a society remarkable for its diversity and for its multicultural reinvention."[1]

Then Kelly declared: "It is as irresistible as it is unfashionable — that the late 1990s had the potential to be a Golden Age for Australia."[2] The potential was there but it was not fulfilled. Instead the late 1990s were turbulent times when political battles raged on several fronts. A new administration at the helm brought old conflicts to the surface.

At federal elections in March, 1996, the Labor Party was defeated after 13 years in office. The victors formed a coalition government of two conservative parties: the Liberals (akin to the U.S. Republican and the British and Canadian Conservative parties) and the National Party (an outgrowth of the old Country Party). John Howard, leader of the Liberal Party, became prime minister.

Howard, who has described himself as the most conservative prime minister the Liberal Party ever had, lost no time in making changes that implemented his beliefs. His administration swiftly cut government funding for services in areas such as health care, higher education and the arts. Programs for the indigenous people felt the pruning shears of the government as did programs that supported a multicultural Australia.

The new prime minister also opposed a referendum to make the country a republic. Two decades earlier a constitutional crisis had given a new surge of life to a movement to end the last formal tie with Britain. To understand what happened in 1999, we need to look first at that earlier period.

During the administration of Prime Minister Gough Whitlam, the governor general was Sir John Kerr, an Australian appointed by Whitlam with the consent of Queen Elizabeth, Australia's head of state. Kerr served as her representative there. In November, 1975, he suddenly fired Gough Whitlam and dissolved Parliament. When the stunned public asked how this could happen, they were told that the constitution gave the governor general unspecified reserve powers which allowed such action. The firing and its aftermath brought two different views of Australia to the fore.

The Labor Party had been out of power for twenty-three years when it won the national election in December, 1972. Gough Whitlam, the new prime minister, launched a series of sweeping reforms. During Whitlam's three years in office, "The Federal Government assumed responsibility for Aboriginal health, education, and welfare, and the first land rights legislation was drafted; the Aboriginal people were drawn into administration of their own affairs for the first time," journalist John Pilger recounted.[3] "Racially selected sports teams were banned from entering Australia. Equal pay for women was introduced. Wages, pensions, and unemployment benefits rose. A national health service was established, open to all.... The arts were elevated; and the already resuscitated film industry was given the flesh and blood of extensive Government funding."[4]

Changes in Australia's immigration policies and attitudes towards other countries were also far reaching. "Gough Whitlam was determined to reverse support for White Australia, to reduce the British connection, and to oppose racist ideas and practices," multicultural specialist James Jupp pointed out. "His brief government officially ended White Australia, declared Australia to be a multicultural society, created a Community Relations Commission and Racial Discrimination Act, granted independence to Papua New Guinea in 1975 [and] ... recognized the Chinese Communist government in Beijing."[5]

"It is no exaggeration to say Australia changed overnight," journalist Geraldine Brooks declared. "Whitlam immediately ended conscription, freed jailed draft dodgers, and ordered the troops home from Vietnam.... The voting age was lowered to eighteen from twenty-one. The arts began to receive an unprecedented infusion of government funding.... [Whitlam] doubled education spending, abolished university fees, and established generous allowances for students who needed them. 'God Save the Queen' ceased to be our national anthem, and we stopped shunning countries like Cuba and China just because the Americans told us to.... Every day under Whitlam, Australia seemed to become more itself and less a pale imitation of elsewhere."[6]

The opposition viewed these spiraling changes with shock and alarm. From their perspective the country they knew, and had controlled for more than two decades, was being torn apart by a cyclone that would destroy the way of life they held dear. By the fall of 1975 there was gridlock in Parliament, with Whitlam's opponents in the Senate blocking his budgetary Supply Bills. Historians can point to several reasons for the unprecedented dismissal but one stands out: Gough Whitlam tried to change too much too quickly. His opponents must have felt that drastic action was needed to stop him. The irony here is that a number of changes ushered in by the Whitlam government eventually became standard Australian policy with bipartisan support. Gough Whitlam served as a catalyst in the making of modern Australia.

The shock over Whitlam's dismissal reinvigorated the desire to make Australia a republic. The movement grew over the next twenty years. Paul Keating, prime minister from December, 1991 to March, 1996, strongly favored becoming a republic: his administration set in motion the procedure for a referendum on the issue. But when the time to hold it drew near, John Howard, who adamantly opposed a republic, had become prime minister.

A brief look at the country's form of government makes clear what was at stake. Australia's parliamentary democracy has two top offices. The prime minister, who heads the government, runs the country and has political power. The head of state, by contrast, is a ceremonial post. Britain's Queen Elizabeth, as mentioned earlier, is Australia's head of state. Her duties are performed by her on-site representative, the governor general, an Australian appointed by the prime minister with the queen's consent. A respected figure, he presides at state dinners, confers with officials and diplomats, and makes patriotic speeches on national holidays and special occasions. If an Australian became head of state outright, and the British monarch no longer had a formal role in Australia, the country would be a republic.

When delegates assembled in 1998 for a constitutional convention to plan the referendum, so many factions were promoting so many different changes that at first it seemed unlikely they would ever reach an agreement. But in the end they agreed on a "minimalist" first step: to make the head of state an independent Australian office, ending the last official link with the British crown. Other needed changes could be worked out in time, they decided.[7]

Delegates did not alter the functions of head of state. But they did change the title of the office to "president," to get away from the colonial connotations of the term "governor general." Here they followed many republics with British-type parliamentary systems that have a prime minister and a ceremonial head of state called president (for example, Ireland, Israel, and India). Delegates at Australia's convention also decided that instead of being appointed by the prime minister as before, the president should be elected by a two-thirds vote of both houses of Parliament.

As a republic Australia would still retain cultural ties with Britain through membership in the Commonwealth of Nations, an organization of the U.K. and most of its former colonies. Of its 53 members, five have their own monarchs, 15 retain Queen Elizabeth as their head of state, and 33 have become republics. "Queen Elizabeth could still be an honored guest in Australia as Head of the Commonwealth," the Republican Movement's website pointed out.

But when Australians heard the word "president" they assumed that any official with that name would wield substantial power. Instead of thinking "ceremonial figurehead," Australians thought of presidents who were frequently in the news—America's president in particular but also dictators who are called presidents. They were encouraged in such thinking by the Constitutional Monarchists who wanted to preserve the status quo.

The cry went out that an Australian president must be elected directly by the people or goodbye democracy. Opponents of a republic denounced the proposed two-thirds vote for president by Parliament as an egregious power grab by political elites—the "chardonnay sippers"—who were trying to deprive the people of the right to choose their leader. "Don't vote for the politician's republic" became their mantra.

As the campaign heated up, Australians were besieged with prophecies of dire consequences—all fictitious—if the measure passed. One media pundit said it would smooth the way for "the desperate man and the rogue" to seize power as well as removing protections for freedom of the press. A president not directly elected might become a dictator. Others warned that if the country became a republic, its athletes might be ineligible to participate in the Commonwealth Games, ignoring the fact that nearly two-thirds of Commonwealth members were already republics. Still others said that the changeover would cost hundreds of millions of dollars, money the country could better spend in other ways. On the other side, the Republican Movement failed to respond vigorously to such specious charges or to effectively hammer home the ways in which a republic would benefit Australia.

The Constitutional Monarchists painted the republic referendum as an invention of Paul Keating and the Labor Party, which people in other parties opposed. In fact the referendum had supporters and opponents in both major parties; for example, a group of Liberal Party members, mainly business executives and former officials, formed "Conservatives for an Australian Head of State." They argued that a fully independent Australia would benefit people in all political parties. Bank executive Charles Goode thought becoming a republic would help the country's relations with Southeast Asian nations and bolster its position in the region. Mining executive Robert Champion de Crespigny said other countries would consider Australia backward and out-of-date if voters rejected a republic.[8] But the prime minister brushed aside such concerns.

John Howard worked hard to save the constitutional monarchy. He succeeded. When the referendum was held on November 6, 1999, 55 percent of Australians voted "no" and 45 percent "yes." Britain's Queen Elizabeth remained the country's head of state. Howard flew to London to receive thanks, and in March the queen and Prince Phillip toured Australia.

Was the vote an affirmation of loyalty to the British crown? In a poll taken just before the referendum, only nine percent of voters expressed strong support for retaining the queen. Many people in their twenties and thirties thought the whole issue was irrelevant to their lives. In another poll, 70 percent of voters said they favored a republic but not that model.

Confusion over the meaning of the word "president" played a role in the defeat. Kay Lawson, emeritus professor of political science at San Francisco State University and a specialist in political parties, commented on this aspect of the referendum: "Most parliamentary systems with presidents have strong legislatures and prime ministers, and weak presidents," Lawson wrote. "Naming a 'president' is just a way of getting rid of the crown, which is what they wanted to do in Australia. The case is interesting because it suggests that the role of the U.S. president is now so powerful and so well followed internationally that the more common kind of (weak) president is not known or understood by most people. This is too bad; I think it's a good kind of government, keeping most power where it belongs, in the hands of the people's representatives in Parliament. Maybe a new title is needed instead of 'president' such as 'ceremonial head of government' (plus a reminder: don't pay too much attention to this guy)."[9]

Another major controversy that erupted during the last four years of the twentieth century concerned immigrants from Asia, and the country's indigenous population, who had long been known as the Aborigines. It reflected the old divide between those who favored an increasingly multiethnic Australia and those who wanted the country to remain oriented toward Britain and the West. Back in 1988 John Howard had come out strongly in favor of assimilation and called multiculturalism an "aimless, divisive policy," as we saw in Chapter Nine. In 1996 he made no such statement — it would have ignited a firestorm — but his actions showed where he stood. Agencies that served immigrants or furthered multiculturalism were cut back or lopped off entirely: "within months of coming into office," the London *Economist* reported in December, 1996, "Mr. Howard has abolished both ... the Office of Multicultural Affairs and the Bureau of Immigration and Population Research."[10]

In the changed political climate, voices that had been heard faintly in the background moved front and center. The loudest was that of Pauline Hanson, a new member of Parliament from Queensland. In her maiden speech in September, 1996, she dropped a verbal bomb: "I believe we are in danger of being swamped by Asians," she warned her colleagues. "They have their own culture and religion, form ghettos and do not assimilate." Hanson called for the immediate abolition of the country's multicultural policy and a temporary halt to immigration while the country "radically reviewed" its policies.[11]

Her condemnation of Aboriginal policy was no less sweeping: "I am fed up to the back teeth with inequalities that are being promoted ... under the assumption that Aboriginals are the most disadvantaged people in Australia."[12] She urged the abolition of ATSIC, the Council for Aboriginal Reconciliation, and every program set up to help indigenous people.

Hanson's speech stunned Australians. So did its immediate aftermath. Her words were a green light for those with pent-up resentments against Asian immigrants and indigenous people, and for those dissatisfied with their lives and looking for someone to blame. The country had just been through a stubborn recession as well as a prolonged drought in some regions, so many Australians were hurting. In the days after Hanson's speech there was a sharp upsurge of incidents in which indigenous people and Asian Australians, as well as other immigrants and Jews, were insulted verbally. Buoyed by her sudden ability to attract attention, Hanson continued issuing provocative statements and the media lapped them up.

Those Australians who took pride in their country's solid track record as a multiethnic society were shocked and dismayed. Aboriginal groups organized rallies against Hanson, using Internet websites to publicize events where blacks and whites marched together in several cities to proclaim their opposition to her views. Organizations that help immigrants issued statements condemning her for racism and calling for bipartisan efforts against her.

Protests soon came from a different quarter as well. The Wool Exporters Council said Hanson's speech was inflammatory and could damage trade if it went unchecked. Tour operators in Melbourne and on the Gold Coast, a popular beach resort area in Queensland, "reported cancelled tours by groups from Singapore and Taiwan in response to the negative headlines about Australian racism in regional newspapers."[13]

Trade groups, along with politicians from the major political parties, urged the prime minister to repudiate Hanson's assertions and affirm Australia's commitment to multiculturalism. He refused. Such a statement was unnecessary, he believed, because everyone knew that most Australians were tolerant.[14] In the end he agreed to a bipartisan declaration by Parliament affirming Australia's tolerance and commitment to multiculturalism. But the statement did not mention Pauline Hanson.

"In the past week newspapers, magazines, and radio stations in Thailand, Singapore, Indonesia, the Philippines and Hong Kong have been giving prominent coverage to the row," the Melbourne *Age* reported in late October. "And while most media have dismissed Ms. Hanson as a fringe extremist, there has been almost universal condemnation of Mr. Howard for weak leadership."[15]

In April, 1997, Hanson launched her own political party, One Nation. When polls showed that the bulk of the new party's supporters were defectors from the coalition's Liberal or National parties, Foreign Minister Alexander Downer did speak out. "Australia's future lies with Asia ... that is why we have made engagement with Asia our highest foreign policy priority," he told a group of key diplomats and top officials on May 1. Australian values "such as tolerance and respect for cultural diversity" were important elements of the country's foreign policy. But there were "dissonant voices," he said, "most notably Pauline Hanson and the One Nation Party, which do not see Australia's future with the region."[16] These voices were not the views of the government or the vast majority of Australians, Downer stressed.

A week later John Howard told the Asia Society that "the Hanson cure would be worse than the disease.... She is wrong to seek scapegoats for society's problems."[17] By then she was attacking both Howard and the Liberal Party and had become a first-class headache. Support for One Nation gradually declined over the next several months, falling to a low of five percent. Meanwhile the indigenous Aborigines, who had been pushed into the background by the Asia debate, began to dominate the headlines because of a controversial legal decision on land rights.

The Wik decision, as the ruling became known, was a clarification of Mabo, a landmark case in 1992 where the High Court said indigenous people could file claims to land that their people had occupied continuously. (See Chapter Six.) In 1993 the Keating government had passed the Native Title Bill, which in part set up machinery for the orderly filing of claims. But one aspect of Mabo remained unanswered — the question of leaseholds.

Much of the land used by farmers and pastoralists in rural Australia is owned by the federal government, which leases it to users for a fee. Mining companies also lease land. Leaseholds, which collectively occupy 42 percent of Australia and can be quite large, are often in areas where the same indigenous peoples had lived for thousands of years. Could their descendants who still live there claim the land of leaseholders? The Wik and Thayorre peoples of Cape York Peninsula in Northern Queensland filed such a claim. In December, 1996, the High Court ruled that pastoral leases did not automatically extinguish native title; in some cases the two parties might coexist on the same land.

Coexistence, the judges ruled in 1996, meant that the indigenous people might be granted such rights as hunting, fishing, and camping on part of the property, or the right to look after their religious sites. It also meant that if minerals were found on the land, indigenous people could claim a portion of the profits. But in the event of a conflict, the leaseholder's right would prevail.

Panic broke out among farmers and ranchers as word went around that the indigenous people could come in now and take away anyone's land. Aboriginal leaders issued a call for a national summit on Wik so that high-level government officials and leaders of indigenous groups, farmers, pastoralists, and miners could discuss the conflicts and try to resolve them. "The Government should be trying to create an atmosphere for negotiations," said Mick Dodson, Aboriginal Social Justice Commissioner. "The political response has been hysterical. They should calm down and sit down and begin negotiations."[18]

A summit on Wik took place in Cairns on January 22 and 23, 1997.[19] It attracted high-level Aboriginal leaders—Gatjil Djerrkura, an Aboriginal businessman who was the new head of ATSIC, and Noel Pearson, legal adviser to the Cape York Land Council and ATSIC. The major organizations of farmers, ranchers, and mining companies all sent representatives. But top government officials were absent.

On the day that the Cairns summit opened, the prime minister was in Sydney meeting with state premiers who opposed the Wik decision.[20] A few days earlier the premiers of Queensland, Western Australia, and the Northern Territory had met and developed a submission to the PM "which would demand Federal legislation to extinguish native-title on leasehold land."[21] Queensland's premier, Rob Borbidge, was active in this effort.

Indigenous leader Mick Dodson. In the 1990s he coauthored the report about the "stolen generations," Aboriginal children once forcibly taken from their parents in an effort to wean them from their traditional culture; he also served as Aboriginal Justice Minister. Dodson is now a professor (by permission of the National Library of Australia, photograph by Terry Milligan).

A year of acrimony followed as the government drafted a 10-point bill to dilute the effects of Wik, while Aboriginal groups, with backing from several churches and civic organizations, opposed the bill. Tensions over the Wik decision escalated, especially in rural Queensland. Farmers and ranchers, whose families in some cases had worked the same land for generations, feared they might lose everything now. Officials bent on overturning Wik fed these anxieties, not mentioning that in case of conflict, the leaseholder's claim would prevail. Then Premier Borbidge announced that a state parliamentary election would be held on June 13, 1998.

This was good news for Pauline Hanson's One Nation Party. While the fight over Wik was raging, One Nation had lined up candidates across Queensland. It is the only state where more people live in country areas than in cities, so there were a number of seats up for election in rural and semi-rural districts. Hanson found voters there responsive when she campaigned to extinguish all land rights for indigenous people, and also promised to solve farmers' economic woes. A reporter who watched her in action described her appeal: "she is a canny, albeit highly simplistic politician. She captivates her audience with short messages—often nasty and blatantly untrue—and then says she will fix their problem."[22] On election day One Nation got 23 percent of the vote in Queensland and won eleven seats in the state's Parliament. The results shocked the country and the government, because the prime minister's Liberal Party won only nine seats.

But in another twist to the election, it brought the Labor Party back into power in Queensland. To defeat One Nation, some people who might have voted for smaller parties such as the Democrats or Greens cast their vote for Labor. By combining with one Independent MP, the Labor Party gained enough seats to form a government. Its leader, Peter Beattie, replaced Ron Borbidge as premier. One of Beattie's first actions was to announce visits with Asian leaders to assure them that Queensland was neither racist nor anti–Asian. He described reports abroad about the recent election as "absolutely outrageously inaccurate."[23] He had good reason to be concerned.

In other countries, news of the Queensland election was reported as a groundswell against Asian immigrants and a resurgence of racism. The *Jakarta Post* warned that "for Asians in particular, the rapid rise of One Nation ... could forebode a return to that continent's old and antiquated White Australia policy," while an editorial in *The Bangkok Post* said: "We don't think Australia is a racist country but there will be many who are still wondering." An editorial in the *Hong Kong Standard* spoke of worldwide fears of a return to the White Australia policy.[24]

In fact Asian immigration was secondary in the Queensland election. The Wik decision dominated the debate. Embedded prejudice against the indigenous people certainly was a strong part of the reaction of many farmers and pastoralists; but the hot button issue was who controlled the land? It was a classic battle between two peoples over the same land, a situation now seen in one form or another in countries around the globe. Even if both sides had had the same skin color, the decision to share land would have been potentially divisive. If the state and federal governments had done all they could to explain what the decision actually said, and to help make it work, a crisis might have been averted. By instead feeding the rumor mill and increasing leaseholders' anxieties, the government, in effect, paved the way for One Nation's gains.

One Nation's triumph was short-lived. At elections a few months later Pauline Hanson lost her seat in Parliament. By December, 1999, all eleven people elected to the Queensland Parliament under the One Nation ticket had switched parties or resigned. Internal conflicts plagued Pauline Hanson's party continually. After Queensland she hired two men to help her run the national office; the three became known as "the troika" because of their authoritarian style, which brooked no input or dissent from local branches. Branch members revolted. The two men of the troika departed, as did a series of staff members before and after them. Some were fired; others resigned in protest. Working with a team of people on a sustained basis seems to have been difficult for Hanson.

She was best on the hustings, tapping into the frustrations of poor white people who viewed their government as a power elite that ignored their needs and only helped minorities. The situation was somewhat similar to that of people in the United States who join militia movements and other extremist groups. In the United States, the anger has usually focused on "affirmative action" for African Americans or Hispanics (Native American remain largely invisible). In both countries the bases of these movements lie outside big cities, attracting people in rural areas who are barely making it financially. Their dissatisfaction also resonates for some people in cities with low-paying jobs or no jobs, who likewise feel overlooked. One Nation supporters, *The Age* reported in 1998, were largely "poor, semi-skilled rural folk whose subsistence farms are struggling ... or people who have lost their jobs.... They see Hanson as one of them."[25]

Robert Manne, associate professor of politics at La Trobe University, saw support for Hanson as "the howl of protest of those who were suffering materially ... and who felt that 'their' country was being stolen from them by condescending, well-heeled city-based elites who were far more interested in the problems of Aborigines or Asian immigrants than they were in what was happening to battlers like themselves."[26] In Australia as in the United States, poor white people are unlikely to support extra help for minorities and immigrants unless they feel their own needs are also being met. But the emphasis lately in both countries has been on cutting government services and curtailing domestic spending, not on meeting needs.

During the same period that One Nation and the Wik decision were making headlines, yet another disagreement came to the fore. This was the controversy over the "Stolen Generations," up to 100,000 Aboriginal children who had been taken away from their parents over several decades in an effort to wean them from their traditional culture and "assimilate" them. (See Chapters Five and Six.) A report about the Stolen Generations had been commissioned during the Keating years, with Sir Ronald Wilson, a former High Court judge and a board member of the Council for Aboriginal Reconciliation, and Mick Dodson, an Aboriginal leader, as co-chairs. Several years in the making, the report was published in May, 1997, just one month after the One Nation Party was formed, and it became a political hot potato.

"Bringing Them Home," as the 700-page report was called, documented case after case of physical, sexual or emotional abuse of Aboriginal children after they were taken away from their parents. The authors concluded that in view of the wrong done to these children, states and the federal government should apologize to the indigenous people, and some form of reparations should be given to those who were taken away.

Initially Australians were shocked by the descriptions of cruelty and mistreatment of Aboriginal children. Several states quickly passed apology resolutions. But the federal government did not. It downplayed the findings, insisting that they were exaggerated. Before long some people on the far right declared that the Stolen Generations had never happened: this was a myth concocted by leftists. Others said that if some Aboriginal children had been taken from their parents in the past, this was a boon for these youngsters because the excellent educations they received enabled them to do well as adults.

Canada, in contrast, reacted differently after a Commission report gave details of 1880 native children who had been forcibly removed to residential schools, where they were subject to physical and sexual abuse, At a ceremony on January 7, 1998, Jane Stewart, Minister of Indian Affairs, said: "The Government of Canada today formally expresses to all aboriginal people in Canada our profound regret for past actions of the federal government which have contributed to these difficult pages in the history of our relationship together." Speaking about the abuse of children forcibly sent away to school, she said: "To all of you who suffered this tragedy at residential schools, we are deeply sorry."[27] Stewart announced that a "healing fund" of $384 million (US $245 million) was being set up to compensate the victims. If the Australian government had apologized soon after the report appeared, the declaration likely would have been newsworthy for a day or two, as in Canada. The refusal escalated the issue into a major controversy. But this in turned fueled support for Aboriginal justice.

At the Corroboree 2000 People's Walk for Reconciliation on May 28, more than 200,000 people showed up, the largest political gathering in Australian history. They walked across Sydney Harbour Bridge together to say "yes" to reconcilation, including an apology to the Stolen Generations. There was a large contingent of indigenous people and noticeable numbers of Asian Australians but the majority of marchers were white, reflecting the country's population. Similar walks in Melbourne and Brisbane over the next few weeks also attracted crowds.

But in the years that followed, ATSIC (the Aboriginal and Torres Strait Islander Commission), the federally funded organization set up by the Hawke government to give indigenous people a say in their own development and the money to administer programs, was plagued by conflicts. Accusations of cronyism and fiscal mismanagement came from Aboriginal leaders outside of ATSIC, as well as from the government. By 2003 both major political parties called for changes although their approaches differed. Labor's indigenous affairs spokeswoman, Julia Gillard, said of ATSIC that "the status quo is not an option. However, Labor believes that any new future for ATSIC should be determined through a transparent process in which indigenous Australians get to have a clear say."[28]

In April, 2004, John Howard "solved" the problems of ATSIC by abolishing it. New programs would spend as much as before, he said, and Indigenous Coordinating Councils would give local Aborigines input into the process. But new council members would be appointed by the government. "Many Aboriginal people are suspicious of the new arrangements because they feel betrayed by a Government that has robbed them of their elected voice, ATSIC," wrote Rob Welsh, chairperson of Sydney's Metropolitan Local Aboriginal Land Council. But "Given the enormous gulf that still exists between Aboriginal and other Australians," Welsh was ready to give the new system a chance to show what it could accomplish.[29]

The new approach featured Shared Responsibility Agreements (SRAs) stressing "mutual obligation" between communities and goverments. When Ruth McCausland, senior researcher at Jumbunna Indigenous House of Learning at University of Techology Sydney, evaluated the SRAs in 2005, she found them "resonant of past policies of assimilation.... Evidence that is publicly available suggests that the government is more concerned with furthering its 'mutual obligation' policy agenda than genuinely addressing Indigenous disadvantage." The SRAs also gave priority to "remote communities over urban communities, where the majority of Indigenous people live."

The policy of promising rural communities needed equipment or buildings if its residents changed their ways disturbed Aboriginal leader Mick Dodson. "The Government should not be saying to Indigenous people: 'You need a shared responsibility agreement for us to deliver normal citizenship entitlements that other Australians take for granted. We will give you a school, if you behave in a particular way.' That's discriminatory," said Dodson, who now directs the National Centre for Indigenous Studies at Australian National University.[30]

Many changes were made outside this system by indigenous groups at the local level, sometimes in partnership with local governments. For instance, in March, 2006, the Metropolitan Local Aboriginal Land Council signed an agreement with the North Sydney Council that "opens the way for possible future projects to improve employment, educational and training opportunities for Aboriginal people, including tourism management."[31]

Along with the domestic conflicts discussed in this chapter, another issue surfaced during these turbulent years. This was the question of Australia's relations with nearby countries. The government insisted that all was well on that score but growing numbers of Australians were pressing for more interaction. People with this outlook saw themselves as citizens of a multiethnic nation of the Asia Pacific region. For them, building solid relationships with their neighbors emerged as the new imperative.

Twelve

Asian Connections

Australia woke up to find itself in the right place at the right time. As countries such as Japan, South Korea, Taiwan and Hong Kong prospered, Australia's location at the tip of Southeast Asia meant it could readily supply them with many of the raw materials, products and services they needed for their development. Singapore, Malaysia and Indonesia also became buyers. The financial collapse of some Asian nations in 1997 caused a slowdown in sales but not as much as expected; by 2000, these countries were on the road to recovery and Australia was selling to many of them, especially its mining and agricultural products.[1] In time China emerged as the biggest buyer of them all.

In building relationships with countries in the region, however, Australia faces a delicate situation because of the past. Memories of the former European occupation of much of that region, and of Australia's past exclusion of immigrants from Asia, have made nearby countries sensitive to any signs of the old colonial attitudes and prejudices. Mistrust decreased in the decades after the Second World War as immigration from Asian countries swelled, Australia's policies stressed tolerance and inclusion and the government made special efforts to cement friendships with neighboring nations. But events in the second half of the 1990s, especially the backlash against Asian immigrants fomented by MP Pauline Hanson soon after a new administration came to power in 1996, put some nations on guard; and the country's treatment of boat refugees seeking asylum has brought international criticism. Still, the momentum has been toward Asia.

After World War II, many political analysts, economists, historians and other specialists in Australia realized that their country's future would be tied to that of its neighbors. When the government opened Australia National University (ANU) in Canberra in 1947, Professor Brij V. Lal pointed out, a major reason for the new university was to provide a research center where Australians could learn more about their region. Lal, director of the Centre for the Contemporary Pacific at ANU's Research School of Pacific and Asian Studies, is one of many academics specializing in Asian countries. His input has helped Australia interact with its region. An Indian Fijian Australian, his grandfather came to Fiji from India in 1906 as a *girmitiya* (indentured servant) and Lal grew up in Fiji. His continued interest in that country led the Fijian government to invite Lal to help write its 1997 constitution.[2]

If government interest in Asia waned in the 1950s after Robert Menzies returned to power, at the nation's universities that interest continued. Librarians kept building up their Asia collections, while scholars quietly initiated contacts and exchanges with professors and students in the Asian countries they studied. More universities opened Asian studies departments and the number of Asian languages offered at Australian universities continued to grow. By 2003 ANU's National Institute for Asia and the Pacific offered

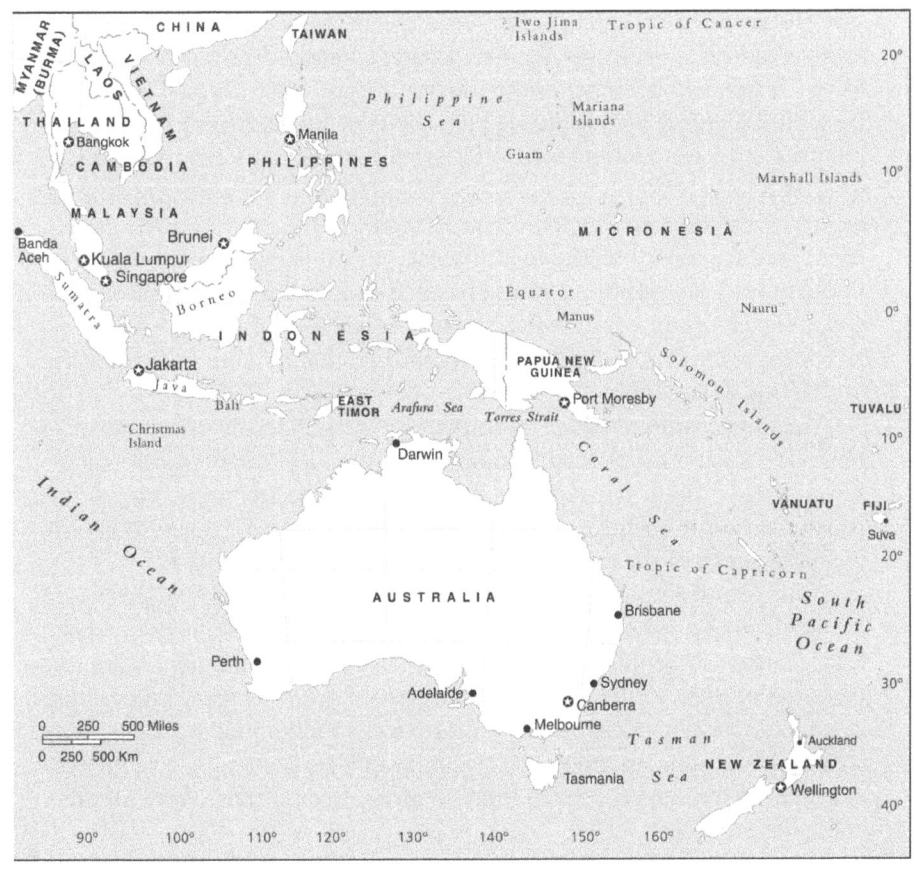

Australia in the Asia Pacific (map by Ben Pease, Pease Press).

intensive language study in Arabic, Chinese, Hindi, Indonesian, Japanese, Javanese, Korean, Lao, Persian, Sanskrit, Thai, Urdu, and Vietnamese.

Some Asian countries, in turn, began studying about Australia. Japan, a major trading partner, was the first. In 1967, Otemon Gakuin University outside Osaka opened a Center for Australian Studies; more followed in Tokyo and other cities. In China, which has had considerable interaction with Australia for 30 years, by 1998 there were Australia Studies Centres at universities in Beijing, Shanghai and Guangzhou, and courses on Australia in half a dozen provinces. In Indonesia, Petra Christian University in Java has an Australian Studies Centre, while Nanyang Technical University in Singapore offers several courses on Australia.

The Australian government began actively reaching out to Asian nations in the 1970s. The pace accelerated after Bob Hawke became prime minister in 1983. Noting the success of the European Economic Community (forerunner of the European Union), Hawke helped organize a trade alliance of Pacific countries, the Asia Pacific Economic Cooperation Forum (APEC), now a 21-member group of countries on both edges of the Pacific Rim. Paul Keating, who succeeded Hawke as prime minister in 1991, made building stronger relationships with Asian nations a top priority. During his first year in office, he visited Indonesia, Papua New Guinea, Japan, Singapore, Cambodia and the Solomon Islands.[3] His foreign minister Gareth Evans told the *New York Times*: "What has got to change in Australia's relationship with Asia is not just the substance, but the perception. We have to create the environment in which we are perceived by our Asian neighbors as having made that psychological transition," that is, away from identifying mainly with Britain and Europe.[4]

Keating championed the movement for a republic. He told a Canadian reporter: "Australia will be taken more seriously as a player in regional affairs if we are clear about our identity. I think that in the area in which we live, which is an area of ancient cultures, there'll be a greater willingness to include us in the affairs of the region if we are of an independent mind."[5]

The country's new policies and practices bore fruit. After it promoted ethnic diversity and encouraged services to help immigrants, many Asian leaders and their people began changing their image of Australia. Asian students attended Australian universities in record numbers and Asian tourists came in droves. By the early 1990s, more than a million tourists a year were coming from Asian countries. If one excludes New Zealand, whose citizens come and go frequently, Asian tourists outnumbered those from all other countries combined.[6]

Australia also forged strategic agreements with nearby countries such as Indonesia, Malaysia, Singapore, and Papua New Guinea. "As never before

Australia's economic, strategic, and political interests now coalesce in the region around us ... and importantly, finding a place for ourselves in Asia is also about finding our own identity," Paul Keating wrote in *Asiawatch*.[7] Then early in 1996, after a campaign that centered more on domestic than international issues, the Labor Party was defeated in federal elections. John Howard became prime minister of a coalition government of his Liberal Party and the National Party. Their opponents feared that Howard might revert to the old policy of ignoring Asia.

Howard, however, swiftly scheduled meetings with leaders of several nearby Asian countries to reassure them that his government wanted continued trade and friendly relations. An astute politician, he surely realized that ignoring Asia in 1996 would be tantamount to political suicide. Large blocs in both coalition parties relied increasingly on sales to Asian countries: the Liberal Party had a strong city-based business constituency while the National Party, whose stronghold was in rural areas, attracted ranchers, farmers, and miners.

At the same time, the new prime minister made no secret of his strong support for retaining Britain's monarch as Australia's head of state. He looked for ways to bolster friendships with Britain, other European countries and the United States, while summarily dismissing any suggestion that Australia was part of Asia. His opponents, however, saw danger in this approach, coupled as it was with his distaste for multiculturalism. As James Jupp, Director of the Centre for Immigration and Multicultural Studies, has pointed out: "It is impossible to have fruitful trade, tourism, and foreign relations with neighboring states while discriminating against their citizens on a racial or ethnic basis."[8] There was another consideration as well, Jupp wrote: "It is already hard enough to persuade some states of the region that 'Australia is part of Asia.'"[9] Just as a remnant of the old guard in Australia remained fixated on the past, so some Asian leaders could not put the colonial period in perspective and see the whole region as part of a new geopolitical bloc in the world.

Malaysia's prime minister Mahathir Mohamad was one such leader. After several Asian and European Union nations formed the Asia-Europe Meeting (ASEM), a group that met annually to discuss common interests, Mahathir insisted that Australia and New Zealand were not Asian countries. He managed to bar them from the first two meetings and urged their permanent exclusion.[10] Likewise his opposition was crucial in excluding Australia and New Zealand from a meaningful role in the Association of Southeast Asian Nations, or ASEAN, the region's most important coalition group.[11] But a new breed of leaders in Asia appeared to have a different view. "We regard Australia and New Zealand as Asian," Thailand's foreign minister Prachuab Chaiyasan said in 1997. Thailand pledged to sponsor the country's admission to the next meeting of ASEM.[12] A year later, Surin Pitsuwan, the new Thai foreign minister, described Australia as the third leg of a tripod supporting the Southeast Asian economies.[13] (The other two legs were Japan and China.) "You belong to the region," he told participants at a business seminar in Sydney.[14]

After the Asian economic plunge, some other countries looked to Australia. On a visit early in 1998, British trade minister Lord Clinton-Davis said Australia was a critical link between Asian and European countries.[15] In June, the *Herald* reported, "The World Bank yesterday called on Australia to take a leading role in communication between crisis-ridden Asian countries and major industrialized nations." Jean-Michel Severino, the Bank's vice-president for the Asia Pacific region, said: "There are very few countries that can be credibly heard in the region.... The role for Australia is critical."[16] And in October, Chris Patten, the last British governor of Hong Kong, who became the EU's minister for external affairs, told a group of foreign correspondents in Singapore: "Australia is in a better position than almost anybody to help give a lead in Asia ... (it) can provide a very useful bridge for Asia and can march over that bridge a lot of ideas about good government and sensible economic management."[17]

Nearby Indonesia also weighed in. After One Nation's gains in the 1998 Queensland election, Indonesia's new president downplayed its significance. B. J. Habibie, who had recently replaced Suharto, told reporters that the election "will not damage Australia's standing in Asia." He had visited Australia, he said, and did not believe its people, who were "very cultivated, very open" would choose the isolationism advocated by Hanson.[18]

The next year, however, troubles in East Timor caused a rift between Australia and Indonesia. Timor, an eastern island of the Malay Archipelago, has been divided for more than four centuries. The Dutch held the western half until 1950 when it became part of the new Republic of Indonesia, while East Timor was under Portuguese rule from the sixteenth century until 1975 when Portugal withdrew. The country declared its independence but as rival factions fought for control, the Indonesian army annexed the country in a bloody coup. But violence continued. The East Timorese, more than 90 percent Roman Catholic, resisted becoming part of predominantly Muslim Indonesia.

After a United Nations–brokered referendum was held in East Timor in 1999 and its people voted overwhelmingly to become an independent nation, Indonesian military forces and their local supporters went on a rampage there. When Australia led a United Nations peacekeeping mission into East Timor, Indonesians reacted with anger. Although Habibie had agreed to both the referendum and the peacekeepers, Australia's participation set off protests in Jakarta. The Indonesian government canceled a joint security agreement between the two nations. Gradually the countries mended fences.

Over the years, as more Australians became engaged with Asian countries through diplomacy, business, development projects, academic studies and tourism, the call for closer identification with the region has increased. Stephen FitzGerald has been one of the strongest advocates of this view. He served as ambassador to China during the Whitlam administration and later became chair of the Department of Far Eastern History and the Contemporary China Centre at ANU. He has also headed the Asia-Australia Institute at the University of New South Wales in Sydney and worked as a consultant for Australian companies doing business in Asian countries, principally China.

FitzGerald's book, *Is Australia an Asian Country?* (1997), gave a new picture of Asian nations. After getting to know top political, intellectual, and business leaders in several Asian countries, he saw a growing consciousness there "of confidence and pride in achievement, a sense of being 'empowered,' of being 'Asian' in the way that elites in Europe have of being 'European.'"[19] He used the term "elites" to mean a country's government and business leaders as well as its professionals and specialists. FitzGerald, who is fluent in Mandarin Chinese, urged Australians to learn the languages of its neighbors along with more about their cultures. He saw these steps as crucial prerequisites to effective participation in the region.

He also pointed out that Australia's input into Asia's development had been "quietly helpful" in projects in several countries. And he noted that Australian universities have provided education and training to students "who have gone back to their Asian countries and become agents of the dynamic which is making Asian economies the focus of the global economy." FitzGerald saw Australia as an Asia Pacific player. But when his book appeared in 1997, the new administration in Canberra paid scant attention to such views.

In the years that followed, however, it could not ignore China. When tensions between Beijing and Washington heated up over a United States spy plane that landed in Chinese territory in 2001, *The Age* commented: "Nobody wants to get offside with the American superpower.... But neither does the region want to forsake almost three decades of painstaking diplomatic efforts in bringing China into the heart of Asia's political and economic life."[20]

Hugh White of the Australian Strategic Policy Institute suggested that the government should offer to assist the Americans in working out their China policy. "Australia's future security will depend more than anything else on the way China develops and uses its growing power and on the way the rest of the world responds ... on whether America and China can compromise to reach a modus vivendi that accommodates the power and ambitions of both," he wrote. "The US needs to recognise that there can be no peace in Asia without China's cooperation." With America's views on China "markedly more hostile than Australia's," White believed that "no country in the world is better placed than Australia to help shape American policy on China and as America's closest Pacific ally, we have a responsibility to do so. If we can't help, who can?"[21]

But China was not yet at the top of the government's agenda. The focus was on asylum seekers from troubled areas of Middle Eastern and Central Asian countries who were arriving on small boats. Keeping out refugees who came illegally, and discouraging others from trying to gain entry that way, became a priority of the coalition government.

Boatloads of illegal refugees had stopped coming to Australia in 1981, as we saw in Chapter Nine, but they began appearing again in 1989. This time the people in them at first were Cambodians. After the Khmer Rouge under Pol Pot seized control of the country in 1975, his regime murdered more than a million fellow Cambodians and destroyed the nation's institutions and infrastructure. Pol Pot's government fell in 1979 but the destruction it wrought left the country in such dire straits that a decade later it still had not recovered. Concern over boat refugees from Cambodia, and from other troubled countries such as East Timor, rekindled the old fears about Asians inundating the country. The government reacted in 1991 by setting up a detention camp in Port Hedland, Western Australia, where refugees who arrived illegally were held while their eligibility under the UN Convention on Refugees was examined. Gradually more camps were built and the length of incarceration in them increased.

These camps were in place several years later when people from countries such as Afghanistan, Iraq, Pakistan and Iran began arriving as boat refugees. The vast majority of such refugees had gone to camps bordering their own countries but for the minority who went further afield, Australia was one of several popular destinations. Some refugees flew to Malaysia, which offered all Muslims a temporary visa and then made their way to Indonesia. There they paid "boat smugglers" to take them to Australia.

As the number of such boat refugees increased, so did the government's concern. The situation came to a head on August 26, 2001, when a leaky boat from Indonesia, crammed beyond capacity with refugees, began to founder. A Norwegian freighter in nearby waters, the MV *Tampa*, responded to a distress signal and rescued all 433 refugees aboard, who were mainly Afghans and Iraqis. The *Tampa* headed for Christmas Island, a nearby Australian possession.

But Australia refused to let the freighter land there. Prime Minister

A religious observance assembly at an Islamic school in Sydney. Immigrants and refugees from several countries have increased the numbers of Muslims in Australia, and they have built new schools and mosques. This school was about to move into new quarters (by permission of the National Library of Australia, photograph by John Immig).

Howard went on radio and on national and then world television to explain why Australia could no longer accept boat people. The country was being swamped with so many refugees that it simply could not handle more; it had to call a halt. He appealed to the United Nations and other countries to help out with this "awful problem."[22] The only positive response came from New Zealand, which agreed to take up to 150 refugees. When Howard phoned Indonesia's president she did not call back, but a spokesman said: "We will not allow these illegal immigrants into the country."[23]

The prime minister remained adamant that none of the refugees would be allowed to land on Australian soil. When the United Nations High Commissioner for Refugees (UNHCR) said these people had no place else to go, the government began looking around for some other country that could house them while their claims for refugee status were examined. Meanwhile some lawyers in Melbourne took the government to court to force it to let the refugees in. While the case was pending, the 433 refugees remained in the sun on the deck of the *Tampa*, which was designed to hold 58 people. The Norwegians were furious and accused Australia of being a bully. When the judge ruled that the refugees must be admitted, the government immediately appealed to a higher court, and transferred the refugees to an Australian troop ship, where once more they waited.

In Europe, reaction was scathing. France's *Liberation* said Howard appealed to "xenophobic" instincts similar to those of the country's old White Australia policy.[24] The London *Guardian* thought his "hardline stance ... demonstrated the country's continuing discomfort with multiculturalism."[25] At that time immigrants in transit in France were descending on the Channel Tunnel nightly in hopes of riding a train into England. Boatloads of Albanians continued reaching Italian shores, while North Africans were flooding into Spain and France. Collectively, Western Europe had absorbed 400,000 asylum seekers the previous year, as well as an estimated 150,000 illegal immigrants who slipped across borders. Europeans, *The Age* reported, were "bemused by Australia's claims that it was being 'swamped' by boat people." On a per capita basis Australia's intake of refugees measured "reasonably well" against that of European countries, a UNHCR official told a reporter, but it was neither high nor unusual: "Using words like swamped in regard to this, well, I mean, Pakistan and Iran between them have about 3.7 million Afghans who have been there for years. Frankly, that's when the word swamped comes readily to mind."[26]

Nauru, a tiny Pacific island with less than 11,000 people, finally agreed to house the *Tampa* refugees temporarily for a price, reportedly $20 million, but in any case more than it would have cost to house them in Australia while their claims were processed. While quarters were being prepared there, another event influenced the fate of the refugees.

In the United States on September 11, hijackers from Arab nations crashed one plane into the Pentagon in Washington, D.C., and two into the World Trade Center in New York, killing nearly three thousand people and demolishing the trade center towers. People all over the world reacted with horror and with the gut-level fear that they, too, were in danger of being killed if terrorism was not stopped. When the appeal of the *Tampa* case was heard two days later, lawyers argued that terrorists posing as "friendly aliens" might gain entry to Australia if the government had no power to keep out asylum seekers. The government won. By early October, all the *Tampa* refugees, plus others on boats that had since been intercepted, were in camps on Nauru. Later some were sent to Manus, an island of Papua New Guinea, and to a camp on Christmas Island.

The government's refugee policy continued to be hit with verbal brickbats from abroad as well as from vocal opponents at home. But Howard and his ministers could blithely ignore them because the boat refugee crisis, coupled with the 9/11 attack on the United States, rescued their sinking political fortunes.

Six months before the *Tampa* incident, the coalition government's approval rating had dropped to 35 percent while the Labor Party, led by Kim Beazley, had edged up to 43 percent.[27] Five of the six states already had Labor governments. Australian bookmakers were laying odds on Labor. A federal election was due to take place before the end of December, but the prime minister, who sets the date, had not yet done so. The moment that Howard refused to allow the Tampa to land, his approval rating went up. September 11 drove his ratings higher as fear gripped the nation. The coalition moved ahead of the Labor Party.

After setting the election date for November 10, Howard proved a savvy campaigner. He told reporters in Melbourne: "There is a possibility that some people with links to organisations that we don't want in this country might use the path of asylum seeker to get here." The *Herald*, translating the innuendo, ran a headline: "Howard links terrorism to boat people."[28]

Labor leader Kim Beazley initially favored letting the *Tampa* land on Christmas Island; he urged the government to admit more Afghans because of the troubles there. But as he watched his own approval ratings slide while his opponent's went up, he cautiously backed down, supporting the government's policy on refugees, while stressing the need for humane treatment. This equivocal stance worked to the prime minister's advantage: "Mr. Howard claimed a Labor government would lead to an escalation of illegal immigrants ... because Mr. Beazley was sure to change the policy."[29]

Some columnists and commentators supported the government's policy but larger numbers decried it. "Is this exercise worth the expense?" author Thomas Keneally wrote. "To what extent is it a gesture to Howard's re-election? What will be the real cost of Australia's decreased international credit?"[30] Overseas observers also weighed in. The London *Economist* came out in favor of Labor, which it expected to continue the path of economic modernization begun by Bob Hawke. Labor, it said, would also "almost certainly" be more successful than Mr. Howard's team "in helping to bring an end to the attitudes of the past, many associated with the White Australia policies that characterized the country for so long."[31]

The government's campaign was further buoyed in early October by stories that some boat refugees had thrown their own children overboard in a cynical ploy to gain sympathy and force Australia to let them in. When the government released photos showing refugee children in the water, Australians were appalled; polls a week later found the coalition 15 points ahead of Labor, its highest lead yet. Three months after the election proof emerged that no children had been thrown overboard by their parents. The photos of children in the water had been taken a day after the alleged incident, when their boat sank. Uncropped photos showed parents in the water with their children, all wearing lifejackets and waiting to be rescued.

But on November 10, fortune smiled on the coalition. A considerable number of Labor Party regulars, angry at what they saw as Beazley's abandonment of their party's principles, voted instead for the Democrats or for the Greens, who gained a second seat in Parliament.[32] Pauline Hanson complained: "Mr. Howard took my policies."[33] She was right: many who had supported One Nation earlier voted for the National or Liberal Parties. Hanson failed to win the Senate seat she sought; a few months later she resigned from One Nation. When the final election tallies came in, the coalition had a slim majority over Labor. John Howard remained prime minister.

The detention camps remained, both the new ones offshore and the larger number within Australia, often in remote outback locations. In the year before the *Tampa* incident, stories in the press gave heart wrenching descriptions of families who were kept behind barbed wire for years and young children who were devastated by the experience. In 2000, for example, at least 300 detainees at the Curtin detention center had gone on a hunger strike and sewed their mouths closed with needles and thread. Alarmed officials called in an Iraqi Australian doctor to convince strikers that such protests would not bring their release. He succeeded but later told a journalist that conditions at the camp were deplorable; even worse than the poor physical conditions was the despair they felt "at being cut off from the rest of Australia and the rest of the world — there was no telephone, no access to the media and no ability to send or receive mail."[34] When the doctor relayed a message from one detainee to his friends in Sydney, "they wept tears of joy and relief."[35] Hearing no word from him or about him, they assumed their friend had drowned on the crossing from Indonesia and had already held a funeral service for him.

What caused Australia to inaugurate refugee policies that placed it among countries with the most restrictions? As we saw in Chapter Eight, after World War II Australia took in a quarter of all immigrants leaving war-torn Europe. For nearly forty years the country regularly took in refugees from trouble spots around the globe and made special efforts to help them through the transitional years.

Overseas, one reason still given for the current policy is that Australia is a racist country. Prejudice does exist there of course but it is not more prevalent than in most other countries. At the height of the media blitz about Pauline Hanson's anti–Asian, anti–Aborigine sentiments, her One Nation Party got less than 10 percent of the vote in one national election; in 2001 it fell to 4.5 percent. In France, after Jean-Marie Le Pen, leader of the far-right Popular Front Party, campaigned against immigrants in 2002 and got 18 percent of the vote in a national election, Le Pen and his followers were labeled racist, not all of France. But foreign critics, remembering the old White Australia policy and knowing little about changes in the country's ethnic makeup and policies, may still paint the entire country of Australia with the brush of intolerance the minute a movement against immigrants becomes visible.

Such critics assume that the two sides in the *Tampa* and detention camp controversies were divided neatly by race and skin color. This was not the case. Those who favored getting refugees off Nauru and out of other detention camps included numerous Australians of British and other European ancestry. On the other hand, large numbers of citizens who cheered the prime minister when he refused to let the *Tampa* land came from countries in Asia and Africa.

A major reason for the latter group's displeasure was the belief that boat people were "queue jumpers." Far from being genuine refugees fleeing political persecution, this line of reasoning went, those arriving by boat were pushy people with plenty of money to pay boat smugglers who expected to become even richer in Australia. Instead of waiting their turn in the immigration queue like everyone else, they demanded special treatment. This argument was made regularly by officials to support their policy of putting all boat refugees in detention camps.

"But there were no queues to jump," Professor John S. Conroy, former educationist at Macquarie University, points out.[36] The countries refugees fled often had no Australian consulate or immigration office where they could apply for visas, he said. Journalist Peter Mares, author of *Borderline: Australia's Responses to Refugees and Asylum Seekers in the Wake of the Tampa*, found that even where such offices and those of the UNHCR did exist, other barriers might stand in the way of obtaining a visa.[37] In some countries the bureaucratic tangle of regulations and restrictions, the long waits, the difficulty of getting an appointment without bribing the local employee who controlled access, and the likelihood of being shown the door if you were not sophisticated enough to know how the system worked, caused many to give up and flee the country without a visa. No doubt some people did abuse the system, but considering the hazard of coming to Australia by boat (some refugees drown when their boats capsize and no ship comes to their rescue) few but the desperate would choose that route.

Mares found a second reason why recent immigrants to Australia might regard boat people as queue jumpers. During the Keating administration, immigration minister Nick Bolkus had separated the annual slots reserved for refugees who applied "offshore" (overseas) and "onshore" (they arrived by boat, or by plane but without a visa). His successor, Phillip Ruddock, merged the two categories. This meant that for every boat refugee granted asylum there was one less place available for refugees who applied for this status abroad: "a Somali family waiting for a needy relative to be granted a visa in Nairobi could feel understandably resentful towards an Afghan who comes by boat and is granted refugee status onshore. Yet both are refugees in fear of persecution and in need of resettlement." The situation "pits communities against one another," wrote Mares, who concluded that "the notion of a 'queue jumper' is something largely manufactured by government."[38]

What about religious prejudice as a factor in detaining boat people? There can be little doubt that widespread publicity about Muslim suicide bombers has increased prejudice against Muslims in Australia as elsewhere, even though only a minute fraction of the billion and a half people who follow Islam are suicide bombers or "terrorists." But to conclude that because most boat refugees in recent years have been Muslims, their detention is due to their religion is specious: it ignores not only the government's immigration policy but also Australian history. As we have seen, the earlier arrival of boat refugees from Vietnam, Cambodia, and China triggered a similar panic among many Australians. In a book published in 1996, Professor Nancy Viviani wrote: "the fact that just over 2000 boat people arrived on the northern shores of Australia from 1976 to 1989 has been wildly distorted by the media on every occasion that a boat arrives."[39] She pointed out that well over a million people emigrated legally to Australia during this period, as both immigrants and refugees.

Some immigrants who arrived legally during that period were Lebanese fleeing the civil war that ravaged their country from 1975 to 1991. Lebanese, who are Arabs, have lived in Australia since the 1880s though the earliest immigrants had been predominantly Christian. This time a good portion who came were Muslims; but their increased presence, and the new mosques they built in Sydney and Melbourne, set off no alarm bells. They were absorbed into the country.[40]

From the government's view, loss of control was another factor in its hostile reaction to boat people. Australia had long exercised considerable control over who it allowed to enter. The old White Australia Policy was one example but a more sustained and pervasive control came through assisted passage. These schemes allowed the government to pick not only the country but also the age and occupation of entrants. Young male farm workers and laborers and female domestic servants were sought in the past; in the twenty-first century the government wanted workers with specialized skills, professionals and technicians, and business people with enough money to set up new businesses. Officials could not pre-select the refugees who arrived unexpectedly in small boats.

Although some Australians might still yearn for "a White Australia, in which the absolute mastering and dominating element shall be British" (as

Twelve • *Asian Connections*

a prime minister in 1901 declared), few citizens a century later could have expected a return to such a past.⁴¹ More likely they were driven by the historical fear that the country might be taken over by Asians. "There is a deeply-held, yet irrational anxiety that Australia is perpetually in danger of being overrun," Peter Mares wrote in his book on refugees. When Pauline Hanson declared in 1996, "I believe we are in danger of being swamped by Asians," her words struck a responsive chord in many.

As Professor Robert Manne put it: "The collective psyche here is still possessed by ancient fears experienced by a newly arrived small British settler society, of being overwhelmed by an invasion from the millions of exotic others to our north."⁴² This fear was used to sway public opinion against boat refugees. Immigration minister Ruddock spoke of an "assault to our borders," while some media reports described the arrival of Asian immigrants on boats as "an invasion," "an armada" and "a flood tide" that threatens to "inundate" the country.⁴³

When John Howard said in 2001, "We decide, and no one else, who comes into this country," public response was enthusiastic.⁴⁴ The general public probably did not know that having signed the U.N. Convention on

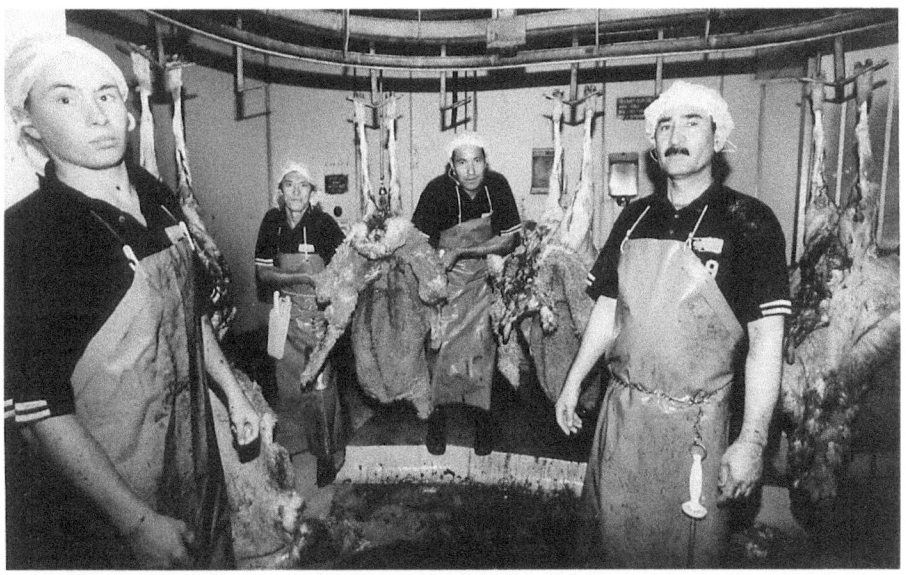

Refugees from Afghanistan skinning sheep in an abbatoir in 2002. These men are Harzara Shiites, a minority group persecuted by the Taliban. Many Hazara were placed in detention camps on the island of Nauru after the prime minister refused to let the boat they were on, the *Tampa*, land on Australian soil (by permission of the National Library of Australia, photograph by John Immig).

Refugees in 1954, Australia was obligated to take in genuine refugees fleeing a regime that put their lives in danger. The Convention specified, however, that signers must keep such refugees until the danger was past and refugees could return home. In 1951, when the Convention was set up, it was assumed that repressive governments would not last long. Australia had allowed all people who qualified as genuine refugees to apply for citizenship if they wanted to stay; but in 1999 the Howard government changed the rules: now refugees who arrived illegally could not stay on permanently. They were given three-year temporary visas, which were reviewed when this time was up; if the country they came from was deemed "safe," they were deported back to it, even though in some countries, such as post–Taliban Afghanistan, minority groups such as the Hazaras were still in danger there.[45]

But alongside those who favor detention centers and temporary visas, there has been a counter offensive of Australians who side with the refugees and consider detention camps an abomination. Immigrant advocacy groups who defend the rights of boat refugees have held conferences, published reports, and called for a federal judicial inquiry into conditions at the camps. They urged the government to let most asylum seekers live in the community while their cases were pending, and to improve conditions in the camps for those considered a security risk. Woomera, a detention camp in an isolated outback region of South Australia, came in for special criticism. But immigration minister Ruddock insisted that conditions there and in other camps were excellent. When Malcolm Fraser, a staunch critic of the camps, described Woomera as a "hellhole," Ruddock said the former prime minister was out of touch.

Ruddock insisted that these detention policies were necessary, humane, and similar to what other countries were doing. But UNHCR figures showed that among the 29 developed nations that accept refugees and asylum seekers, only four put all of them into camps: Greece, Turkey, Poland, and Australia. The United States and Britain detained some in camps, but in the other 23 countries asylum seekers could live in the community while their cases were being evaluated.

As escalating publicity about the detention camps brought them to public attention, more Australians spoke out against them. The Refugee Action Committee held a rally in the capital, Canberra in September, 2001, with a large banner saying "Free the Refugees." The next year in June, a coalition of national groups supporting the end of mandatory detention held rallies in Sydney, Melbourne, Perth, Newcastle, Brisbane, Adelaide, and Hobart. "The soul of Australia is what is under assault and only the voices of the people can restore our humanitarianism," Margaret Reynolds, president of the United Nations Association of Australia, told a crowd in Sydney.[46] The

The dominant banner used in a Free the Refugees rally in September 2001 in Canberra, the nation's capital. The rally, organized by the Refugee Action Committee, protested the policy of putting asylum seekers who arrive by boat without visas into offshore detention camps (by permission of the National Library of Australia, photograph by Loui Seselja).

Refugee Council of Australia, an NGO umbrella coalition, urged communities to pass resolutions designating their city as a "refugee welcome zone." By the end of June, Brisbane, Enfield, Fremantle, Melbourne, Monash, Port Adelaide and Port Phillip had passed such resolutions, along with some smaller towns. The Catholic Commission for Justice Development and Peace accused the federal government of "psychological child-abuse" in the camps.

In seeking other reasons why Australia overreacted to boat refugees, the country's location was surely a factor. Australia is a separate continent and has no land borders contiguous with other nations. In countries where refugees sneak across borders at night, bribe guards on duty to let them through or evade immigration officers on trains crossing national frontiers, the public may be less aware of how many people are coming in illegally. And in parts of Europe, Asia and Africa where adjoining countries may also have a steady stream of refugees arriving, one's own country does not seem unique in this regard. By contrast, refugees who come ashore in Australia from small, overloaded boats invariably received publicity, reinforcing the belief that they posed a significant threat.

The actual picture is different. First, the number of newcomers accepted through traditional immigration programs far exceeds those admitted as refugees. Australia took in 105,000 migrants in 2001–2002, up 11.7 percent from 2000–2001. This figure is the total of all programs including humanitarian categories of which refugees fleeing political persecution is one slot. During that period 8418 people qualified as refugees.

Second, the perception that most people seeking refugee status arrive by boat is erroneous. Far more arrive by plane with visas in hand that designate them as refugees. In addition large numbers of would-be emigrants come in on student or tourist visas and then apply for refugee status. They can live in the community while their applications are being processed. This group makes up 66 percent of applicants for refugee status, according to the Refugee Council, but only 20 percent are successful because on examination they fail to meet the criteria. By contrast, only one third of people seeking refugee status arrived by boat, but they make up 80 percent of those granted asylum.

Malcolm Fraser used these figures to lash out at the policy of automatically incarcerating all who arrive by boat but letting those who come in by plane live in the community while their applications are being considered. "Why is the one-third, who have suffered most, who are far more likely to be genuine refugees, who have risked greater danger, penalised so harshly and placed in detention centers?" he asked. Such policies "defile the best Australian standards and our own concepts of a fair go."[47]

Hugh McKay, a researcher and columnist, lambasted the coalition government for being "worried about the tiny handful that try to come here in small boats." He pointed out that some boat refugees became stellar Australians: "People like John Yu, chancellor of the University of New South Wales and one of our most distinguished pediatricians— a man who arrived in just such a boat but, luckily for him, did so in more humane times."[48]

Finally, earlier immigrants may have reacted negatively to boat people for another reason. They saw Australia as a safe haven far from a troubled world, the "Lucky Country" where they could live a happy life in a free, uncrowded land. (*The Lucky Country* was the title of a popular book about Australia by journalist Donald Horne. He later said he meant the title to be ironic but it was taken literally by those who hadn't read the book. The phrase came to mean a land of unparalleled opportunity and freedom for those lucky enough to live there.) But if foreigners kept flooding in, placing a strain on the country's resources and introducing "alien" cultures, some worried, their personal paradise could be lost. Likewise some Australians may have feared that masses of refugees might crowd the beaches and put a damper on the lifestyle they cherished.

The belief that Australia was far from the conflicts plaguing other parts of the world was shattered early in the twenty-first century. On October 12, 2002, powerful car bombs exploded on the Indonesian island of Bali in the nightclub district of Kuta, a beach resort popular with young tourists. The bombs killed 202 people. They came from 20 countries but 88 of the dead were Australians. Bali, a tropical island whose population is 95 percent Hindu, has long been a favorite holiday destination for Australians.

Investigators linked the bombing to Jamaah Islamiah (JI), a militant group operating in a few Southeast Asian nations, whose goal is to establish an Islamic super state that includes Indonesia, Singapore, Malaysia, Brunei, Cambodia, Thailand, and the southern Philippines.[49] An Islamic cleric in Indonesia, Abu Bakar Bashir, was identified as the spiritual leader of JI.

Bashir, an activist since his student days in the 1960s, was influenced by an earlier movement, Darul Islam, which emerged in the late 1940s; it was the earliest group in Indonesia to call for an Islamic state under Sharia law. In the mid–1970s Bashir and another cleric, Abdullah Sungkar, opened an Islamic boarding school, or "madrasa," in the village of Ngruki, outside Solo in central Java. When President Suharto cracked down on Islamic militants in 1985, the two men fled to Malaysia. There Bashir "helped recruit fellow Indonesians to join the Mujahideen in Afghanistan. He traveled to Saudi Arabia on fund-raising missions and sent followers to Pakistan." In Malaysia the clerics met a younger Indonesian, Riduan Isamuddin, known as Hambali, who fought against the Soviet Union in Afghanistan and then, experts say, went on to become JI's top coordinator of terrorist activities in Southeast Asia. He is thought to be a member of Al Qaeda's consultative council.[50] Hambali was arrested in Thailand in August, 2003.

After the Suharto government fell in 1998, Bashir and Sungkar returned to their boarding school. Sungkar died the next year and Bashir continued alone. The Brussels-based International Crisis Group reported in 2002: "One network of militant Muslims has produced all the Indonesians so far suspected of links to Al-Qaeda."[51] The ICG identified the network's hub as a religious boarding school in the village of Ngruki in central Java outside Solo.

By 2002 Malaysia, Singapore, and the Philippines were all trying to weed out leaders of Jamaah Islamiah in their midst. When these countries, along with the United States, urged Indonesia to do the same, the government declined, saying it lacked evidence.[52] But soon after the Bali bombing, Indonesia raised no objection to the arrival of intelligence experts from several nations, or to a new international police and intelligence taskforce, with Australia playing a prominent role. Several days later the government arrested Bashir. At his trial, although one witness claimed that Bashir had given his blessings to the bombing of several churches on Christmas Eve of 2000, which killed 19 people across Indonesia, no direct links with the Bali bombing were proven. He was convicted of immigration violations and given a three-year sentence. Two years later the government again tried Bashir, after handing down a 65-page indictment alleging his involvement in the Bali bombings and a later attack on the Marriott Hotel in Jakarta. But they were unable to prove the most serious charges, his young supporters protested against his arrest, and although convicted again, Bashir was given a 30-month sentence.[53]

Although Indonesia has the world's largest Muslim population, they are "indeed moderate and among the most religiously tolerant Muslims globally," a leader there wrote. But a rash of stubborn economic and political problems, compounded by growing anger over America's actions in the Middle East, and by extension anger at Australia for supporting U.S. policies, has eroded some of that tolerance.

In November, 2002, after investigators in Australia learned that Bashir had preached periodically at a mosque in Perth, special forces there raided the home of an Indonesian Australian who had hosted Bashir. When they arrested the man, a good part of the Indonesian media reacted with outrage. A cartoon in the popular news magazine *Tempo*, for instance, showed a huge gun-toting kangaroo in military garb bending menacingly over a tiny cowering figure: "Are you Muslim?" the caption read. The *Herald*, which reported the reaction, commented: "An extremely difficult balancing act will be required between Australia's role in the anti-terrorism alliance and rebuilding its relationship with Indonesia and helping encourage moderate Islam."[54]

Soon after the Bali bombing, Australians in both major parties stressed the importance of maintaining good relations with Indonesia and other Asian countries. Analysts saw indications that Asia was emerging as a significant power bloc on the international scene and China was its rising star.

Thirteen

Which Way Ahead?

"Australia is in a unique position to straddle both civilizations." He Yafei, an official in China's Foreign Ministry in Beijing, made this comment while talking with a reporter about an upcoming event in the capital city of Canberra.[1]

It was a double header. On October 23, 2003, the United States president, George W. Bush, addressed a joint session of Australia's Parliament. The next day China's president, Hu Jintao, addressed the same body. Both leaders had just attended a meeting in Bangkok of the Asia Pacific Economic Cooperation Forum, known as APEC. The dual invitations said much about the changing configuration of world power and Australia's place in it. They indicated that the country saw China and the United States as the giants whose actions would affect their region. Conversely the dual acceptances showed that these countries regarded Australia as a country whose support was important to them.

Whatever role Australia plays will involve world as well as regional issues. The two presidents' speeches made this clear although they emphasized different issues. George W. Bush listed the many times when Australian and American troops had fought together in previous wars: "And in the war on terror, once again, we are at each other's side."[2] The body of his speech stressed the need to fight world terrorism; it could have been given in any country. Using the words "terror," "terrorists," and "terrorism" 15 times, as in "The terrorists cannot be appeased — they must be found and fought and defeated," Bush declared, "We call evil by its name and stand for the freedom that leads to peace."[3]

When Hu Jintao spoke the next day, he also mentioned the need to fight terrorism but briefly near the end of his speech. His main topic was about expanding trade and development in their region and how the two countries could work together. "I believe that China and Australia will shape a relationship of all-round cooperation that features a high degree of mutual trust, long-term friendship and mutual benefit, a relationship that makes our two people both winners.... China welcomes and supports a constructive Australian role in regional and international affairs," he said.[4]

Hu's speech showed that his staff had done their homework about Australia, supplying him with an array of facts and statistics. He mentioned, for example, that "China is now the biggest source of foreign students in Australia," and "by June, 2003, Australia has invested in accumulative 5,600 projects in China ... [and] China has invested in 218 projects in Australia."[5]

Trade was an important issue for both presidents. Bush and Howard discussed setting up a free trade agreement between their two countries, while Hu and Howard finalized an agreement where Australia would sell liquid natural gas to China, a deal estimated to be worth $30 billion over the next 25 years.[6] "Australia, with its political stability, is seen by the Chinese leadership as an ideal long-term supplier of raw materials," wrote Zhang Jian of the Australian Defense Force Academy in Canberra.[7]

A number of Asian nations experienced heady growth in the early years of the twenty-first century. After China, India has the fastest-growing economy in the world. It is exporting software, cars, motorcycles, and more — and buying from other nations including Australia. The majority of people in India and China remain poor and thus far the economic booms in their countries seem to have bypassed most of them. But because these countries have more than a billion people apiece, the size of their new "consumer classes" with money to spend is substantial. India, for instance, now sells "more than one million new mobile phone subscriptions each month."[8] Australia and Japan have been trading partners for decades as have Indonesia, Singapore, Malaysia and other countries in the region. But China has emerged as a prime export market — and the regional powerhouse.

"While many of us have been focusing on terrorism," Hugh White, director of the Australian Strategic Policy Institute, wrote, "China has just kept growing." He recognized the necessity of fighting terrorism but thought it was overemphasized by the United States: "I'd bet that in 20 years it will be the way the tower blocks are going up in Shanghai, rather than the way they came down in New York, that will be seen as the true symbol of the decisive global dynamic of the decade."[9]

China's buoyant trade with countries in its region did not go entirely unnoticed in the United States. The *New York Times* contrasted President Hu's upbeat words about trade and prosperity with President Bush's "dour message" about terrorism. A photo of a smiling Hu Jintao surrounded by smiling Australian lawmakers after his speech had the caption: "With Washington riveted on the antiterror campaign, Beijing is making hay with neighbors in Southeast Asia and the larger region."[10] A Malaysian lawyer and writer, Karim Raslan, told the *Times* "the American 'obsession' with terror seems tedious to Asians. We've all got to live, we've all got to make money. The Chinese want to make money and so do we."[11]

In Beijing, He Yafei, the Chinese foreign minister, told *The Age*: "Our goal is to join hands with other countries in the region, so that the whole region can prosper at the same time." He stressed that: "We do not see a scenario in which only one system or civilisation ... would dominate the region."[12] This was, said *The Age,* "an implicit riposte" to Malaysian prime minister Mahathir Mohamad whose long-standing hostility to Australia and New Zealand has kept them from a meaningful role in the Association of Southeast Nations, known as ASEAN.[13] But Mahathir was about to retire.

He Yafei believed that Australia's links with Western and Eastern countries were good for the region and could "enrich not only Australia but benefit other countries, too."[14] Commentators in Australia and England pointed out that Australia's current close relationship with the US was seen by China as a plus, with "the potential to play a constructive role in China's dealings with Washington," as the *Financial Times* put it.[15]

One of Australia's links with Asia is through its universities. In addition to attracting Asian students on its home turf, Australia has 38 offshore universities serving 60,000 students. A few are in other parts of the world such as Canada but "85 per cent of the overseas programs are in China (including Hong Kong), Singapore and Malaysia and demand is greatest for degrees in business and information technology."[16] For parents worried about the cost of overseas study for their children, these facilities offer "a cheaper option: an Australian degree without leaving home."[17]

Many Asian students also attend universities in Australia. The country, along with Britain, Ireland, Canada and New Zealand, is receiving additional students who once would have chosen an American university. After the 9/11 attack the United States, for security reasons, made it much more difficult for students from Asian as well as from Middle Eastern countries to study there. As Joseph S. Nye, Jr., a professor of government at Harvard, put it: "In an effort to keep out the dangerous few, we are keeping out the helpful many."[18] Former U.S. secretary of state Colin Powell has said: "I can think of no more valuable asset to our country than the friendship of future world leaders who have been educated here."[19] Australia, physically closer to Asia than any of the countries mentioned above, is well-situated to benefit from friendships with Asian leaders who studied there.

Australia's invitations to the two presidents reflected a change in its prime minister's view of Asia during the early years of the twenty-first century, as he reacted to unfolding events and trends. In 2002 John Howard had described Australia's bilateral relationship with the United States as "the most important we have with any single country."[20] This brought a protest from Laurie Brereton, then foreign affairs spokesman for the Opposition Labor Party. Brereton saw four key bilateral relationships—with Indonesia, Japan, China and the United States. He accused the prime minister of "classic Menzian foreign policy posture: the conscious step away from Asia and the soulful look across the water to great and powerful friends ... the Government's pointed rejection of special relationships with Asian countries, and its deliberate emphasis on our cultural differences from Asia" sent the message that Asia was not important, he said.[21]

The next year, after the United States invaded Iraq, Howard quickly sent Australian troops there even though "the war was deeply unpopular" in his country.[22] As John Hill, a retired school counsellor in Queensland, lamented to the author: "We are once again the handmaiden of another nation." Writer and historian Don Watson used satire to express his disapproval of the Howard administration's foreign policy, suggesting tongue in cheek that Australia should apply to become the 51st American state: "Far better than playing America's deputy in South-East Asia, a region from whose forums we are comprehensively excluded," he wrote in *Quarterly Essay*, "let us petition for inclusion in the American union. Demand it." This would be a "win-win" situation, he said, because the United States would get "a state instead of a colony," while Australians "won't have to go on pretending our soul's our own."[23]

Yet in the fall of 2003 the prime minister invited the presidents of both the United States and China to address Parliament, as we have seen, and his government has increasingly reached out to Asian countries. After the devastating Asian tsunami in December, 2004, Australia pledged $60 million immediately and $1 billion in long-term aid to help the devastated province of Aceh rebuild: "Our home is this region and we are saying to the people of our nearest neighbour that we are here to help you in your hour of need," the PM said.[24] A few months later, after China agreed to send a signal to ASEAN countries "supporting Australia becoming a part of emerging east Asian regional structures," the prime minister told a business lunch at home that Australia "sees herself naturally and properly as being a part of evolving regional political arrangements and political structures—not as a supplicant, but as a contributing player."[25]

This gradual shift in policy toward Asia obviously reflected changing political and economic realities as did China's growing interest in Australia. But on China's side there was another factor as well. President Hu spoke about more than trade and cooperation; he also stressed the importance of diversity among nations and an acceptance of differences. "Diversity in the world is a basic characteristic of human society, and also the key condition for a lively and dynamic world as we see today," he said. "The proud history, culture and traditions that make each country different from others are all parts of human civilisation."[26] After speaking of China's 5000-year civilization, he turned to Australia, saying: "Cultural pluralism is a distinct feature of Australian society, a feature that embodies ethnic harmony in the country."[27] He also paid tribute to the many Australians of Chinese ancestry who contributed "their proud share to Australia's economy, society and its thriving pluralistic culture."

Other aspects of President Hu's message can be gleaned from words he repeated several times in his speech; they give a sub-rosa look at concerns he did not address openly. He used the word "respect" (or respected) seven times, the word "equal" (or equality), four times, and the word "mutual," in phrases such as "mutual respect" seven times. What comes through is, first, his concern that Australia accept China's Communist government; that is, "the political system and path of political development chosen by the people of each country should be respected."[28] But beyond this, the frequent use of such words give a hint that President Hu, like other Asians, has not forgotten the period when European powers including Britain colonized or dominated much of Asia and looked down on its people as inferior.

Nor is Hu Jintao, who appeared to know a lot about Australian history, likely to be unaware that the country once had a policy of keeping out Asians (especially the Chinese), that its official head of state is still the British monarch, and that during the referendum campaign in 1999 to make Australia a republic, John Howard was one of the staunchest supporters of retaining this formal tie with Britain (see Chapter Eleven).

If support for multiculturalism waned at the federal level under the coalition government, one official on the periphery was consistently enthusiastic. He was Sir William Deane who served as governor general during the early years of the Howard administration; that is, he was the Australian appointed to be the on-site representative of Queen Elizabeth, the country's head of state. Deane's speeches were a ringing endorsement of the cultural pluralism that Hu Jintao praised. In 1997, while the country was reeling from Pauline Hanson's speech against Asian immigrants and the indigenous Aborigines, Deane offered a different vision for the country. Australians must be vigilant in defending the achievements of multiculturalism, he declared: "The essence of that multi-culturalism is mutual respect and tolerance for all our different cultural, ethnic, national and religious backgrounds and lawful practices."[29] The next year he said: "Our multiculturalism is not only decent, just and right. It is not only our Australian way. It is what we are." And on Australia Day in 1999, he responded to the charge that multiculturalism was divisive, asserting that to the contrary, "it inspires and sustains our modern Australia.... It has enabled us to blend the many into a pretty harmonious whole without bringing to this new land old hatreds, old prejudices and old conflicts ... [it was] not a vision of imposed uniformity but of true and worthwhile unity and mutual acceptance."[30]

Throughout his tenure, Deane was perhaps most eloquent in speaking about the need for reconciliation with the Aborigines. In 2000 he said that the most important practical effect of reconciliation "will be to create an environment of trust and mutual respect and acceptance in which indigenous and non-indigenous Australians can work together." Until that was achieved, "our nation will remain diminished, unable to fulfill its enormous social, cultural and moral potential. For our search for national reconciliation is not a matter of charity or generosity. It is a matter of basic justice and national decency."

Governor General Deane articulated a vision for Australia that was in keeping with the tradition it had developed over the past 40 years. Yet his speeches apparently had scant impact on the direction the country took while he was in office, even though he was popular with the public and highly respected. This is not surprising. For every newspaper article that mentions the governor general, there are perhaps 300 to 400 articles that feature or bring in the prime minister. He is the leader who heads the government, presides over Parliament, and is involved in the day-to-day running of the country. The voice of the representative of the country's head of state, a ceremonial post, is heard infrequently and has no political clout.

This division underscores the irony of the 1999 republic referendum campaign when the majority of Australians were persuaded that a head of state called "president" instead of "governor general," and serving Australia in his or her own right, would somehow be invested with awesome powers. Yet the duties of the office itself would not have changed.

The outcome of the referendum also showed the power of the "bully pulpit." This term was coined by an earlier U.S. president, Theodore Roosevelt, who thought the presidency provided a strong platform, akin to a preacher's weekly sermon, from which to convince citizens to support what he believed was right for the nation. The same holds for prime ministers and other national leaders. The last four prime ministers before John Howard — Gough Whitlam, Malcolm Fraser, Bob Hawke, and Paul Keating — used their bully pulpits to promote acceptance of multiculturalism, Aboriginal reconciliation, and increased engagement with nearby Asian nations. They believed in these policies.

John Howard came to office with beliefs that were closer to those of an earlier prime minister, Robert Gordon Menzies (1950–1966; see Chapter Ten).

Menzies thought "the world" meant Western nations, that Asian nations were irrelevant, and that a white Australia which recreated the British way of life in the antipodes was the ideal. "Menzies," said one analyst, "set his face almost totally against Asia. He was a man on a life-support system from a receding world."[31] Howard was more accepting of immigrants with dark skins than Menzies and more open to interaction with Asian nations. But he was an avid supporter of the Menzies-era assimilation policy: that is, all immigrants must drop their "foreign" ways and emulate the Anglo–Australian way of life.

During his first three years as prime minister, John Howard never used the word "multiculturalism" in public; but starting in 1999 he did use it. Asked about this change later by an interviewer, he said, "You have to go with the flow."[32] By 2002, he "disagreed with Blainey's critique of multiculturalism, argued that Muslims could integrate into Australian society and supported a modest increase in the migrant intake."[33] "It was unfortunate that he had not been converted to these views fifteen years before," Jupp commented.[34]

Australia's multicultural policy succeeded in part because it built on the country's progressive social heritage. As we saw in Chapter Three, the belief that every Australian should have a fair go, a chance for a pleasant life without poverty, became embedded in the national fabric. In the late nineteenth century the country passed legislation and wrote sections of the Constitution designed to encourage public policies and services that would make the government receptive to the needs of its citizens. Middle-class reformers played a role here, but the working classes, initially through their labor unions and later through a political party geared to their needs, were a driving force for an egalitarian society.

C. Hartley Grattan noted the role of labor in Australia. Grattan, an American journalist who became interested in the country during his first visit there in 1927, had a penchant for Australian literature but wrote on many aspects of the country.[35] For his book, *Introducing Australia*, published in the United States in 1942, he asked a number of prominent Australians about their country and related their responses in one chapter. "Practically all my correspondents had something to say about the place of the labor movement in the national life," he reported. "Almost to a man, they stated their conviction that that place made Australia in some way unique. Some thought that the far-famed social legislation and the court system for handling employer-employee relations somehow made Australia a paradise for the workingman. Some expressed the view that the standard of living was high and that no extreme contrasts of wealth and poverty existed."[36]

Government was expected to play a role in providing needed social services and benefits that workers could not afford. Sixty years later this viewpoint is muted but belief in the fair go tradition remains strong. It helped bring about what we now call a "safety net." Welsh writer Jan Morris saw the legacy of that net in Australia in the 1990s: "There are no such obvious emblems of class distinction as there are in England, no fearful contrasts between rich and poor as one sees in the United States," she wrote. "Slums are rare, the standard of living is high."[37] An Australian correspondent based in Washington, D.C., wrote in 1997 that "the working poor in the US face a much harsher edge to their lives than is common in Australia."[38]

In the 1990s one rarely saw poor people sleeping on city streets in Australia, as was commonplace by then in the United States. The minimum wage was higher in Australia and there were wide-ranging supports then such as subsidized child care and some type of medical coverage for everyone. There was a difference in the way Australia and the United States have traditionally looked on the role of government in promoting the welfare of its people. This American thought her country could pick up a few practical ideas about good government from Australia in this regard. She was also impressed that a country which once tried to keep out people of color had not only opened its door but also provided them with the kind of practical services that became a hallmark of the country. Other countries might benefit from knowing how Australia absorbed five million people from over 200 countries without violent upheavals.

Nick Bolkus thought so too. Bolkus, who served as minister for Immigration and Ethnic Affairs during the second half of the Keating administration, reported to a conference in late 1993: "I returned from overseas visits this year — to Asia, the US, Germany, Switzerland, Greece and Turkey — more convinced than ever that Australia has a lot to offer other parts of the world in terms of sharing our experience of immigration and multiculturalism." Germany had expressed "great interest" in Australia's policies in these areas "and plans to hold a Symposium comparing the two countries' experiences, in February next year," Bolkus reported.[39] He also announced a forthcoming international conference on global cultural diversity, sponsored by Australia.

That conference was suggested by then U.N. Secretary General Boutros Boutros-Ghali when he visited Australia and was impressed at how the country had absorbed immigrants from so many places without turmoil.[40] Held in Sydney in April, 1995, the conference attracted delegates from around the world; many presented papers on their own nations' efforts to accommodate diversity, as did a number of Australians. Less than a year later, however, a conservative coalition came to power and as we have seen, efforts of the federal government to promote acceptance of diversity ceased.

But the country's multicultural policy remained intact. Although Howard and some other top ministers showed no enthusiasm for it — and made cutbacks in funding and closed a couple of offices that promoted it — they did not abolish the national multicultural policy set up in 1989, as Hanson had urged. An Immigration Department website for potential immigrants stated in 2004: "Australian multiculturalism is the philosophy, underlying Government policy and programs, that recognises, accepts, respects and celebrates our cultural diversity ... all Australians benefit from productive diversity, that is, the significant cultural, social and economic dividends arising from the diversity of our population. Diversity works for all Australians."[41]

Practical services, a core component of Australian society, are also described in a website for immigrants; it advises recent migrants to visit their nearest Migrant Resource Centre, which can "help people who migrate to Australia find housing, join English-language classes, find child-care, look for work and enroll children in schools." Their staff members, who speak various languages, can "provide basic information on health, employment, education and the law and can refer you to government services dealing with these matters. They also give useful information about Australian society, customs and institutions."[42]

The delivery of services is carried out by the states which, along with the Northern Territory, have all had Labor governments since 2001.[43] State agencies "gave a direct voice to immigrants communities in defining the services which their members needed; ... from 1996, they became the main public sector defenders of multiculturalism."[44]

Person-to-person services happen at the local level. Fairfield, an outer metropolitan area of southwest Sydney, has an active Migrant Resource Centre. Its services are well-used because Fairfield has "the largest and densest concentration of migrants in the State" and thus also the most languages spoken.[45] Cabrametta, with its hefty Vietnamese population, is a suburb of Fairfield. Over the years new immigrants from various countries have come to the Fairfield Centre for services until they got settled, and then were replaced by recent arrivals. A picture of who the Centre was serving in 2004 could be gleaned from photos taken at an open house for new immigrants. A few people from Ethiopia or Vietnam attended but most had come recently from the Congo: they all looked under 35 and were refugees from that troubled nation in central Africa.[46]

Over the past two decades increasing numbers of Africans have settled in Australia. The current number of black Africans now living there is around 50,000.[47] About 6000 refugees came from Sudan during that county's long civil war, and refugees or immigrants have come from many countries in conflicts such as Somalia, Ethiopia and Eritrea. There are Africans of other colors in Australia as well: white immigrants from South Africa; about 27,000

Egyptians, the majority of them Coptic Christians; and people from North African countries who are Berbers or Arabs, and usually Muslims. The Federation of African Communities Council was established in 2002 with the goal of "responding to the needs of the Australians of African origin."[48] It has African community members from every part of the country except Tasmania and the Northern Territory and listed 48 countries—in West, East, North, Southern and Central Africa—from which it members came.

Australia continues to admit refugees from several continents as long as they apply overseas for entry and arrive with the necessary visa in hand; and some who came in illegally are eventually determined to be genuine refugees. On June 20, 2005, for example, 90 refugees became citizens: they came from Sudan, Iraq, Afghanistan, Iran, Sierra Leone, Bosnia, Russia, Pakistan, Croatia, Turkey, Mongolia, Sri Lanka, Lebanon and Nicaragua.[49] But hundreds of refugees who came a few years earlier on unauthorized

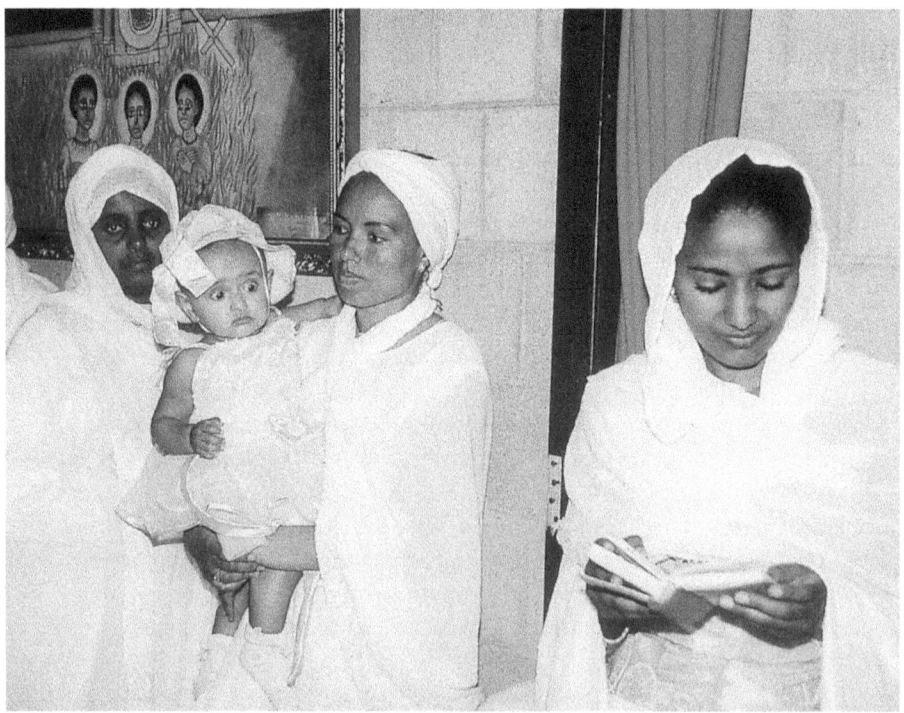

Ethiopian women and a young child at their Coptic Orthodox church in Melbourne. There have been Africans in Australia for decades, but their numbers have increased in recent years. Africans from dozens of countries now live there (Centre for Immigration and Multicultural Studies, photograph by Elizabeth Gilliam).

boats are still housed in camps that feel like prisons, because mandatory detention of illegal asylum seekers has continued. Some people with status problems have been incarcerated in these camps for several years.

The government has justified the policy by invoking the need to protect its borders. It claimed victory in this regard because several months after it stopped the *Tampa* and instigated the "Pacific Solution" of placing boat refugees in offshore camps, the unauthorized arrivals stopped. This is true. But it is equally true that boatloads of refugees also stopped coming in 1981 after a previous government used a different approach. As we saw in Chapter Nine, once the Fraser government negotiated with the UNHCR to let a specified number of Vietnamese refugees enter legally each year, virtually no illegal boats arrived for almost nine years.

And some Australians argue that it was not mandatory detention that caused refugees to stop coming in small boats; instead it was the fate of people on one of those boats. Less than two months after the *Tampa* incident, an overloaded boat known as SIEV X (Suspected Illegal Entry Vessel) left Indonesia for Australia. It sunk in the Indian Ocean on October 19, 2001. When no ship came to rescue its passengers in time, 353 people drowned.[50] Tony Kevin, who has written a book about SIEV X, said one need only "ask former boat people why their relatives stopped trying to come here, to get the true answer — that after SIEV X, people rightly feared for their lives in these perilous voyages."[51]

For many years a number of organizations have campaigned to end mandatory detention. The government paid no attention until 2005 when a challenge came from one of its own. Petro Georgiou, a member of Parliament who belongs to John Howard's Liberal Party, told his colleagues it was time to change the policy. (The son of Greek immigrants, he was the member of the Galbally Committee who in 1978 influenced it to recommend funds for ethnic organizations that provided services for their people.) When the government flatly rejected his suggestions, Georgiou teamed up with a few other Liberal Party MPs who supported him. After further rebuffs, on May 24 Georgiou announced that he would offer two private bills on mandatory detention if necessary.[52] In the tightly controlled parliamentary party system, this was the equivalent of an insurrection.

The prime minister said he wouldn't budge: "There won't be any basic alterations to the policy. It's the right policy," he said on ABC television.[53] But the public mood had changed since 2001. Some Anglican bishops supported Georgiou and newspapers spoke of support from "doctors' wives," a term that came to symbolize Liberal Party members in affluent suburbs who were sympathetic to the plight of refugees sitting in camps for years, especially young children and their parents.

Naomi Leong and her mother fit that description. This 3-year old Malaysian girl was born in a detention center and had spent her life there. The case came to public notice after a psychiatrist reported that she would bang her head against a wall repeatedly and often stopped talking. On the same day that the Georgiou rebellion was reported, so was the news that Naomi and her mother had been released from detention.[54] The story made the front page in the *Malay Mail* with the headline, "Naomi's Free," indicating that people in Malaysia were well aware of her situation.[55]

Before long the prime minister was meeting with the four key rebels to negotiate a deal and on June 17 a compromise was reached. All families with children would live in the community while their cases were being evaluated; the Immigration Department would report to an ombudsman twice a year on the cases of people who had been in detention for more than two years and there would be a limit of six months on the processing of new visa applications and appeals. Although the prime minister refused the demand that all people on temporary visas be given permanent ones, not wanting to set a precedent, unless there were individual special problems, the several thousand currently in that category would be given permanent visas by October.[56]

In July, bomb attacks in London killed 52 people and in October another bomb erupted on Bali. This blast was much smaller than the bomb set off three years earlier, but it rekindled fears in Australia of an attack at home by Muslim terrorists. A few weeks later, on November 3, the prime minister announced he had received "specific intelligence ... which gives cause for serious concern about a potential terrorist threat."[57] In the early hours of November 8, hundreds of police raided dozens of properties and arrested ten young men in Melbourne and seven in Sydney. All were alleged to be followers of a Muslim cleric in Melbourne, Abdul Nacer Benbrika, who was among those arrested. Most were identified as Lebanese Muslims. Police said that they had found enough chemicals to make 15 bombs.[58]

As attorneys for both sides collected material to bolster their cases, repercussions were felt in Sydney. In Cronulla, a suburban town at the southern edge of metropolitan Sydney, part of the beach had been a surfers' hangout since the 1960s. "It has a tribal surf culture shaped by violence and substance abuse," the *Herald* reported, and was long "the scene of battles with outsiders."[59] Dedicated surfers resented the presence of people who were not part of their group.

In the fall of 2005 the surfers' resentment focused on groups of Lebanese Australian youths who often came to the beach from nearby western suburbs where immigrants cluster. Early in December, two volunteer life guards asked a group of young Lebanese who were playing soccer to stop their game and leave because it was disturbing others on the beach. They refused and two of them attacked the lifeguards.

In the days that followed, surfers sent out text messages on their cell phones urging their mates to come to Cronulla the next weekend and take revenge for the attacks on the lifeguards. Leaders of anti-immigrant groups heard about these messages and urged their members to come out, too. Announcers and talk-show hosts on some Sydney radio stations encouraged listeners to come to Cronulla Beach on Sunday.[60] On December 11, more than 5000 young people converged on Cronulla and began attacking anyone they thought looked Lebanese, Middle Eastern or Muslim. The media soon arrived and descriptions and film footage of the riot on this hot summer day went out around the world.

The police also came out in force: they helped rescue people being pursued by attackers, arrested a number of rioters and asked bars and drink shops in the area to stop take-away sales because many surfers were drinking heavily. The beach was sealed off the next day but many angry Muslim youth took revenge in other suburbs, breaking windows and trashing cars. In the end many people were hurt but no one was killed. Property damage was moderate. The biggest damage was to Australia's reputation.

The prime minister strongly condemned the riots but kept insisting that Australia was not a racist society. This led to two days of outpouring on blogs, talk-show radio and other media on the question: is this country racist or isn't it? Meanwhile, in the area where the riots occurred, leaders came together to try and defuse the tensions. Kevin Schreiber, mayor of Sutherland Shire where Cronulla is located, held peace talks on December 15 with 28 community leaders. They sent invitations to Lebanese representatives "to attend the launch of a surf boat at Cronulla on Sunday. The talks also paved the way for young men of Middle Eastern descent to train as lifesavers with the Cronulla surf lifesaving clubs, and for young Lebanese teachers to help out at the surf schools."[61]

During the riots, on the bare back of one 13-year-old were the words: "We grew here; you flew here."[62] But the young Lebanese who took part in the melee also grew up in Sydney. Their parents had fled the civil war that raged in Lebanon from 1975 to 1991 between Muslims and Christians, the two largest religious groups there. Lebanese Australians, who have been an established community for more than a century, come from both groups (though more are Christians than Muslims) as well as from smaller sects. Joseph Wakim, founder of the Australian Arabic Council, pointed out that the community in Australia included "Maronites, Orthodox, Sunnis, Alawis, Shiites and Druze ... Lebanese embrace the full range of hair, eye and skin color."[63]

Salam Zreika, a Sydney freelance journalist of Lebanese descent, criticized "young, angry violent Lebanese men" as well as "young, angry violent Cronulla locals." Both were "heading down a dangerous and destructive path," she said. Zreika also described her own feelings and frustrations. In the Cronulla area, "I do get odd looks at my headscarf, long skirt and Mediterranean complexion. But if you spoke to me for just a minute or two you would discover through my very Aussie accent that I love my country, I love the Aussie way of life at the beach with fish and chips for lunch ... and I'm very proud to be Australian. But how can I can get this message across when no one gives me the time of day ... when talk-back radio presenters speak on racial issues and incite more hatred than anyone else?" She concluded that "Sutherland Shire may be predominantly Anglo-Australian, but the beach — and this country — belongs to us all."[64]

Writing about the riots in the *New York Times*, Australian author Eva Sallis said: "Our government has done little to substantively allay fear of Muslim and Middle Eastern Australians generally or to increase public understanding and appreciation of their culture and contribution to Australian life."[65] Wakim saw recent government input as negative: "This fear has been compounded by the Howard Government's dog-whistle politics regarding home-grown terrorist cells."[66]

The Cronulla Beach riots raised questions about Australia's future immigration policy and direction. Would the country continue to become increasingly multiethnic or would it try to restrict immigrants to people from cultures similar to those of its Anglo-Celtic majority? In fact Australia has only one viable option: to continue down the path of inclusion it chose 40 years ago. The country's economic future, as well as its place and security in the region, depends on it.

In recent years Australia's economy has expanded considerably, causing shortages of highly-trained technical and professional workers, and of other workers as well. "For Australia, allowing large numbers of people into the country every year is not a choice but a necessity," the London *Financial Times* reported in November, 2005; "without an ongoing, plentiful supply of fresh workers, the economy would seize up." The country was already accepting more immigrants than it did during the 1990s; one analyst said that by 2010 the country would need at least 180,000 immigrants a year.[67]

Where will all these people come from? Back in 1947 when Australia launched a campaign to attract large numbers of immigrants (see Chapter Eight), the immigration minister said he hoped to bring out ten Britons for every "foreign" migrant. That didn't happen. Instead the majority of immigrants came from places where a lot of people wanted to move to another country, for economic, political or other reasons. Similarly today's immigrants will come from every continent.

Along with educated professionals the country also needs unskilled workers. Newly-arrived immigrants perform the messy jobs that other Australians, including second-generation migrants, usually don't want. And immigrants also fill slots for other low-paying, low-status jobs. The Howard government has sided consistently with management over labor and has been dismantling some historic labor legislation that shaped the nation and helped give workers a fair go. But even if this hadn't happened, and even if Australia had put more money into higher education in recent years, home-grown workers alone would be unlikely to meet the country's needs for workers in the coming years.

Immigration minister Amanda Vanstone said: "We do need to fill job vacancies but immigration has to match community sentiment.... If people feel their jobs are threatened, they will not support it." [68] This statement shows the need for national leaders who will use the bully pulpit of their office to explain to the people how the country's situation has changed and why some old concerns are no longer relevant.

This foreign observer sees a few areas where future leaders might help the populace accept the current reality. The first is the area just mentioned: show people why they no longer need to fear that immigrants will take their jobs. The second concerns Australia's multiethnic society: to build popular acceptance for it, leaders need to re-emphasize that multiculturalism means everybody in the country, including the Anglo-Celtic majority. And they need to ease fears, whipped up by those on the far right, that Asians, and now Middle Easterners, may take over the country or destroy it.

To the contrary, "by all projections based on Australia's migration program, Australia will remain a predominantly Anglo-Celtic-Irish country into the foreseeable future," Australian professors Laksiri Jayasuriya and Kee Pookong found. The country will become increasingly multiethnic but this will happen gradually. In their book *The Asianisation of Australia? Some Facts about the Myths* (1999) Jayasuriya and Kee also pointed out that "in the last two and a half decades, Australia has benefited greatly from the large number of Asian immigrants with special skills, qualifications, and, more recently, capital and entrepreneurial know-how."[69]

The country's multicultural policy means that arriving immigrants are no longer urged to discard their own customs and embrace the Anglo-based culture of early British settlers. Today immigrants have a choice. Many of their children and grandchildren partake of traditions from more than one culture, as in the case of the Lebanese Australian who wore a headscarf while enjoying a lunch of fish and chips at the beach.

In a poll taken soon after the Sydney riots, 81 percent of those contacted said they favored a multicultural policy for Australia.[70] This indicates far more acceptance of the country's ethnic mix than media coverage of the riots might lead one to believe.

Australia has developed a distinctive culture of its own based on input from numerous sources. It encompasses many aspects of the British way of life but also reflects influences from the different peoples who live there, as well as outsides influences such as the impact of popular American culture on the young. Australian culture has also been shaped by nature of the land itself, the area where it is located and the country's history.

The general populace needs to understand how much the country's security and economic prosperity depend on good relationships with Australia's many neighbors to the north, that is, southeast and continental Asia. The country finally was invited to the East Asian summit, a new group whose inaugural one-day meeting was held in Malaysia on December 14. The prime minister arrived ready to talk about trade and cooperation; but the Sydney beach riots had just occurred, so that was the only topic other delegates would talk to him about. What happened, they wanted to know, and why?[71] The summit took place at the end of a meeting of the Association of Southeast Nations, whose ten members are Brunei, Cambodia, Indonesia, Laos, Malaysia, Myanmar (formerly Burma), the Philippines, Singapore, Thailand and Vietnam. For several years China, Japan and South Korea have also been included and the organization is know as ASEAN plus three. But Australia, New Zealand and India are still excluded.

These days some retired Australian diplomats who spent years posted to Asian countries and came to know their peoples and cultures are in the forefront of those advocating closer ties with countries in the region. Richard Woolcott urged strengthening relationships with Indonesia, where he served as ambassador, and modifying the style of diplomacy. To achieve this, he suggested, "We should consult and listen more and lecture less."[72] Stephen FitzGerald, the former ambassador to China mentioned in Chapter Twelve, wrote that engaging with Asia "involves, while maintaining the integrity of our own political and social system, coming to terms intellectually with Asia and Asians. Not on American or 'Western' ground, but on our ground and on Asians' ground ... taking account of their cultural and historical backgrounds."[73]

Finally, another area where input from leaders, and from the media, might be helpful concerns Australia's achievements and its ties with Britain. The two topics are related. In the cultural realm, Britain will remain important to Australia because the majority of its citizens or their forebears came from there. Its membership in the (British) Commonwealth of Nations provides a link with those traditions. But the issue of Australia's head of state is another matter.

It seems unlikely that Asian nations will accept Australia fully as part of the region as long its official head of state is the monarch of a Western nation. Retired diplomat Richard Woolcott, who has served as Australia's ambassor to four southeast Asian nations said that "prominent Indonesians, Filipinos, Malaysians and Singaporeans found it curious and confusing that, even in a formal sense, our Head of State was the Queen of England. In their eyes this diminished to some extent Australia's sovereignty as a nation."[74] This anachronistic arrangement also leaves Australia open to the charge that its heart is still in the West and it only participates in regional affairs for economic gain.

This book has described several innovations that Australians can be proud of yet a good part of the world knows little about them. One reason is that Australia has not projected an image abroad that includes its accomplishments. For 200 years the nation looked westward for models and innovations, with Britain as its prime role model, while downplaying or even disparaging its own successes. The country could use a new appraisal that describes and values Australia's considerable achievements.

If future leaders can encourage Australians to take pride in the policies and services that enabled the country to successfully absorb several million immigrants from around the globe in less than two generations, people overseas will also become aware of these accomplishments. If Australia can accept its destiny as a nation that geographical and historical forces are pushing toward the international stage, it may yet serve as a small bridge between cultures that have frequently been at odds. The potential is there; the outcome remains to be seen.

Chapter Notes

For two publications frequently cited in these notes, the following shortened versions have been used:

Encyclopedia of Aboriginal Australia: Aboriginal Australia
Sydney Morning Herald: Herald

One. Before the British

1. F. G. Clarke, *Australia: A Concise Political and Social History*, pp. 18–20.
2. Alan Moorehead, *The Fatal Impact*, and Geoffrey Blainey, *The Tyranny of Distance*. Both describe Cook's visit in 1770.
3. Robert Hughes, *The Fatal Shore*, pp. 54–5.
4. Ibid., p. 55.
5. "The Instructions to Captain Cook for his First Voyage, July, 1768," excerpted in Manning Clark, ed., *Sources of Australian History*, p. 36.
6. Moorehead, *Fatal Impact*, p. 36.
7. Ibid., p. 4.
8. "Captain Cook sums up his Impressions of New Holland, August, 1770," exerpted in Clark, *Sources*, p. 55.
9. Charles Corn, *The Scents of Eden: A History of the Spice Trade* (1998).
10. Ibid., p. 176.
11. "The Instructions to Tasman for his First Journey, August, 1642," reprinted in Clark, *Sources*, pp. 5–6.
12. Author's interview with Mary E. White.
13. Mary E. White, *The Greening of Gondwana*, pp. 34–37.
14. Ibid., pp. 43–47.
15. Geoffrey Blainey, *Triumph of the Nomads*.
16. Abbott Emerson Smith, *Colonists in Bondage*.
17. Warren B. Smith, *White Servitude in Colonial South Carolina* (Columbia: University of South Carolina Press, 1961), p. 39.
18. Quoted in Ronald W. Clark, *Benjamin Franklin: A Biography* (New York: Random House, 1983), p. 254.
19. Blainey, *Tyranny of Distance*, pp. 23–27. Blainey recounted the views of K. M. Dallas.
20. Jonathan King, *The First Fleet*.
21. Ibid., pp. 165–166.
22. Quoted in Hughes, *Fatal Shore*, p. 87.

Two. Convicts and Colonists

1. Russel Ward, *Concise History of Australia*, pp. 51–52.
2. F. G. Clarke, *Australia: A Concise Political and Social History*, pp. 41–42; Geoffrey Blainey, *The Tyranny of Distance*, pp. 45–46.
3. Robert Hughes, *The Fatal Shore*, p. 68.
4. Ibid., p. 91.
5. Ibid., pp. 88–89.
6. A. G. L. Shaw, "1788–1910," in Frank Crowley, ed., *A New History of Australia*, p. 11.
7. Hughes, *Fatal Shore*, p. 145.
8. Ibid., pp. 145–146.
9. Ibid., p. 105.
10. Geoffrey Sherington, *Australia's Immigrants*, p. 4.
11. Ibid.
12. J. J. Auchmuty, "1810–1830" in Crowley, *New History*, p. 64.
13. Quoted in Malcolm D. Prentis, *The*

Scots in Australia, p. 48. The speaker was Alexander Majoribanks.
14. Portia Robinson, *The Women of Botany Bay*. This book lists every woman who was transported, giving the date and ship she came out on.
15. Hughes, *Fatal Shore*, pp. xv–xvi.
16. Shaw in Crowley, *New History*, p. 21.
17. Sherington, *Australia's Immigrants*, p. 7.
18. Blainey, *Tyranny of Distance*, pp. 76–78.
19. Auchmuty in Crowley, *New History*, p. 81.
20. Ward, *Concise History*, p. 87.
21. Marcus Clarke, *His Natural Life*. The introduction by Stephen Murray-Smith gives the history of the two editions of this book.
22. Ross Fitzgerald and Mark Hearn, *Bligh, Macarthur and the Rum Rebellion*.
23. Ibid., pp. 19–20.
24. Ibid., p. 33.
25. Ibid., p. 19.
26. Ibid., p. 37.
27. Ibid., p. 56.
28. Ibid.
29. Shaw in Crowley, *New History*, p. 41.
30. Fitzgerald and Hearn, *Rum Rebellion*, p. 87.
31. Clarke, *Political and Social History*, pp. 59–61; Chapter Five, "The Rum Rebellion," in Fitzgerald and Hearn, *Rum Rebellion*, pp. 81–101.
32. John Ritchie, *Lachlan Macquarie: A Biography* (Melbourne: Melbourne University Press, 1984).
33. Manning Clark, *A Short History of Australia*, p. 44.
34. Ibid., pp. 54–56.
35. Clarke, *Political and Social History*, p. 71.
36. Quoted in Russel Ward, *Australia*, p. 33.
37. Ibid., 35.
38. Robinson, *Women of Botany Bay*.
39. Ibid., pp. 250–256.; Hughes, *Fatal Shore*, pp. 247–248.
40. Robinson, *Women of Botany Bay*, p. 255.
41. Ritchie, *Macquarie: A Biography*.
42. Clarke, *Political and Social*, pp. 105–106.
43. Blainey, *Tyranny of Distance*, p. 90.
44. Ibid., pp. 93–95.
45. Author's visit to Port Arthur in Tasmania.
46. Author's visit to the old prison barracks in Sydney.
47. Authur's tour of The Rocks with a guide who explained the area's history.
48. Ibid.
49. Charles Darwin, *The Voyage of the Beagle*, ed. Leonard Engel (New York: Doubleday/Anchor, 1962), pp. 444–445.

Three. Class Conflicts with Unexpected Outcomes

1. Quoted in Russel Ward, *Australia*, p. 23.
2. Manning Clark, *A Short History of Australia*, p. 99; F. C. Clarke, *Australia: A Concise Political and Social History*, p. 100; Geoffrey Sherington, *Australia's Immigrants*, p. 48.
3. Sherington, *Australia's Immigrants*, p. 48.
4. Ibid., p. 70.
5. Paul Johnson, *Ireland: A Concise History from the Twelfth Century to the Present Day*.
6. Quoted in Margery Barnard, *A History of Australia* (Sydney: Angus & Robertson, 1963), p. 236.
7. Quoted in Sherington, *Australia's Immigrants*, p. 11.
8. Ibid.
9. Clarke, *Political and Social History*, p. 73.
10. Ibid.
11. Jan Morris, *Sydney*, p. 82.
12. Quoted in Clarke, *Political and Social History*, p. 79.
13. Quoted in Ilsa Sharp, *Culture Shock! Australia*, p. 9.
14. James Jupp, *The English in Australia*, p. 35.
15. Ibid., p. 52.
16. Ibid., p. 53.
17. Ibid., p. 35.
18. Ibid., p. 53.
19. Ibid., p. 54.
20. Ibid., p. 70.
21. Jupp, *English in Australia*, p. 114.
22. Jupp, ed., *The Australian People:An Encyclopedia of the Nation, its People and their Origins*, p. 457.
23. Jupp, *English in Australia*, p. 54.
24. Quoted in Ward, *Australian Legend*, p. 60.
25. Jupp, *English in Australia*, p. 82.
26. Ian Turner, *In Union Is Strength: A History of Trade Unions in Australia, 1788–1978*.
27. Ibid., p. 34.
28. Ibid., pp. 26–27; Jupp, *Australian People*, p. 457.
29. W. G. Spence, *History of the A.W.U.*, 1911 (Reprint: Sydney, The Workers' Trustee, 1961), pp. 6–8.
30. Ibid., p. 9.
31. Ibid., p. 8.
32. Ibid.
33. Ibid., p. 7.
34. Quoted in Turner, *In Union Is Strength*, p. 32.
35. John Bartlett, *Bartlett's Familiar Quotations* (Boston: Little, Brown, 1980), p. 421.
36. Cecil Woodham-Smith, *Florence Night-*

ingale, 1820–1910 (London: Constable, 1950), pp. 239–241.
  37. Clarke, *Political and Social History*, p. 77; Robert Hughes, *The Fatal Shore*, pp. 448–449.
  38. Ward, *Australia*, pp. 85–86.
  39. Resolutions of the Pan Australasian Conference of Employers, *Sydney Morning Herald*, September 13, 1880. Reprinted in Manning Clark, *Sources of Australian History*, p. 424.
  40. Quoted in Turner, *In Union Is Strength*, p. 40.
  41. Ibid., p. 42.
  42. Clarke, *Political and Social History*, p. 166.
  43. Turner, *In Union Is Strength*, p. 42.
  44. Anthony Trollope, *Australia*, vol. 1, p. 28.
  45. Ibid., p. 29.
  46. Ibid., p. 36.
  47. Quoted in Jim Hagen and Andrew Wells, eds., *The Maritime Strike: A Centennial Retrospective* (Wollongong, Five Island Press Assoc., 1992), p. 84. The writer was F. W. Coneybeer, a future Labor MP.
  48. B. K. de Garis, "1890–1900," in F. K. Crowley, ed., *A New History of Australia*, p. 244.
  49. Clarke, *Political and Social History*, pp. 164–165, 168.
  50. Quoted in Turner, *In Union Is Strength*, p. 52.
  51. For information on the Chartist movement in Australia, see Jupp, *English in Australia*, pp. 161–162.
  52. Peter J. Coleman, "New Zealand Liberalism and the Origins of the American Welfare State," *Journal of American History*, September 1982, pp. 372–391.
  53. Ibid., p. 387.
  54. de Garis, "1890–1900," p. 244.
  55. Jupp, *English in Australia*, p. 172.
  56. Norway had a Labor Party a few years earlier.
  57. Clarke, *Political and Social History*, p. 168.
  58. Ibid., p. 171.
  59. Colin Howard, ed., *Australia's Constitution* (Ringwood: Penguin Books, 1978), p. 182.
  60. De Garis, "1890–1900," p. 243.
  61. David Pope, and Peter Shergold, *ASEAN-Australian Immigration and the Demise of White Australia*, p. 9.
  62. Clarke, *Social and Political History*, p. 188.
  63. Charlie Fox, *Working Australia*, p. 103.
  64. A. G. L. Shaw, *The Story of Australia*, p. 200.
  65. Ibid. Shaw gave details of the case to paint Higgins as an impractical dreamer "noted for his sympathy with the under-dog" (p. 199) while Fox's presentation was more sympathetic.
  66. Fox, *Working Australia*, p. 104.
  67. Celeste MacLeod, *Horatio Alger, Farewell: The End of the American Dream* (New York: Seaview Books, 1980), p. 9, lists more than twenty books published in the United States between 1850 and 1900 that promised to show poor people how they could become rich. See also Irwin G. Wyllie, *The Self-Made Man in America: The Myth of Rags to Riches* (New York: Macmillan/Free Press, 1960).
  68. Ward, *Australian Legend*, p. 244.

Four. Spreading Across the Land

  1. Anthony Trollope, *Australia*, vol. 2, p. 107.
  2. Ibid., p. 105.
  3. Quoted in Manning Clark, *A Short History of Australia*, p. 86.
  4. Michael Roe, "1830–50" in F. K. Crowley, ed., *A New History of Australia*, pp. 84–5.
  5. Ibid., p. 84.
  6. "Henry Lawson, 1867–1922" in Graeme Kinross-Smith, *Australia's Writers*, pp. 47–56.
  7. Jill Ker Conway, *The Road from Coorain*, p. 11.
  8. Clark, *Short History*, pp. 140–141.
  9. F. G. Clarke, *Australia: A Political and Social History*, pp. 128–133.
  10. Quoted in Russel Ward, *Australian Legend*, p. 162.
  11. Clarke, *Political and Social History*, p. 131.
  12. Quoted in Kinross-Smith, *Australia's Writers*, p. 49.
  13. "Steele Rudd, 1865–1935" in ibid., pp. 81–87.
  14. Steele Rudd, *On Our Selection*.
  15. Ibid., p. 113.
  16. Ibid., p. 5.
  17. Ibid., p. 31.
  18. Geoffrey Blainey, *Tyranny of Distance*, p. 165.
  19. Trollope, *Australia*, 2 vols. The original edition, published in 1873, was called *Australia and New Zealand*, but the edition quoted here only reprinted the Australian chapters.
  20. Ibid., vol. 1, p. 165.
  21. P. D. Edwards, *Anthony Trollope's Son in Australia*.
  22. Quoted in Victoria Glendinning, *Anthony Trollope* (New York: Knopf, 1993), p. 483.
  23. Clark, *Short History*, p. 91.
  24. Russel Ward, *Australia*, p. 68.

25. "Class and Society" in Alan Brissenden and Charles Higham, eds., *They Came to Australia*, p. 168. The excerpt is from Pringle's book, *Australian Accent*.
26. Edwards, *Trollope's Son*.
27. Clark, *Short History*, p. 104.
28. Thomas Keneally, *The Chant of Jimmy Blacksmith*, p. 51.
29. Ward, *Australia*, p. 70.
30. Chapter 10, "The Riverina," in Trollope, *Australia*, vol. 1, pp. 198–211.
31. Ibid., p. 203.
32. Ibid., p. 206.
33. Ibid., p. 205.
34. Ibid., p. 209.
35. Matthew Josephson, *The Robber Barons, 1861–1901* (New York: Harcourt Brace, 1962), p. vi. Josephson took the term "robber barons" from a manifesto written by angry farmers in Kansas who were protesting the high prices charged by the railroads once the railroads had a monopoly.
36. See Nels Anderson, *The Hobo: The Sociology of the Homeless Man* (Chicago: University of Chicago Press, 1961) for a realistic picture of America's seasonal migrant workers in the late nineteenth and early twentieth centuries.
37. Mary Durack, *Kings in Grass Castles*, p. 19.
38. Hamlin Garland, *A Son of the Middle Border* (New York: Collier, 1927), which is a memoir of his childhood on a homestead in South Dakota.
39. Henry Nash Smith, *Virgin Land: The American West and Symbol and Myth* (Cambridge: Harvard University Press, 1970), pp. 196–200.
40. Ibid. For more about Powell, see Wallace Stegner's biography, *Beyond the Hundredth Meridian: John Wesley Powell and the Second Opening of the West* (New York: Penguin Books, 1992).
41. See Ward, *Australian Legend*.
42. Ibid., p. 198.
43. Ibid., p. 199.
44. For more about the *Bulletin* and its role in publishing writers from the bush, see "J. F. Archibald, A. G. Stephens and the *Bulletin*" in Kinross-Smith, *Australia's Writers*, pp. 76–80.
45. "Andrew Barton Patterson, 1864–1961" in Kinross-Smith, *Australia's Writers*, pp. 57–62; "Henry Lawson" in ibid., pp. 47–56.
46. "Joseph Furphy, 1843–1912" in ibid., pp. 40–46.
47. Ibid., p. 43.
48. Russel Ward discusses mateship in several places in his book *The Australian Legend*. See also Ilsa Sharp, *Cultural Shock! Australia*, pp. 19–20 and pp. 121–123.
49. Ward, *Australian Legend*, p. 203.

50. Elspeth Huxley, *Their Shining El Dorado: A Journey through Australia*, p. 348.
51. Ibid.
52. Miriam Dixon, *The Real Matilda: Women and Identity in Australia*.
53. Ibid., p, 25. The quote is from Norman MacKenzie, *Women in Australia* (Melbourne: F. W. Cheshire, 1962), p. xi.
54. Anne Summers, *Damned Whores and God's Police*, p. 79.
55. Portia Robinson, *The Women of Botany Bay*, p. 243.
56. Ibid., p. 239.
57. Heather Radi, ed., *200 Australian Women: A Redress Anthology* (Women's Redress Press, Inc., 1988).
58. "Catherine Spence," in ibid., pp. 24–26. See also the biography by Susan Magarey, *Unbridling the Tongues of Women: A Biography of Catherine Spence* (Sydney: Hale & Iremonger, 1985).
59. "Mary Lee," in Radi, *200 Australian Women*, pp. 20–21. See also the biography by Helen Jones, *Nothing Seemed Impossible: Women's Education and Social Change in South Australia, 1875–1915* (St. Lucia: University of Queensland Press, 1985).
60. Quoted in the brochure of exhibition, "Trust the Women: Women in the Federal Parliament," Parliament House, Canberra, 1994, p. 2.
61. Ibid., p. 1.
62. Summers, *Damned Whores*, p. 9.

Five. Dispossessed

1. Henry Reynolds, *The Other Side of the Frontier*, p. 65.
2. Robert Hughes, *The Fatal Shore*, p. 276.
3. Reynolds, *Other Side*, pp. 121–123.
4. "Aboriginal People of the Northern Territory" (Canberra: Council for Aboriginal Reconciliation and ATSIC, 1992), p. 3.
5. Louise Levathes, "A Geneticist Maps Ancient Migrations," *New York Times*, July 27, 1993, Sec. B, p. 5.
6. "Aboriginal Settlement," in "Koorie History in Australia," 1996, www.ciolek.com/wwwvlpages/aborigpages/koori.html, p. 2.
7. Uluru-Kata Tjuta National Park Notes, "Tjukurpa," 2001.
8. "Koorie History," p. 2.
9. David Horton, ed. *Encyclopaedia of Aboriginal Australia*, p. xii.
10. "Captain Cook Sums Up His Impressions of New Holland, August 1770," excerpt from *Journal of the First Voyage of Captain James Cook*. Reprinted in Manning Clark, *Sources of Australian History*, p. 54.
11. "Jean-Jacques Rousseau" in *The New*

Columbia Encyclopedia (New York: Columbia University Press, 1995), p. 2365.
  12. "Captain Cook" in Clark, *Sources of History*, p. 52.
  13. "The Reaction of the Indigenous People to a Flogging, May, 1791," an excerpt from Watkin Tench, *A Complete Account of the Settlement at Port Jackson in New South Wales* (London, 1793), p. 111. Reprinted in Clark, *Sources of History*, p. 97.
  14. Quoted in Hughes, *Fatal Shore*, p. 275.
  15. Ibid., p. 277. The letter was from Benjamin Hurst to Charles La Trobe, July 22, 1871.
  16. For information about the Myall Creek Massacre, see Clarke, *Australia: A Concise Political and Social History*, pp. 115–116; Hughes, *Fatal Shore*, pp. 277–278; Russel Ward, *Concise History of Australia*, pp. 127–130.
  17. Quoted in John Pilger, *A Secret Country*, p. 43.
  18. Ward, *Concise History*, p. 128.
  19. Ibid., pp. 181–182. See also the book about the Burke and Wills expedition, Alan Moorehead, *Cooper's Creek* (New York: Harper and Row, 1963).
  20. Mary Durack, *Kings in Grass Castles*, pp. 89–90.
  21. Ibid.
  22. Albert Facey, *A Fortunate Life*, p. 157.
  23. Ibid., pp. 162–163.
  24. Quoted in Geoffrey Blainey, *Triumph of the Nomads*, p. 22.
  25. Charles Bartlett, *Bartlett's Familiar Quotations*, 15th ed. (New York: Little, Brown, 1980) pp. 514 and 579.
  26. "Herbert Spencer" in *Columbia Encyclopedia*, 4th ed. (New York: Columbia University Press, 1975), pp. 2593–2594.
  27. Quoted in Peter L. Brent, *Charles Darwin: A Man of Enlarged Curiosity* (New York: Harper & Row, 1981), p. 432.
  28. "Aboriginal Protection Association" in Horton, *Encyclopedia of Aboriginal Australia*, p. 27.
  29. Coral Edwards and Peter Read, eds., *The Lost Children*, pp. xiii–xiv.
  30. Ibid.
  31. Ibid., p. xi.
  32. Part of Mary Durack's family biography *Kings in Grass Castles* tells the story of her grandfather "Patsy" Durack's move from Queensland to the Kimberly mountain region of Western Australia in 1880 and 1881, a journey that involved both a sea journey and a trek.
  33. Sally Morgan, *My Place*, p. 38.

Six. A Place in Two Cultures

  1. "Australia Day Protest 1988" in David Horton, ed., *Aboriginal Australia*, pp. 74–75.
  2. Quoted in Richard Glover, "Henry Reynolds: The Past Master," *Herald*, April 18, 1992.
  3. "Australian Aborigines Progressive Association" in Horton, ed., *Aboriginal Australia*, pp. 75–76.
  4. "Australian Aborigines League" in ibid., p. 75.
  5. Ibid.
  6. "Aborigines Progressive League" in ibid.
  7. "Australia Day Protest 1938" in ibid., pp. 73–74.
  8. "Politics" (photo caption) in ibid., p. 882.
  9. "Aborigines Progressive Association" in ibid.
  10. "The International Bill of Human Rights" (pamphlet, 1985), p. 5.
  11. "FCAATSI" in *Aboriginal Australia*, pp. 359–60.
  12. "Aboriginal Australian Fellowship of NSW" in ibid., p. 8.
  13. Quoted in F. G. Clarke, *Australia: A Concise Political and Social History*, p. 303.
  14. Richard Broome, *Aboriginal Australians: Black Response to White Dominance, 1798–1980* (Sydney: Allen & Unwin, 1982).
  15. Elspeth Huxley, *Their Shining El Dorado*, p. 283.
  16. Recounted in a documentary film about the Pilbarra strike, *How the West Was Lost* (1987). Copy in Alexander State Library, Perth.
  17. Charlie Fox, *Working Australia*, p. 164.
  18. "Gurindji," p. 443 and "Wave Hill," pp. 1164–65 in Horton ed., *Aboriginal Australia*.
  19. "Aboriginal Land Rights Commission" in ibid., pp. 20–21.
  20. "The Native Title Act of 1993: A Plain English Introduction."(Canberra, ATSIC, 1994), unpaged pamphlet; author's interview with Tony Haritos, Northern Land Council, Darwin; "Aboriginal Land Rights Act 1976" in *Aboriginal Australia*, p. 20.
  21. "Gurindji" in *Aboriginal Australia*, p. 443.
  22. "Mabo and Australia's Native Title Act" (Canberra: Dept. of Foreign Affairs & Trade, International Public Affairs Branch, 1994), fact sheet, 6 pp.; "The Mabo Judgement" (Canberra: ATSIC, 1994); author's interview with Gary Highland, legislative assistant to Senator Margaret Reynolds. For more details about Mabo, see Bain Attwood, ed., *In The Age of Mabo: History, Indigenous People & Australia* (1996) and Henry Reynolds, *Why Weren't We Told?* In Chpt. 13 "Mabo and Land Rights," Reynolds's book describes what led Mabo and a few other indigenous people from Murray

Island, who were living in Brisbane, to bring the suit.
23. "Rebutting the Myths: Some Facts about Aboriginal and Torres Strait Islander Affairs" (1994).
24. Author's interview with Bev Davies, ATSIC staff member, Perth.
25. "Archie Roach — Singer-songwriter" in Wayne Coolwell, *My Kind of People: Achievement, Identity and Aboriginality*, pp. 127–141.
26. Quoted in "The Vlam Family" in Maryon Allbrook, *Journeys of Hope*, p. 114.
27. Cartoon reprinted in M. Dugan and J. Szwarc, *There Goes the Neighbourhood!* p. 168.
28. C. Edwards and P. Read, eds. *The Lost Children*.
29. Author's interview with Peter Smith.
30. Author's interview with John "Sandy" Atkinson; see also "J. Atkinson" in *Aboriginal Australia*, pp. 70–71.
31. Ibid.
32. Lois [now Lowitja] O'Donoghue, "The Indigenous Experience," speech at Global Cultural Diversity Conference, Sydney, April 27, 1995.
33. "Aboriginal Development Commission" in *Aboriginal Australia*, pp. 10–11.
34. "What Is ATSIC?" (Canberra: ATSIC, 1994); "ATSIC" in *Aboriginal Australia*, pp. 71–71.
35. Ibid., p. 3.
36. "Miss Lois O'Donoghue, CBE, AM," biographical information about participants in program of Diversity Conference, Sydney, 1995.
37. "What Is ATSIC?," p. 2.
38. *Council for Aboriginal Reconciliation: An Introduction* (Canberra: AGPS for CAR, 1993), 14 pp.
39. CAR, *Exploring for Common Ground: Aboriginal Reconciliation and the Australian Mining Industry* (Canberra: AGPS, 1993, 1994).
40. Ibid., p. 4.
41. "Urbanisation of Aboriginal and Torres Strait Islander People," Table 1.14, Australian Bureau of Statistics, "Australians in Profile, 1991," p. 11. The numbers of indigenous people in cities and towns have likely increased since then. See also "Indigenous Australia Today" (Canberra: ATSIC, 1994), pp. 22, 23.
42. Australian Bureau of Statistics, Census of Population and Housing, 2001.
43. Ibid.
44. "Indigenous Experience ... Culture of the First Australians." Fact sheet, Department of Foreign Affairs and Trade, Overseas Information Branch, 1994.
45. Coolwell, *My Kind of People*.
46. "Noel Pearson — Land Rights Activist" in ibid. pp. 42–51.

47. Penelope Debelle, "Clash of Cultures," *The Age*, July 30, 2005.
48. Author's interview with Barbara Shore, faculty member at CATSIS. Prof. Shore, an indigenous person from Alice Springs, teaches in the community development program.
49. Author's interview with Isaac Brown. Dr. Brown, an indigenous person whose family came from an island in the Torres Strait, grew up in Darwin.
50. Author's interview with Eric van Dissell at Batchelor College.
51. "Sandra Eades — Doctor" in Coolwell, *My Kind of People*, pp. 29–41.
52. Ibid.

Seven. Immigrants and "White Australia"

1. Manning Clark, *A Short History of Australia*, p. 119.
2. Geoffrey Blainey, *The Tyranny of Distance*, p. 140.
3. F. G. Clarke, *Australia: A Concise Political and Social History*, p. 119.
4. Quoted in G. L. Buxton, "1870–90" in Frank Crowley, ed., *A New History of Australia*, p. 206.
5. "German Settlement in South Australia until 1914," in Jupp, ed., *The Australian People*, pp. 360–365.
6. "Poles: Settlement in South Australia," in ibid., p. 621; "Exhibit on Dissenters and Nonconformists," Old Parliament Building, Adelaide, 1994.
7. Dissenters and Nonconformists Exhibit, Adelaide; Geoffrey Sherington, *Australia's Immigrants, 1788–1978*, pp. 42–44.
8. "Seeds of a Multicultural Society — 19th Century Emigrants," an exhibit in the Migration Museum, Adelaide, South Australia, 1994. See also the ethnic database on immigrants to Australia, on the museum's top floor.
9. "Cornish ... Mining in South Australia," in Jupp, ed., *Australian People*, pp. 227–228.
10. "Welsh ... South Australia," in ibid., p. 740.
11. Christine Stevens, "Afghan Camel Drivers: Founders of Islam in Australia," in Mary L. Jones, ed. *An Australian Pilgrimage*, pp. 49–62.
12. Ibid., p. 52.
13. Ibid., pp. 53–54.
14. Anthony Trollope, *Australia*, vol. 1, p. 22.
15. Caernarfon *Herald*, Nov. 29, 1856. Reprinted in Lewis Lloyd, *Australians from Wales*, p. 174.
16. Information about the "Kanakas" comes

from author's interview with Prof. Brij V. Lal; Clive Moore, "The Counterculture of Survival: Melanesians in the Mackay District of Queensland, 1865–1906," in B. V. Lal, ed., *Plantation Workers: Resistance and Accommodation*; Russel Ward, *Concise History of Australia*, pp. 144–146.
17. Lal, ed., *Plantation Workers*.
18. Author's interview with B. V. Lal.
19. D. Pope and P. Shergold, *ASEAN-Australian Immigration and the Demise of White Australia*, pp. 9–10.
20. Information about Chen Ah Kew (later Jimmy Kew) comes from the author's interview with his granddaughter, Elizabeth Chong.
21. Robert Travers, *Australian Mandarin: The Life and Times of Quong Tart*.
22. Malcolm D. Prentis, *The Scots in Australia*.
23. Travers, *Australian Mandarin*, p. 187.
24. Quoted in Clark, *Short History*, p. 109. Stephen was the grandfather of English author Virginia Woolf.
25. M. Dugan and J. Szwarc, *There Goes the Neighbourhood!* p. 34.
26. Quoted in Timothy Jones, *The Chinese of the Northern Territory*, p. 88.
27. Quoted in James Jupp, *From White Australia to Woomera*, p. 11.
28. Quoted in Jones, *Chinese of Northern Territory*, p. 89.
29. "Natal" in *New Columbia Encyclopedia* (1975), p. 1883.
30. Clarke, *Political and Social History*, p. 172.
31. Clark, *Short History*, pp. 197–198.
32. Quoted in Jones, *Chinese of Northern Territory*, p. 90.
33. Brian Murphy, *The Other Australia*, p. 34. She was Ellen Fitzgibbon.
34. Reply from Atlee Hunt, November 6, 1911. From the Emma Goldman Collection in the Howard Gotlieb Archival Research Center at Boston University. The letter was addressed to a friend of Goldman's in Sydney, E. Penfold. Goldman's projected lecture tour, which would have included Australia, never took place.
35. Author's interview with Brij V. Lal.
36. Ibid; Moore in B. V. Lal, ed., *Plantation Workers*.
37. Jean Stone, *The Passionate Bibliophile*, pp. 78–81.
38. Author's interview with Elizabeth Chong, daughter of Mrs. Wing Young.
39. Sherington, *Australia's Immigrants*, p. 94.
40. Clarke, *Political and Social History*, pp. 154–155.
41. E. P. Hutchinson, *Legislative History of American Immigration Policy, 1789–1965* (Philadelphia: University of Pennsylvania Press, 1981), pp. 483–484.
42. Dugan and Szwarc, *Neighbourhood*, p. 58.
43. Ibid.
44. "Italians," sections on immigrants before World War II in Jupp, ed., *Australian People*, pp. 486–493.
45. "Greeks," sections on immigrants before World War II in ibid., pp. 387–392.
46. Murphy, *Other Australia*, p. 40.
47. Quoted in Sherington, *Australia's Immigrants*, p. 118
48. Ibid.
49. Ibid.
50. Both illustrations are reproduced in black and white in Jupp, ed, *Australian People*, p. 57, while Dugan and Szwarc, *Neighborhood*, has the "Domestic Girl" drawing in its original colors, p. 113.

Eight. A Multiethnic Nation

1. Author's interview with Joe DeLuca.
2. Ibid.
3. Russel Ward, *Concise History of Australia*, p. 277.
4. Ibid., p. 276.
5. James Jupp, ed. *The Australian People: An Encyclopedia of the Nation, Its People and their Origins*, pp. 65–66.
6. Jupp, *White Australia*, p. 12.
7. Jupp, ed. *Australian People*, pp. 66–67.
8. Ibid., p. 68.
9. Ibid., p. 67.
10. Ibid., p. 68.
11. Geraldine Brooks, *Foreign Correspondence*, p. 87.
12. Quoted in Geoffrey Sherington, *Australia's Immigrants*, p. 128.
13. Sherington, *Australia's Immigrants*, pp. 132–138; Michael Dugan and Josef Szwarc, *There Goes the Neighbourhood!*, pp. 134–191; Wendy Lowenstein and Morag Loh, *The Immigrants*, pp. 7–12.
14. Quoted in Dugan and Szwarc, *There Goes the Neighbourhood!*, p. 169.
15. Quoted in Maryon Allbrook, ed., *Journeys of Hope: Six Stories of Family Migration to Western Australia 1937–1968*, p. 92.
16. Department of Immigration and Multicultural Affairs. "Abolition of the 'White Australia' Policy," 1998. Migration Fact Sheet 5. http://www.immi.gov.au/facts/05policy.htm.
17. David Pope and Peter Shergold, *Demise of White Australia*, pp. 12–13.
18. Jerzy Zubrzycki, "The Evolution of the Policy of Multiculturalism in 1968–1995." Speech given at Global Cultural Diversity Conference, Sydney, April 26, 1995.

19. Quoted in Jupp, *White Australia*, p. 86.
20. Mark Lopez, *The Origins of Multiculturalism in Australian Politics, 1945–1975*, pp. 76–80.
21. Ibid., pp. 93–97; James Jupp, *Arrivals and Departures* (Melbourne: Chesire-Landsdowne, 1966).
22. Pope and Shergold, *Demise of White Australia*, p. 14.
23. Lopez, *Origins of Multiculturalism*, p. 200.
24. Ibid., p. 201.
25. Jupp, *White Australia*, p. 87.
26. Ibid.
27. Ibid., p. 121.
28. Ibid.
29. "Evaluation of Post-Arrival Programs and Services by the Australian Institute of Multicultural Affairs," 1982, in "Summaries of Policy Reports about Australian Multiculturalism," http:www.immi.gov.au/australian/summaries/htm.
30. Office of Multicultural Affairs (in Prime Minister's Office), *National Agenda for a Multicultural Australia—Sharing Our Future* [NAMA], (1989), pp. 57–60.
31. Ibid., p. vii.
32. Ibid., p. 7.
33. Ibid., p. 3.
34. Ibid., p. vii.
35. Dugan and Szwarc, *There Goes the Neighbourhood!*, p. 165.
36. Jupp, *White Australia*, p. 13. See also "Nina Stojanovic (geologist)" in Susan Mitchell, *Tall Poppies: Nine Successful Australian Women Talk to Susan Mitchell* (Ringwood: Penguin Books, 1990), p. 73.
37. Sherington, *Australia's Immigrants*, p. 136.
38. Author's interview with Edna McGill.
39. Ibid.
40. Ibid.
41. Author's interview with Hakan Akyol.
42. "Index by Cuisine" in Claude Forell and Rita Erlich, *The Age Good Food Guide* (South Yarra: Anne O'Donovan, 1994), pp. 211–213.
43. Timothy G. Jones, *The Chinese in the Northern Territory*.
44. Author's interview with Joe DeLuca.
45. Author's interview with Judith Ventic.
46. Jupp, *The Australian People*.
47. Tim Pegler, "Australia speaks for itself—in 240 ways," *The Age*, September 26, 1997.
48. Joseph de Riva O'Phelan, paper describing Australia's language programs, given at Regional Seminar on Foreign Language Teaching in Asia and the Pacific, in Tokyo, June 22–July 8, 1994.
49. Author's visit to the Museum of Chinese Australian History in Melbourne.
50. Janet Worden, "Public Libraries and Ethnic Communities in Queensland," *Link up* (a library publication), September, 1994.
51. Ibid.
52. Ethnic Affairs Commission of NSW, *Annual Report*, 1992–1993, pp. 23–24.
53. NAMA, 1989, p. 5.
54. Author's interview with Hakan Akyol.
55. Ilsa Sharp, *Culture Shock!*, p. 20.
56. Author's interview with Rita Erlich.
57. Author's interview with Sandra Theseira.

Nine. Diversity and Dissent

1. Maryon Allbrook, *Journeys of Hope: Six Stories of Family Migration to Western Australia, 1937–1968*.
2. Ibid., pp. 72–73 and 75.
3. Ibid., p. 96.
4. Letter from Anne-Marie Catalano to the author.
5. Ibid.; additional information from Ethel Ruymaker, a friend of the Catalano family.
6. Author's interview with Edmund Teo and Janet Seagh Teo.
7. Ibid.
8. Ibid.
9. Author's interview with Ramdas Sankaran.
10. Michael Casey, "Action Urged to Break Cycle," *West Australian* (Perth), Oct. 1, 1994, p. 11.
11. "Indonesian Wedding in Sydney." Press release from the Australian News and Information Bureau, May, 1972, 2 pp.
12. Vannary Imam, *When Elephants Fight*, p. 265
13. Ibid., p. xi.
14. Nancy Viviani, *The Indochinese in Australia from 1975–1995: From Burnt Boats to Barbecues*, pp. 8 and 9.
15. Ibid.
16. Ibid.
17. Ibid., p. 31.
18. Ibid.
19. Ibid., pp. 31–32.
20. Ibid.
21. Ibid., p. 47.
22. James Jupp, ed., *Australian People*, p. 68.
23. Geoffrey Blainey, *All for Australia*, p. 131.
24. Ibid., pp. 131–134.
25. Quoted in Jupp, *White Australia*, pp. 110–111.
26. Ibid.; Viviani, *Indochinese in Australia*, pp. 40–41.
27. Quoted in Jupp, *White Australia*, p. 109.
28. Blainey, *All for Australia*, pp. 155–156.
29. Quoted in Allbrook, *Journeys of Hope*, p. 65.
30. Ibid.

Ten. Embedded Legacies

1. Quoted in Hazel Rowley, *Christina Stead: A Biography*, p. 64.
2. Ibid., p. 174.
3. Jill Ker Conway, *The Road from Coorain*, p. 98.
4. Ibid.
5. Ibid., p. 182.
6. Ibid., p. 206.
7. Malcolm Muggeridge, "Australia in Asia," radio speech, 1958; reprinted in Brissenden and Higham, eds., *They Came to Australia: An Anthology*, pp. 150–51.
8. Ibid., p. 151.
9. Quoted in Thomas Keneally, "The Australian Republican Movement," address to the National Press Club, Canberra, July 15, 1992. The columnist was Andrew Taylor.
10. D. H. Lawrence, *Kangaroo*.
11. Ibid. p. 11.
12. Ibid., p. 14.
13. Ibid., p. 27.
14. Ibid.
15. Quoted in Robert Darroch, *D. H. Lawrence in Australia*, p. 24.
16. Jill Roe, ed., *My Congenials: Miles Franklin and Friends in Letters*. vol. 1, 1879–1938, pp. 291–292.
17. Quoted in Darroch, *D. H. Lawrence*, p. 24.
18. Quoted in Brenda Maddox, *D. H. Lawrence: The Story of a Marriage* (New York: Simon & Schuster, 1994), p. 298.
19. Ibid.
20. Darroch, *D. H. Lawrence*.
21. Ibid, p. 91.
22. Maddox, *D. H. Lawrence*, p. 303. Maddox mentioned some other men who have been suggested as models for Kangaroo and pointed out that the actual General Rosenthal was not Jewish, as some have suggested.
23. Simon Leys, "Lawrence of Australia," *New York Review of Books*, April 21, 1994.
24. Paul Theroux, *The Happy Isles of Oceania: Paddling the Pacific* (New York: Putnam, 1992), p. 37.
25. Quoted in Russel Ward, *The Australian Legend*, p. 5.
26. Excerpt from John Douglas Pringle, *Australian Accent* (London: Chatto & Windus, 1958); reprinted in Brissenden and Higham, eds., *They Came to Australia*, p. 160.
27. Ibid., pp. 161–162.
28. Michael Davie, "The Fraying of the Rope," in Stephen R. Graubard, ed., *Australia: The Daedalus Symposium,* (North Ryde: Angus & Robertson, 1985), p. 385.
29. Ibid.
30. Jan Morris, *Sydney*, pp. 82–83. Morris's comments would also be applicable to other Australian cities such as Melbourne.
31. Manning Clark, *A Discovery of Australia*, p. 45.
32. Manning Clark, *The Puzzles of Childhood*, p. 169.
33. Clark, *Discovery of Australia*, p. 16.
34. Manning Clark, *The Quest for Grace*, p. 59.
35. Ibid., p. 61.
36. Ibid., p. 64.
37. "Vance Palmer" in Graeme Kinross-Smith, *Australia's Writers*, p. 158.
38. Jean Stone, *The Passionate Bibliophile*, p. 72.
39. Ibid., p. 79.
40. Ibid., p. 268.
41. Rowley, *Christina Stead*, p. 61.
42. Jill Roe, ed., *My Congenials*.
43. Stone, *Passionate Bibliophile*, p. 175.
44. James Morris, *Farewell to the Trumpets* (New York: Harcourt Brace, Harvest, 1978), p. 187.
45. F. G. Clarke, *Australia: A Concise Political and Social History*, p. 197.
46. Ian Turner, "1914–1919" in Crowley, ed., *New History*, pp. 345–346.
47. Russel Ward, *Concise History of Australia*, p. 239.
48. Clarke, *Political and Social History*, p. 199.
49. David Day, *The Great Betrayal: Britain, Australia and the Onset of the Pacific War, 1939–1942*.
50. Ibid., p. 136.
51. Ibid., p. 160.
52. Ibid., p. 241.
53. Ibid., p. 247.
54. Ibid., p. 254.
55. Ibid., p. 250.
56. Quoted in Clarke, *Political and Social History*, p. 254.
57. Day, *Great Betrayal*, p. 255.
58. Ibid., p. 267.
59. Clarke, *Political and Social History*, pp. 255–256.
60. James Jupp, "From 'White Australia' to 'Part of Asia': Recent Shifts in Immigration Policy Towards the Region," *International Migration Review* (Spring, 1995).
61. Geraldine Brooks, *Foreign Correspondence*, p. 11.
62. Ilsa Sharp, *Australia: Culture Shock!* (2000 ed.), p. 16. "Yobbo," a British slang word based on "boy" spelled backwards, roughly means a young, uncouth working-class punk.
63. Ross Terrill, *The Australians*, p. 306.
64. Bill Bryson, *In a Sunburned Country*, p. 127.
65. Theroux, *Happy Isles of Oceania*, pp. 36, 44.

66. Author's interview with Ethel Ruymaker.
67. Paul Kelly, "The Paradox of Pessimism," in *Future Tense: Australia Beyond Election, 1998*, p. 5.
68. Katie Lahey, "We of Little Faith," *The Age*, June 30, 2002.
69. James Jupp, *The English in Australia*, pp. 136, 144.
70. Ibid., p. 143.
71. G. A. Wilkes, *A Dictionary of Australian Colloquialisms*, p. 258.
72. Ibid.
73. Author's interview with Lewis Lloyd.
74. Lewis Lloyd, *Australians from Wales*, p. 10.
75. Terrill, *The Australians*, p. 308.
76. Ibid., p. 309.
77. Sharp, *Culture Shock!*, p. 16.
78. Author's visit to the Migration Museum in Adelaide, South Australia.

Eleven. Turbulent Times

1. Paul Kelly, "The Paradox of Pessimism" in Kelly and the National Affairs Team, *Future Tense: Australia Beyond Election 1998*, pp. 4–5.
2. Ibid., p. 5.
3. John Pilger, *A Secret Country:The Hidden Australia*, pp. 143–144.
4. Ibid., p. 144.
5. James Jupp, "From 'White Australia' to 'Part of Asia': Recent Shifts in Immigration Policy Towards the Region," *International Migration Review*, (Spring, 1995), p. 19 online.
6. Geraldine Brooks, *Foreign Correspondence*, p. 96.
7. The Constitutional Convention was held in Canberra from February 2–4 and 9–13, 1998. There were 152 delegates, half elected and half appointed. They were asked to consider whether Australia should become a republic, what model to offer to voters, and when the vote should occur. See "Constitutional Convention: How It Works," *Herald*, January 30, 1998.
8. Margo Kingston, Damien Murphy and AAP, "PM 'Has Misled Australia,'" *Herald*, November 6, 1999.
9. Dr. Lawson made these comments in a letter to the author.
10. "Australia: A National Identity Crisis," *Economist* (London), Dec. 14–20, 1996, p. 41.
11. Pauline Hanson's maiden speech to the Australian Parliament, September 10, 1996.
12. Ibid.
13. F. Farouque, L. Tingle and L. Murdoch, "Kennett in Tough Stand on Racism," *The Age*, November 1, 1996.
14. Tony Wright and James Woodford, "Howard Dithers over Joint Racism Reproof," *Herald*, October 15, 1996.
15. Mark Baker, "The Tiger Awakens," *The Age*, October 30, 1996.
16. Alexander Downer, "Australia's True Role in Asia" (Address to the Asialine Launch); printed in *The Age*, May 2, 1997.
17. Innes Willox, "PM Slams Hanson's Divisive Policies," *The Age*, May 9, 1997; Michael Millett, "'Sour, Bitter,' Hanson Exploiting Fear, says PM," *Herald*, May 9, 1997.
18. Ben Mitchell, "Call for Summit on Wik Title Judgment," *The Age*, December 30, 1996.
19. James Woodford, "Summit to Calm Fears of Farmers," *Herald*, January 21, 1997.
20. Michael Millet and James Woodford, "PM's Urgent Summit to Resolve Wik," *Herald*, January 21, 1997.
21. Greg Roberts, "What the States Want," *Herald*, January 21, 1997.
22. Paul Daley, "Lessons from the People's Pauline Conversion," *The Age*, June 14, 1998.
23. Sid Maher, "Beattie Acts to Reassure Asia," *Australian*, June 28, 1998.
24. Owen Brown (of AAP), "Asian Press Laments Hanson's Rise," *The Age*, June 15, 1998.
25. Daley, "Pauline Conversion," *The Age*, June 14, 1998.
26. Robert Manne, "Centenary Writ Small," *The Age*, February 5, 2001.
27. "Ottawa Statement of Reconciliation," *Herald*, January 9, 1998.
28. Cynthia Banham, "Ruddock Takes Away Cash from ATSIC," *Herald*, April 18, 2003.
29. Rob Welsh, "Government Must Listen and Act on Aboriginal Disadvantage," Sydney: Metropolitan Local Aboriginal Land Council, December 7, 2004. First published in *National Indigenous Times* (www.nit.com.au).
30. Quotes from Ruth McCausland and Mick Dodson are from two articles by McCausland: "Shared Responsibility Agreements: progress to date," December 8, 2005, and "Shared Responsibility Agreements: Reconciliation or Paternalistic Rhetoric?" *Indigenous Law Bulletin*, July, 2005, vol.6, issue 12. Both are online: www.jumbunna.uts.edu.au.
31. Gary Highland, "North Sydney Confirms Leadership in Reconciliation." Media Release for Metropolitan Local Aboriginal Land Council, March 17, 2006 (www.antar.org.au).

Twelve. Asian Connections

1. Richard Baker, "Economists Tip Better Times Ahead," *The Age*, March 1, 2000.
2. Author's interview with Professor Brij V. Lal and biographical information on the jacket of his memoir, *Mr. Tulsi's Store: A Fijian Journey* (Canberra: Pandanus Books, 2001).

3. "Biography of Prime Minister Paul Keating," *The Prime Minister's* home page, February, 1995.
4. Quoted in David Sanger, "Australia Is Striving to Be Asian but How Asian?" *New York Times*, August 16, 1992.
5. Scott Steele with John Howse, "A Battle Royal Down Under," *MacLean's*, May 31, 1993, p. 23.
6. James Jupp, "From 'White Australia' to 'Part of Asia' Recent Shifts in Immigration Policy towards the Region," *International Migration Review*, v29, n1 (Spring, 1995), Table 5.
7. Quoted in Peter Smark, "Ill-prepared for the Pacific Century," *Herald*, March 8, 1997.
8. James Jupp, "Selection and Rejection: Twenty Years of Australian Immigration," paper delivered at the Global Cultural Diversity Conference, Sydney, April 26, 1995, p. 7.
9. Ibid.
10. Lindsay Murdock, "Malaysia too Inconvenient," *The Age*, February 10, 1997.
11. Mark Baker, "Malaysia Thwarts Howard's Bid to Join ASEAN Summit," *Herald*, November 6, 2002.
12. Tim Colebatch, "Thailand, Australia Resolve Disputes," *The Age*, February 28, 1997.
13. Geoff Hiscock, "Stick With Us, Thailand MP Urges," *Australian*, July 14, 1998.
14. Ibid.
15. Diane Stott, "Britain Backs Australia Forum," *Herald*, March 10, 1998.
16. Sean Aylmer, "Australia: 'Critical role' in Asia," *Herald*, October 28, 1998.
17. Glena Korporaal, "Australia 'Can Lead Way on Asian Recovery,'" *Herald*, October 28, 1998.
18. "Habibie Dismisses Hanson," AAP, June 21, 1998.
19. Stephen FitzGerald, *Is Australia an Asian Country?* p. 39.
20. Tony Parkinson, "Australia's Seat on the Sidelines Just Got Precarious," *The Age*, April 5, 2001.
21. Hugh White, "Australia's Role Vital in US-China Dialogue, *The Age*, January 23, 2002.
22. P. Hudson, S. Mann and K.Taylor, "Howard Appeals for UN Help," *The Age*, August 31, 2001.
23. Ibid.
24. Mark Forbes, "Treatment of Boat People Condemned," *The Age*, November 17, 2001.
25. Quoted in Simon Mann, "Europe's Deluge," *The Age*, September 1, 2001.
26. Simon Mann, "Many Are Doing Their Bit, but Poor Countries Shoulder Biggest Burden," *Herald*, September 1, 2001.
27. Louise Dodson, "Voters Deserting Howard," *The Age*, February 13, 2001.
28. Tom Allard and Andrew Clennell, "Howard Links Terrorism to Boat People," *Herald*, November 8, 2001.
29. Ibid.
30. Thomas Keneally, "A Fearful Australia Betrays Its Own History," *Guardian Weekly*, September 13–21, 2001, p. 25.
31. Quoted in Pamela Bone, "Why Beazley May Be the Lesser of Two Evils," *The Age*, October 27, 2001.
32. "Immigration Spurs Protest Vote," *Yahoo! News: Australia & NZ*, November 10, 2001, 11:55 p.m.
33. "Pauline Hanson," *The Age*, November 11, 2001.
34. Peter Mares, *Borderline: Australia's Response to Refugees and Asylum Seekers in the Wake of the Tampa*, p. 13.
35. Ibid., p. 14.
36. Dr. Conroy made these comments in a letter to the author.
37. Mares, *Borderline*, pp. 18–26.
38. Ibid., p. 24.
39. Viviani, *Indochinese in Australia*, p. 11.
40. See James Jupp, ed., *Australian People*, pp. 68–69.
41. Quoted in James Jupp, *From White Australia to Woomera*, p. 11. The PM was Alfred Deakin.
42. Robert Manne, "Unthinkable Brutality? Who Cares...." *The Age*, April 29, 2002.
43. Mares, *Borderline*, p. 28.
44. Michael Gordon and Louise Dodson, "John Howard: Plainly a Fighter," *The Age*, November 6, 2001.
45. For more on this subject, see Robert Manne with David Corlett, "Sending Them Home."
46. "Thousands Rally against Mandatory Detention," AAP; reprinted in *Herald*, June 24, 2002.
47. Malcolm Fraser, "Australia, Land of the Unfair Go," *The Age*, October 4, 2002.
48. Hugh McKay, "Look around. Is this really Australia?" *The Age*, July 12, 2003.
49. Rohan Gunaratna, "Ties That Bind al-Qaida's Southeast Asian Groups," *Weekly Guardian* (London), October 17–23, 2002, p. 2.
50. Christopher Kremmer, "Asia's Most Wanted Man," *Herald*, October 26, 2002.
51. Quoted in "The Ngruki Network in Indonesia: I," a reprint of the 2002 report of the International Crisis Group. *Laksamana.net*, Jakarta, June 4, 2004, p. 1.
52. "UN Is Urged to Ban Group," *New York Times*, October 16, 2002, p. A11.
53. Mathew Moore, "Jakarta to Try Again to Convict Bashir," October 28, 2004; Mark Forbes, "Outcry as Bashir Gets 30 Months," both in *The Age*.
54. "Without Extreme Prejudice," *Herald*, November 8, 2002.

Thirteen. Which Way Ahead?

1. Hamish McDonald, "China Supports Our Role in the Region," *The Age*, October 18, 2003.
2. President George Bush's address to the Australian Parliament. October 23, 2003.
3. Ibid.
4. President Hu Jintao's address to the Australian Parliament. October 24, 2003.
5. Ibid.
6. Mark Riley and Steve Pennels, "$30 billion Export Bonanza," *Herald*, October 24, 2003.
7. Virginia Marsh, "Australia Moves to Centre Stage," *Financial Times* (London), October 22, 2003.
8. Amy Waldman, "Sizzling Economy Revitalizes India," *New York Times*, October 22, 2003, p. 1.
9. Hugh White, "This Week We Got a View of Our Future," *The Age*, October 22, 2003.
10. Jane Perlez, "China Is Romping with the Neighbors (U.S. Is Distracted)," *New York Times*, December 3, 2003, p. 1.
11. Ibid., p. 4.
12. MacDonald, "China," *The Age*, October 18, 2003.
13. Ibid.
14. Ibid.
15. Marsh, "Centre Stage," *Financial Times*, October 22, 2003.
16. Janaki Kremmer, "Offshore Services Surge Ahead," *Financial Times* (London), special report on Australia, October 28, 2004, p. 5.
17. Ibid.
18. Joseph S. Nye, Jr., "You Can't Get Here from There," *New York Times*, November 29, 2004, p. A25.
19. Ibid.
20. Laurie Brereton, "Howard's Pro-Bush Policies Need Balance," *The Age*, July 10, 2002.
21. Ibid. See also Hamish McDonald, "Labor Blasts Howard for 'Menzian' US Policy," *Herald*, September 12, 2001.
22. "The Reluctant Deputy Sheriff," *The Economist* (A Survey of Australia), May 7, 2005, p. 9.
23. Don Watson, "Rabbit Syndrome: Australia and America," *Quarterly Essay*, Issue 4 (Melbourne: Blacks, Inc., 2001).
24. "Aid a Sign of Closer Asian Ties: PM," *Yahoo! News: Australia & NZ*, January 6, 2005.
25. Michelle Grattan, "China to Put Australia on East Asia Summit," *The Age*, April 20, 2005.
26. Hu Jintao speech to Australian Parliament, October 24, 2003.
27. Ibid.
28. Ibid.
29. Craig Skehan, "Don't Apologize, PM Tells Us," *Herald*, January 27, 1997.
30. Tony Stephens, "Sir William Comes to the Defence of Immigration," *Herald*, July 7, 1998.
31. Stephen FitzGerald, *Is Australia an Asian Country?*, p. 19.
32. James Jupp, *From White Australia to Woomera*, pp. 55 and 121.
33. Ibid., p. 121.
34. Ibid.
35. See Laurie Hergenhamm, *No Casual Traveller: Hartley Grattan and Australia—US Connections*.
36. Ibid.
37. Jan Morris, *Sydney*, p. 78. Morris made these comments in her book on Sydney but they are applicable to Australia in general.
38. Jennifer Hewitt, "Making Hard Work of US Job Figures," *Herald*, December 22, 1997.
39. Report of Nick Bolkus to National Congress of the Ethnic Communities Council, Darwin, 1993.
40. Author's interview with Edna McGill, former president of ECC for NSW.
41. "Australian Multicultural Policy," www.immi.gov.au/multicultural/australian/index.htm.
42. Ibid., p. 3.
43. Information about state governments supplied by the Information Request Service, State Library of New South Wales.
44. Jupp, *White Australia*, p. 69.
45. Ethnic Affairs Commission of New South Wales. Brochure advertising its publication *The People of New South Wales*, a compilation and analysis based on statistics from the 1991 census.
46. Fairfield Migrant Resource Center. "What's New, Current News, Open Day 2004." www.fmrc.net/pagewhatsnew.htm.
47. Information supplied to the author by Dr. James Jupp, Director, Center for Immigration and Multicultural Studies.
48. "Federation of African Communities Council," www.fecca.org.au/Organisations/FACC.html.
49. Malcolm Brown, "Family Torn by War Join in a New Beginning," *Herald*, June 21, 2005.
50. Peter Mares, *Borderline*, pp. 199–203.
51. Tony Kevin, "The Day Howard Bowed to Winds of Change," *The Age*, June 20, 2005. His book is *A Certain Maritime Incident: The Sinking of SIEV X* (Scribe, 2004).
52. Michael Gordon, "Libs Defy PM over Detainees," *The Age*, May 25, 2005.
53. "PM Stands Firm on Mandatory Detention," *The Age*, May 31, 2005.
54. S. Neufled, N. Azzopardi and S. Math-

ieson, "Freedom Tastes Bittersweet to Naomi," *The Age*, May 25, 2005.
55. Ibid.
56. Michelle Grattan, "Howard Yields to Rebels," *The Age*, June 18, 2005.
57. Marian Wilkinson, "Terrorist Suspects No Serious Threat, Say Lawyers," *Herald*, November 5, 2005.
58. J. Silvester, I. Munro and Selma Milovanovic, "Deadly Stash 'Enough for 15 Bombs,'" *The Age*, November 10, 2005.
59. Damien Murphy, "Thugs Ruled the Streets, and the Mob Sang Waltzing Matilda," *Herald*, December 12, 2005.
60. David Marr, "One-way Radio Plays by It Own Rules," *Herald*, December 19, 2005.
61. "As Peace Talks Continue, Cronulla's Beaches Remain Desolate," *Herald*, December 16, 2005.
62. Murphy, "Thugs Ruled."
63. Joseph Wakim, "Lost Between War and Peace, the Leb Wild Westies," *The Age*, December 14,2005. Posted on www.onlineopinon.com.au, December 20, 2005.
64. Salam Zreika, "The Un-Australian Way," *The Age*, December 13, 2005.
65. Eva Sallis, "Australia's Dangerous Fantasy," *New York Times*, December 17, 2005.
66. Wakim, "Lost War."
67. Sundeep Tucker, "Twofold Approach to Addressing the Country's Chronic Skills Shortage," *Financial Times* (London), Special Report on Australia, November 29, 2005, p. 3.
68. Ibid.
69. Laksiri Jayasuria and Kee Pookong, *The Asianisation of Australia? Some Facts about the Myths*, pp. 89 and 88.
70. Jason Koutsoukis, "Howard Got It Wrong on Racism, Poll Found," *The Age*, December 20, 2005.
71. "Asian Leaders Quiz PM over Riots," *Herald*, December 15, 2005.
72. Richard Woolcott, "Australia Must Not Be Afraid of Indonesia," *The Age*, August 4, 2003.
73. Stephen FitzGerald, *Is Australia an Asian Country?*, p. 14.
74. Richard Woolcott, "Away with the Anachronism: A Republic will Serve Australia's Domestic and International Interests," Inaugural National Republic Lecture, delivered at the National Press Club, Canberra, November 26, 200 (http://act.republic.org.au/Woolcott%20transcript.htm, p. 8).

Selected Bibliography

Allbrook, Maryon, ed. *Journeys of Hope: Six Stories of Family Migration to Western Australia 1937–1968.* Wembley/Perth: State Print, Department of State Services, 1994.
ATSIC. *Indigenous Australia Today: An Overview by the Aboriginal and Torres Strait Islander Commission.* Canberra: ATSIC, April, 1994.
———. *What Is ATSIC? The Aboriginal and Torres Strait Islander Commission.* Canberra: ATSIC, May, 1994.
Blainey, Geoffrey. *All for Australia.* North Ryde: Methuen Haynes, 1984.
———. *Triumph of the Nomads: A History of Aboriginal Australia.* Woodstock, N.Y: Overlook Press, 1976.
———. *The Tyranny of Distance.* Melbourne: Sun Books, 1966.
Brissenden, Alan, and Charles Higham, eds. *They Came to Australia: An Anthology.* Melbourne: F. W. Cheshire, 1961.
Brooks, Geraldine. *Foreign Correspondence: A Pen Pal's Journey from Down Under to All Over.* New York: Doubleday/Anchor, 1998.
Bryson, Bill. *In a Sunburned Country.* New York: Broadway Books, 2000.
Cain, Frank, ed. *Menzies in War and Peace.* St. Leonards: Allen and Unwin, 1997.
Chatwin, Bruce. *The Songlines.* New York: Penguin Books, 1988.
Clark, Manning. *The Puzzles of Childhood.* Ringwood: Penguin Books, Australia, 1990.
———. *The Quest for Grace.* Ringwood: Penguin Books, 1991.
———. *A Short History of Australia.* 3rd ed. New York: NAL Penguin, 1987.
———. *Sources of Australian History.* Oxford: Oxford University Press, 1977.
Clarke, F. G. *Australia: A Concise Political and Social History.* Sydney: Harcourt Brace, 1992.
Clarke, Marcus. *His Natural Life.* Edited by Stephen Murray-Smith. (First published in 1870). Middlesex U.K.: Penguin Books, 1987.
Conomos, Denis A. *The Greeks in Queensland: A History from 1859–1945.* Brisbane: Copy-Right Publishing Co., 2002.
Conway, Jill Ker. *The Road from Coorain.* New York: Random House/Vintage, 1990.
Coolwell, Wayne. *My Kind of People: Achievement, Identity and Aboriginality.* St. Lucia: University of Queensland Press, 1993.
Corn, Charles. *The Scents of Eden: A History of the Spice Trade.* New York: Kodansha International, 1999.
Council for Aboriginal Reconciliation. *Council for Aboriginal Reconciliation: An Introduction.* Canberra: AGPS, 1993.
———. *Exploring for Common Ground: Aboriginal Reconciliation and the Australian Mining Industry.* Canberra: AGPS, 1993.

Crowley, F. K., ed. *A New History of Australia*. Melbourne: Heinemann, 1974.
Darroch, Robert. *D. H. Lawrence in Australia*. Melbourne: Macmillan, 1981.
Day, David. *The Great Betrayal: Britain, Australia, and the Onset of the Pacific War, 1939–1942*. Sydney: Angus & Robertson, 1988.
_____. *Reluctant Nation: Australia and the Allied Defeat of Japan, 1942–45*. Oxford: Oxford University Press, 1992.
Department of the Prime Minister and Cabinet, Office of Multicultural Affairs. *National Agenda for a Multicultural Australia ... Sharing our Future*. Canberra: AGPS, 1989.
Dixon, Miriam. *The Real Matilda: Women and Identity in Australia: 1788 to 1975*. Ringwood: Penguin Books, 1976.
Dugan, Michael, and Josef Szwarc. *There Goes the Neighbourhood! Australia's Migrant Experience*. Melbourne: Macmillan, 1984.
Durack, Mary. *Kings in Grass Castles*. Condell Park, NSW: Corgi Books, 1967.
Edwards, Coral, and Peter Read, eds. *The Lost Children: Thirteen Australians Taken from Their Aboriginal Families Tell of the Struggle to Find Their Natural Parents*. Sydney: Doubleday, 1989.
Edwards, P. D. *Anthony Trollope's Son in Australia: The Life and Letters of F.J.A. Trollope (1847–1910)*. St. Lucia/Brisbane: University of Queensland Press, 1982.
Emma Goldman Collection, Howard Gotlieb Research Center, Boston University, US. Reply from Atlee Hunt, November 6, 1911, to letter asking if Goldman would be admitted to Australia to give lectures. In E. Penfold letters (on microfilm, reel 56).
Facey, Albert B. *A Fortunate Life*. Melbourne: Penguin Books, 1981.
Fitzgerald, Ross, and Mark Hearn. *Bligh, Macarthur and the Rum Rebellion*. Kenthurst: Kangaroo Press, 1988.
FitzGerald, Stephen. *Is Australia an Asian Country?: Can Australia Survive in an East Asian Future?* Sydney: Allen & Unwin, 1997 (e-book edition).
Fox, Charlie. *Working Australia*. Sydney: Allen and Unwin, 1991.
Grattan, C. Hartley. *Introducing Australia*. (Revision of 1942 edition.) New York: John Day, 1947.
Hardjono, Ratih. *White Tribe of Asia: An Indonesian View of Australia*. (Monash Asia Institute.) South Yarra: Hyland House, 1993.
"'Has He Got the Ticker?': A Survey of Australia." *The Economist* (London), May 7, 2005.
Hergenham, Laurie. *No Casual Traveller: Hartley Grattan and Australia — US Connections*. St. Lucia: University of Queensland Press, 1995.
Horne, Donald. *The Lucky Country: Australia in the Sixties*. Ringwood: Penguin Books, 1964.
Horton, David, ed. *Encyclopaedia of Aboriginal Australia*. Canberra: Aboriginal Studies Press for the Australian Institute of Aboriginal and Torres Strait Islander Studies, 1994.
Hughes, Colin A. *Mr. Prime Minister: Australian Prime Ministers, 1901–1972*. Melbourne: Oxford University Press, 1976.
Hughes, Robert. *The Fatal Shore: The Epic of Australia's Founding*. New York: Random House/Vintage, 1988.
Huxley, Elspeth. *Their Shining El Dorado: A Journey through Australia*. New York: William Morrow, 1967.
Imam, Vannary. *When Elephants Fight: A Memoir*. Sydney: Allen and Unwin, 2000.
Jayasuriya, Laksiri, and Kee Pokong. *The Asianisation of Australia? Some Facts about the Myths*. Melbourne: Melbourne University Press, 1999.
Johnson, Paul. *Ireland: A Concise History from the Twelfth Century to the Present Day*. Chicago: Academy Publishers, 1984.

Selected Bibliography

Jones, Mary Lucille, ed. *An Australian Pilgrimage: Muslims in Australia from the Seventeenth Century to the Present.* Melbourne: Victoria Press, 1993.
Jones, Timothy G. *The Chinese of the Northern Territory.* Darwin: Northern Territory University Press, 1990.
Jupp, James, ed. *The Australian People: An Encyclopedia of the Nation, Its People and Their Origins.* Cambridge: Cambridge University Press, 2001.
Jupp, James. *The English in Australia.* Cambridge: Cambridge University Press, 2004.
———. *From White Australia to Woomera: The Story of Australian Immigration.* Cambridge: Cambridge University Press, 2002.
Kelly, Paul, and National Affairs Team of *The Australian. Future Tense: Australia Beyond Election 1998.* Sydney: Allen and Unwin, 1999 (e-book edition).
Keneally, Thomas. *The Chant of Jimmy Blacksmith.* New York: Viking, 1967.
Kevin, Tony. *A Certain Maritime Incident: The Sinking of SIEV X.* Carlton North: Scribe Publications, 2004.
King, Jonathan. *The First Fleet: The Convict Voyage That Founded Australia, 1787–88.* South Melbourne: Macmillan, 1982.
Kinross-Smith, Graeme. *Australia's Writers.* West Melbourne: Nelson, 1980.
Lal, Brij V., Doug Munro, and Edward D. Beechert, eds. *Plantation Workers: Resistance and Accommodation.* Honolulu: University of Hawaii Press, 1993.
Landon, Carolyn, and Daryl Tonkin. *Jackson's Track: Memoir of a Dreamtime Place.* Ringwood: Penguin Books, 2000.
Lawrence, D. H. *Kangaroo.* London: Penguin Books, 1980. (First published in 1923.)
Lloyd, Lewis. *Australians from Wales.* Caernarfon, Wales: Gwynedd Archives, 1988.
Lopez, Mark. *The Origins of Multiculturalism in Australian Politics, 1945–1975.* Melbourne: Melbourne University Press, 2000.
Lowenstein, Wendy, and Morag Loh. *The Immigrants.* Ringwood: Penguin Books, 1991.
Macgregor, Paul, ed. *Histories of the Chinese in Australasia and the South Pacific: Proceedings of an International Public Conference held at the Museum of Chinese Australian History, Melbourne, 8–10 October, 1993.* Melbourne: Museum of Chinese Australian History, 1995.
Manne, Robert, with David Corlett. "Sending Them Home: Refugees and the New Politics of Indifference." *Quarterly Essay*, No. 13, 2004, pp. 1–95. Melbourne: Black Inc.
Mares, Peter. *Borderline: Australia's Response to Refugees and Asylum Seekers in the Wake of the Tampa.* Sydney: University of New South Wales Press, 2002.
McKenna, Mark. *This Country: A Reconciled Republic?* Sydney: University of New South Wales Press, 2004.
Moorehead, Alan. *The Fatal Impact: An Account of the Invasion of the South Pacific, 1767–1840.* New York: Harper & Row, 1966.
Morgan, Sally. *My Place.* New York: Little Brown/Arcade, 1990.
Morris, Jan. *Sydney.* New York: Random House, 1992.
Murphy, Brian. *The Other Australia: Experiences of Migration.* Cambridge: Cambridge University Press, 1993.
Nicholson, Margaret. *The Little Aussie Fact Book.* Melbourne: Penguin Books, 1993.
Office of the Minister for Aboriginal and Torres Strait Islander Affairs. "Rebutting the Myths: Some Facts about Aboriginal and Torres Strait Islander Affairs." Canberra: AGPS, 1994.
Pilger, John. *A Secret Country: The Hidden Australia.* New York: Knopf, 1991.
Pope, David, and Peter Shergold. *ASEAN–Australian Immigration and the Demise of White Australia.* Canberra: ASEAN–Australia Joint Research Project, 1985.
Prentis, Malcolm D. *The Scots in Australia: A Study of New South Wales, Victoria and Queensland, 1788–1900.* Sydney: Sydney University Press, 1983.

Reynolds, Henry. *The Other Side of the Frontier: Aboriginal Resistance to the European Invasion of Australia.* Melbourne: Penguin Books, 1995.

———. *Why Weren't We Told? A Personal Search for the Truth about our History.* Melbourne: Penguin Books, 2000.

Robinson, Portia. *The Women of Botany Bay: A Reinterpretation of the Role of Women in the Origins of Australian Society.* Ringwood: Penguin Books, 1993.

Roe, Jill, ed. *My Congenials: Miles Franklin and Friends in Letters,* vol. 1, 1879–1938. Sydney: Angus & Robertson (HarperCollins), 1993.

Rowley, Hazel. *Christina Stead: A Biography.* New York: Henry Holt, 1993.

Rudd, Steele. *On Our Selection.* Sydney: Angus & Robertson (HarperCollins), 1992. (First published in 1899 by *The Bulletin.*)

Sharp, Ilsa. *Culture Shock! Australia.* Portland, Ore.: Graphic Arts Center Publishing Co., 1992.

Shaw, A. G. L. *The Story of Australia.* London: Faber and Faber, 1960.

Sherington, Geoffrey. *Australia's Immigrants: 1788–1978.* Sydney: Allen and Unwin, 1980.

Smith, Abbott Emerson. *Colonists in Bondage: White Servitude and Convict Labor in America, 1607–1776.* Gloucester, Mass.: Peter Smith, 1965.

Stone, Jean. *The Passionate Bibliophile: The Story of Walter Stone, Australian Bookman Extraordinaire.* Sydney: Angus & Robertson, 1988.

Summers, Anne. *Damned Whores and God's Police.* Ringwood: Penguin Books, 1994.

Terrill, Ross. *The Australians.* New York: Simon & Schuster, 1987.

Tiffin, Rod, and Ross Gittens. *How Australia Compares.* Cambridge: Cambridge University Press, 2004.

Travers, Robert. *Australian Mandarin: The Life and Times of Quong Tart.* Kenthurst, NSW: Kangaroo Press, 1981.

Trollope, Anthony. *Australia.* (2 vols.) Gloucester, U.K.: Alan Sutton, 1987. (First published in 1873 as *Australia and New Zealand*).

Turner, Ian. *In Union Is Strength: A History of Trade Unions in Australia, 1788–1978.* West Melbourne: Nelson, 1978.

Viviani, Nancy. *The Indochinese in Australia: From Burnt Boats to Barbecues.* Melbourne: Oxford University Press, 1996.

———. *The Long Journey: Vietnamese Migration and Settlement in Australia.* Melbourne: Melbourne University Press, 1984.

Ward, Russel. *Australia.* Englewood Cliffs, N.J.: Prentice-Hall, 1965.

———. *The Australian Legend.* Melbourne: Oxford University Press, 1993.

———. *Concise History of Australia.* St. Lucia: University of Queensland Press, 1992.

White, Mary E. *The Greening of Gondwana: The 400 Million Year Story of Australia's Plants.* Balgowlah: Reed Books, 1986.

Wilkes, G. A. *A Dictionary of Australian Colloquialisms.* Sydney: Sydney University Press, 1990.

York, Barry. *Empire and Race: The Maltese in Australia, 1881–1949.* Kensington: New South Wales University Press, 1990.

Index

Aboriginal and Torres Strait Islander Commission (ATSIC) 90–92, 158, 160, 164–165
Aboriginal Land Council of the Northern Territory 192
Aboriginal Protection Association (APA) 74
Aboriginal protests and organizations 81–82
Aboriginal Referendum, 1967 83
Aborigines 7, 12, 14–15, 49, 65, 67, 69, 73, 75, 80–81, 86, 89, 91–96, 101, 123, 125, 136, 157, 159, 162, 164, 176
Aceh 131–132
Adelaide 5, 36, 49
Afghan Cameleers (19th century) 99, 100
Afghanistan 8, 98, 114, 123, 172, 174–75, 178–79, 182, 194
Africans 14, 18, 46, 107, 116, 123, 127, 162, 164, 174, 177, 180
agriculture and farming 19, 20, 22, 24, 26, 27, 37, 43–4, 46, 49, 50, 51–3, 55, 58–9; compared 60–3, 66, 91, 98, 102, 108, 111, 129–130, 159, 160–62, 169, 178
Akyol, Hakan 123, 127
Allbrook, Maryon 128–29
American immigration quota system 109–110, 114
Anangu (people of Central Australia) 67–68, 85, 86
Anglican 32–33
Anglo-Saxon 5, 111, 117, 149, 151
Arabs 5, 12, 13, 120, 124, 136, 168, 174, 178, 182
Argentina 114, 123
Asia 5–8, 12–13, 66, 76, 97, 99, 105–106, 114, 116, 119, 121, 124, 127–131, 134–37, 147, 149, 156–59, 161–62, 166–184
Asia Pacific 6, 165, 170, 171
Asia Pacific Economic Corporation Forum (APEC) 168, 185
assimilation theory 116; assimilation 79, 81, 88, 116–118, 120, 122, 157
assisted immigration, assisted passage 33–36, 111–12

Association of Southeast Asian Nations (ASEAN) 169, 187, 188, 200
Atkinson, John "Sandy" 89–90
ATSIC *see* Aboriginal and Torres Strait Islander Commission
Australia: caste 32, 29; cities 48; as commonwealth 45; compared 54; federation (1901) 6, 45; identity 6; as New Holland 11, 26; parched interior 48; pensions 7; post–World War II multiculturalism 5; as potential negotiator between nations 9; as prison colony, migration to 34–7, 40; secret ballot 7; trade unions 41–2; White Australia policy 6, 97–112
Australia National University (ANU) 166–67, 171
The Australian People: An Encyclopedia of the Nation, Its People and Their Origins, 125
Austrian 114, 124

Bali bombings 9, 183–184, 196
Ballarat 36, 97, 100, 103
Bangladesh 123
Banks, Joseph 11, 16
Banta Tjut Najak Hadisah 131–132
Baptists 33, 98
Barossa Valley 55
Barrett, Thomas 19
Bashir, Abu Bakar 183–184
Batavia (Jakarta) 13
Batchelor College 95
Bathurst, Lord 30
Beach riots (Cronulla, 2005) 196–98
Beagle (ship) 31
Beattie, Peter 161
Beazley, Kim 175–76
Belgium 114
Bellamy, Edward (*Looking Backwards*) 43
Bendigo 36, 97, 100, 103
Bigge, John Thomas; Bigge Report 27–29, 34, 50
Blainey, Geoffrey 53, 136, 137, 191

Bligh, Captain William 25–26
Blue Mountains 26, 48
boat people, boat refugees 133–35, 172–82, 195–96
Bolkus, Nick 177, 192
Bosnia 194
Botany Bay (Sydney) penal colony 6–7, 16
Bourke, Richard 33
Boutros-Ghali, Boutros (United Nations Secretary General) 192
Brereton, Laurie 188
Brisbane 23, 36
Britain 5–9, 15–22, 26–9, 32–41, 45–6, 49, 51–52, 54–59, 64, 74, 79, 102, 111, 113, 131, 137–141, 145–158, 169, 180, 187
Broken Hill 109, 115
Brooks, Geraldine 114, 149, 154
Bryson, Bill 150
Buddhist 133
The Bulletin (Sydney) 52
Burmese 114, 116, 27, 128, 147, 148
Bush, George.W. (president of United States) 185

Cabrametta 134, 193
Calwell, Arthur 115–16
Cambodia 113–114, 124, 132–134, 168, 172, 178, 182
Canada 16, 22, 45, 65, 73, 114, 118, 131, 133, 134, 163, 164, 187
Canton (Guangzhou) 13, 25, 105, 125
Cape Town 18
Catalano family 129–130
Catholic 21, 29, 31–33, 36, 75, 116, 132, 137, 147, 149, 170, 180
Celtic 34, 105, 116, 121, 125–127, 181
Centre for Aboriginal and Islander Studies (Northern Territory University, Darwin) 95
Centre for Aboriginal and Torres Strait Islander Studies (Curtin University, Perth) 94
Centre for Immigration and Multicultural Studies (ANU) 125, 159
Champion de Crespigny, Robert 156
Chartists 39, 43
Chile 114
China 6, 8, 13–14, 67, 88, 97, 103–06, 108, 114, 124, 136–37, 154, 166, 168, 170–72, 178, 183, 185–190
Chinatown 31, 42
Chinese 13, 42, 45, 66, 97–108; Chen Ah Kew (Jimmy Kew) 103; opposition to 102–03; Quong Tart 104–06; racially restrictive legislation 45, 107–09; U.S.-Chinese Exclusion Act 109; White Australia policy 97–112
Chisholm, Caroline 37, 38
Chong, Elizabeth 103, 108
Christian 73, 74, 75, 99, 114, 118, 133, 168, 178
Churchill, Winston (prime minister, Britain) 147–148

Clark, Manning 55, 107, 143
Clarke, F. G. 34, 146–7
Clarke, Marcus (*For the Term of His Natural Life*) 23, 30
class divide 32, 145
Coleman, Peter J. 43
Colombo Plan 116, 133
Colonial Land Emigration Commission 37
Commonwealth of Nations, 156, 200
Congo 114, 193
Congregationalist 33, 98
Conroy, John S. 177
conscription, World War I 146–47
convicts 18; labor 27, 30, 33, 36, 40, 49
Conway, Jill Ker 51, 139–40
Cook, James (sea captain) 11–12, 16
Coptic Christian 194
Cornwall, Cornish 34, 98, 151
Corunna, Daisy 77–78
Council for Aboriginal Reconciliation 91, 158, 163
Court of Arbitration and Conciliation 45
Croatia 113, 114, 126, 194
cultural pluralism 116–120
Curtin, John (prime minister) 147–148
Czechoslovakia 114

Darling, Ralph 40
Darling Downs, Queensland 55
Darroch, Robert, 142
Darwin, Charles 31
Davie, Michael 142–43
Davis, Arthur Hoey (Rudd, Steele) 51
Day, David (*The Great Betrayal*) 147
Day, Edward Denny 71
Deakin, Alfred (prime minister) 45, 106, 110
Deane, William 189–190
de Gama, Vasco 12
de Garis, B. K. 44, 45
Della Vedova, Mary 129–130
DeLuca, Joe 113, 124
Denmark 114
deserts (Great Sandy, Great Victoria, Nullabor Plain, Simpson) 55
Dixon, Miriam 62
Dodson, Mick 87, 160, 163–165
Durack, Mary 60
Dutch 10, 13, 17, 18, 106, 123, 125, 125, 126, 128, 170; Dutch East India Company 13; Dutch East Indies 13

Eades, Sandra 95
East India Company (British) 25
East India Company (Dutch) 13
East Sussex, England 37
East Timor 13, 114, 124, 170, 172
Economist (London) 157, 175
economy 16, 21, 24, 41, 42, 45, 55–6, 81–2, 90, 100–101, 119, 121, 128, 130, 137, 161, 166, 168–9, 170, 171, 175, 183

Index

Ecuador 45
Egyptians 194
El Salvador 114
Elizabeth I 15, 33
Elizabeth II 149, 152, 154–157
emancipist(s) 22, 30, 36, 40, 48
Endeavour (ship) 11–12
England 11–13, 15, 16, 17, 19, 21, 22, 24, 25, 28, 29, 30, 32, 35–7, 39, 43, 50, 53, 55, 58, 59, 65, 74, 80, 87, 96, 104, 106, 111, 115, 118, 128, 139, 141, 142, 144, 145, 147, 149, 150, 151, 174
Eritrea 114, 123, 193
Erlich, Rita 127
Ethiopia 5, 114, 123, 193, 194
Ethnic Communities' Councils (ECC) Federation of 113, 121–24, 127
Ethnic Schools Association, parade 5, 125
Europe, compared 52, 55
European Union (EU) 139, 168, 169, 170
exclusives 27–28, 32, 35–36, 56
exports 8, 50, 54–55, 106

fair go policy, following penal period 7
Fairfield 193
farming *see* agriculture and farming
fauna and flora of Australia 14
Federated Seamen's Union 39
Finland, Finnish 114, 126
First Fleet 16
FitzGerald, Stephen 171, 200
Flinders, Matthew 26
Fox, Charlie 45
France, French 16–17, 19, 22, 30, 38, 57, 65, 69, 118, 124, 133, 134, 135, 146, 149, 151, 174, 177
Franklin, Miles 141, 145
Fraser, Malcolm (prime minister) 85, 118–19, 180–81, 190
Freestone, Adam Colin 131–132

Gaelic 34
Galbally, Frank 119
Galbally Report 119, 134
Geelong 55
George, Henry 43
George III 25
George V 80, 82
Georgiou, Petro (MP) 119, 195
Germany 55, 57, 65, 74, 98, 109, 114, 124–127, 131–32, 192
Ghana 123
Gillard, Julia 164
Gipps, George (governor) 56, 71
global cultural diversity conference 192
Goan 124
gold 6, 36, 39, 50
Goldman, Emma 107
Good Neighbour Councils 121–122
Goode, Charles 156

Goulburn 57
Grassby, Al 118
Grattan, C. Hartley 191
graziers (squatters) 55
Great Maritime Strike of 1890 41
Greece 12, 77, 109–111, 114–119, 123–25, 127–129, 137–38, 170, 192
Greenway, Francis (architect) 21, 30
Grose, Francis 23–24
Guangzhou (Canton) 13
Gurindji stockmen (Aboriginal labor strike) 84–85

Habibie, B. J. (Indonesian president) 170–71
Hall, Edward Smith 40, 71, 80
Hanson, Pauline, MP (founder, One Nation Party) 158–162, 166, 170, 176, 179, 189
Harbour Bridge 31
Hargraves, Edward 97
Hawaii (Sandwich Islands) 16
Hawke, Bob (prime minister) 120, 164, 168, 175, 190
Hayden, Bill 152
He, Yafei, China Foreign Ministry 185, 187
Henry VIII 33
Higgins, Henry B. (justice) 45–6
Higinbotham, George (chief justice) 42
Hill, John 188
Hobart City 22
Holland and Spice Islands 13, 128
Holt, Harold (prime minister) 116
Hong Kong 105, 106, 126, 159, 161, 166, 170, 187
Hope, A. D. 141, 145
Horne, Donald 182
Howard, John (prime minister) 20, 153, 155, 157, 161, 164–65, 169, 173, 175, 176, 177, 188, 189, 190, 192
Hu Jintao (president of China) 185, 186, 188, 189
Hughes, Billy (prime minister) 146
Hughes, Robert 22
Hungary 114, 124
Hunter, John 23, 24, 33–4
Hunter Valley 39
Huxley, Elspeth 62

Icelanders, 125
Imam, Vannary 132–33
Immigration, Department of 119, 126, 134, 137, 193
India 5, 77, 99, 105, 107, 131
Indigenous Coordinating Councils (ICCs) 164
indigenous people 6, 7, 11–12, 14–15, 19, 45, 49, 59, 65, 66–78, 79–96, 123–125, 136, 140, 157–165; *see also* Aborigines
Indonesia 9, 13, 14, 67, 99, 116, 123–124, 126, 131–32, 159, 166, 168, 170–73, 176, 182–183, 186, 188
Industrial Revolution, and effect on British crime rate 20

Iran 114, 172, 174, 194
Iraq 8, 114, 120, 172, 176, 188, 194
Ireland 5, 21, 32–34, 36–39, 42, 49, 52, 64, 74, 96, 98, 107–109, 125, 127–130, 137, 146–147, 151, 155, 187
Israel 114, 155
Italy 13, 77, 98, 109, 110, 113, 114, 115, 116, 124, 128, 129, 130, 174

Jakarta (Batavia) 13
Japanese 65, 106–107, 116, 124, 126, 130, 133, 147–148, 166; Australian Studies Centre at Otemon Gakuin University 168, 170, 188
Java 13
Jayasuriya, Laksiri 199
Jemaah Islamiah (JI) 9, 182
Jews, 98, 100, 117, 136 158
Johnston, George 26
Jumbunna Indigenous House of Learning at University of Techology Sydney 164
Jupp, James 37, 44, 114, 118–119, 125, 151, 154, 169

"Kanakas" (Melanesian and Polynesian indentured workers in sugar cane fields) 101–02; 106–08
kangaroos, and dry climate 14, 20, 70, 72
Kartanangaruru-Kurintji 85
Keating, Paul (prime minister) 152, 155, 156, 159, 163, 168–169, 177, 190
Kee, Pookong 199
Kelly, Paul 150, 153
Keneally, Thomas, novelist (*The Chant of Jimmy Blacksmith*) 57, 151, 175
Kent (England) 37
Kerr, John, governor general 154
Kevin, Tony 195
Kew, Jimmy (Chen Ah Kew) 103, 108
King, Philip Gidley 22, 24, 25
Kisch, Egon 108
Koorie or Koori (Aboriginal) 89, 124
Korea 5, 114

labor: free convict 27, 29; paid 36; shortage 37
labor-management relations 45
labor movement and unions: growth of 39–47; impact on country 7, 45, 191
Labor Party 44, 84, 118, 120, 146–47, 153–54, 156, 161, 169, 175–76
Lahey, Katie 150
Lal, Brij V. 102, 166–67
Lancashire 37
Land Rights Act 84–85, 94
Lane, William 43
Laos, Laotian 124, 126, 133, 168
Lawrence, D.H.; novel *Kangaroo* 140–43
Lawson, Henry 51, 52
Lawson, Kay 157
Lebanon (Christian, Orthodox, Maronite) 98–99, 114, 124–25, 133, 178, 194

Leong, Naomi 196
Leys, Simon 142
Lloyd, Henry Demarest 44
Lloyd, Lewis 151
LoBianco, Joseph 125
London 30; colonial rule 47, 49, 50, 56; dock workers 41, 43
Lopez, Mark (*The Origins of Multiculturalism in Australian Politics, 1945–1975*) 118

Mabo decision (Aboriginal land rights) 86–87, 90, 92, 151, 159
Macarthur, John 24–26, 28
Macquarie, Lachlan 26–30
Mahathir Mohamad (prime minister, Malaysia) 169, 187
Malaysian 9, 13, 99, 106, 124, 127, 130, 131, 166, 168–169, 170, 172, 182, 186
Maltese 78, 109, 114, 125
Manhattan, traded for island of Run 13
Manne, Robert 162, 179
Mannix, Daniel 147
Mares, Peter 177, 178, 179
maritime workers 42; strike 44
Marsden, Samuel 29
Martin, Jean 117
mateship 62
McCausland, Ruth 164–65
McGill, Edna 122–123
McKay, Hugh 182
Melbourne 36, 55; border 57; library 23, 39, 41, 43; population 48, 51
Menzies, Robert Gordon (prime minister) 14, 106, 147–49, 167, 190, 191
Meriam people (Murray Island) 86
Methodist 33, 98
Mexican 71, 124
Middle East 6, 99, 121, 148, 172, 183
Migrant Resource Centres 134, 193
miners (coal, copper, minerals) 39, 42, 51, 87, 97–98, 101–103, 108–109, 118, 160, 169
Molesworth, William 30
Moluccas (Spice Islands) 13
Mongolia 124, 125, 194
Morgan, Sally (*My Place*) 77–78
Morris, Jan 35, 192
multicultural Australia; national muticultural policy 7, 113–138, 189–93
multiculturalism 6, 7, 35, 93, 113–127, 131, 136, 153–154, 157–58, 169, 174
Muslims 99, 100, 114, 133, 170, 172–73, 178, 182–83
Myall Creek Massacre 70–71
Myanmar (Burma) 114, 116, 123, 127, 128, 147, 148
Mylonas, Anthony 129
Mylonas, Toula Somas 137–138

Naidoo, Manika 127

Index

Napoleonic Wars, 16
National Agenda for a Multicultural Australia (NAMA) 121, 127
National Indigenous Council (NIC) 164
National Languages and Literary Institute (Canberra) 125
Nauru (Pacific Island) 174
Netherlands 114
New Australia (in Paraguay) 43
New England region of New South Wales 55
New Holland 11, 13, 17; later renamed "Australia" 26, 106
New South Wales 11, 23, 26, 44–45, 50–51, 54–57
New York 43, 47, 57
New Zealand 2, 14, 44, 46, 73, 82, 128, 130, 137, 146, 168, 169, 173, 187
Nicaragua 194
Nightingale, Florence 40
North Africa 174
North America 13, 15, 16, 59
North Queensland 37
Northern Territory 45, 76, 82–85, 92–93, 95, 113–114, 124–126, 160, 193
Norway 114
Nullarbor Plain 55
Nye, Joseph S., Jr. 187

O'Donoghue, Lowitja (Lois) 90–91, 94
Office of Multicultural Affairs (OMA) 120
One Nation Party 159–163, 176; *see also* Hanson, Pauline

Pakistan 99, 172, 174, 182, 194
Palmer, Vance and Nettie 139, 144
Panama 45
Papua New Guinea 86, 124, 154, 168, 174
Paraguay 43
Paris 43, 123
Parramatta Factory 29
pastoralists 27, 29
Pearson, Noel 94, 160
penal colony (1788–1850s) 6, 18–24, 27–30; harshest prisons 23
Perth 30, 55
Peru 45, 71
Philippines (Filipino) 9, 99, 113–116, 124, 159, 182
Phillip, Arthur 16, 18, 23
Pilger, John 154
Poland, Polish 98, 114, 170
Polynesian and Melanesian workers 101–102
Poor Laws (England) 20, 37, 38
population 5; Aborigines, 7; multiethnic 6; urban vs. rural 48
Port Arthur prison, Tasmania 22, 30
Port Jackson 17
Portugal 12–14, 124, 170–171; and Timor Island 13
Powell, Colin 187

Prichard, Katherine Susannah 141
Pringle, John Douglas 55–56, 142
prisoners 18–20; harsh penalties in England and deportations 21, 29; prison colony dismantled 30
Privy Council 25
Protestant judges, Ireland and England 21; British Protestants in Australia 32

Quakers 98
Quarterly Essay 188
Queensland 37, 42, 44; from colony to state 45, 51, 52
Quong Tart 104–05

Raslan, Karim 186–87
Refugee Action Committee 180–181
Republic Referendum, 1999 153, 155–57
Review of Post-arrival Programs and Services to Migrants (Galbally Report) 119, 134
Reynolds, Henry 79–80
Reynolds, Margaret 180
Riverina 55, 57, 61, 115, 118
rivers: Darling 57; Hawkesbury 19, 23; Lachlan 57; Murray 57; Murrumbidgee 57; Parramatta 19, 23; Swan 30; Torrens 5
Roach, Archie 87–88
Robertson, John 51
Robinson, Portia 28
The Rocks 30
Roe, Michael 50
Rudd, Steele (Arthur Hoey Davis) 52–53
Ruddock, Phillip 178–180
Rum Rebellion 26
Run (island traded for Manhattan) 13
Russia 124, 194
Ruymaker, Ethel 150

Sallis, Eva 198
Sandwich Islands (Hawaii) 16
Sankaran, Ramdas 131
Saturday schools 5, 120, 122, 125
Saudi Arabia 182
Scandinavian 98
Schreiber, Kevin 197
Scotland 17, 21, 26, 33–34, 37–38, 40, 87, 98–99, 104–105, 140, 142, 147, 151
Second Fleet 19, 23
Selectors' Act 51-2
Serbs 114, 124
Shared Research Agreements (SRA) 164
Sharp, Ilsa 127, 149, 152
Shaw, George Bernard 36
sheep 49, 55
sheep shearers, itinerant bushmen 39–40, 61–62
Sherington, Geoffrey 33
Sierra Leone 194
SIEV X (ship) 195
Sikhs 126

silver 39
Singapore 117, 130, 131, 147–148, 158–159, 166, 168, 170, 182, 186, 187
Smith, Adam 49
Smith, Peter 88–89
Solander, Daniel Carl 11
soldiers 13, 40, 69, 146
Somalia 114, 193
South Africa 107, 127, 164, 193
South America 14, 98, 121
South Australia 5, 42, 45, 50, 51, 55, 51
South Pacific 13
Spain, Spanish 13, 114, 124, 126, 128, 151, 174
Spence, W. G. 39, 44
squatters 50–56, 105
Sri Lankan 116, 124, 194
Stead, Christina 145
Steamship Owners' Association 41
Stephens, Sir James 105-06
Sterling, James 30
Stewart, Jane 163–64
Stolen Generations (Aboriginal children) 87, 160, 163–164
Sudan 114
Sudds, Joseph 40
Sweden 11, 107, 114, 124
Switzerland 110, 114, 192
Sydney 32, 55; agitation to end transportation and prison colony 29; governor 33–4; and jobs and low crime rate 22, 23, 25; mansions 35; population 48, 51, 57; preservationists 31; social capital 35
Sydney Cove 17, 18, 31
Sydney riots *see* Beach riots (Cronulla, 2005)

Tahiti 11, 25
Tampa, M.V. (ship) 172, 174–77, 194
Tasman, Abel 13
Tasmania (former Van Diemen's Island) 22, 30, 45, 58, 72
Tatars, 125
Tench, Watkin 69
Teo, Edmund, and Janet Seagh Teo 130–31
Terra Australis Incognito 12
Thai, Thailand 123–124, 159, 169–70, 182
Theroux, Paul 142, 150
Theseira, Sandra 127
Tibet 124
Torres Strait Islanders 82, 86, 90, 91, 164
trade unions 32, 39; compared to United States 46; general strike 41–42; tailoresses' strike 39
Trades and Labour Council 39
Trades Hall Council) 39, 41
Trollope, Anthony 42–3, 48, 54, 57–8, 100, 115, 120
Trollope, Fred and Susie 53–56
Turkey, Turkish 114, 115, 124, 127, 146, 180, 192, 194

Turner, Ian 39, 146

Uluru–Kata Tjuta land lease 85–86
Unitarian 98
United Nations Convention on Refugees 114, 172, 179–80
United Nations High Commissioner on Refugees (UNHCR) 134, 135, 173, 174, 180, 195
United States 16, 22, 43, 44, 45, 46, 47, 52, 54, 58, 59, 60, 62, 65, 69, 73, 74, 79, 101, 106, 109, 114, 117, 127, 128, 131, 133, 134, 141, 145, 148, 149, 150, 162, 169, 171, 174, 175, 180, 181, 182, 188, 192
USSR, former 114

Vanstone, Amanda 199
Ventic, Judith 125
Victoria, colony then state 45, 55, 57
Vietnam 5, 79, 113–14, 123–26, 131, 133–36, 154, 168, 178, 193
Viviani, Nancy 134, 178

Wakefield, Edward Gibbon 49
Wakim, Joseph 197–98
Walbiri 75
Wales, Welsh 34, 36–37, 54, 98, 101, 134, 151, 165; Welsh Patagonians 125
Ward, Russel 28, 41, 47, 55, 61, 114, 157
Watson, Don 188
Welsh, Rob 164
Wentworth, W. C. 40
Western Australia 30, 40, 45, 55, 60, 72, 76–77, 82–83, 87, 89, 128, 131, 137, 160, 172
White, Hugh (Australian Strategic Policy Institute) 171, 186
White, Mary E. 13
White, Patrick 145
White Australia policy 89, 97–112, 116, 118, 119, 124, 154, 161, 174–179
Whitlam, Gough (prime minister) 84, 118–119, 153–5, 190
Wik decision 159, 160–161, 163
wine industry 55
women: blamed for riotous evening 19; crimes of poverty 21; female register 29; law-abiding, 28; in New Zealand; shortage of 37–44; Working Party 65,
wool 25; demand 41; production 28, 49–50, 57
Woolcott, Richard 200–201

Yugoslavia 109, 114
Yunupingi, Galarrwuy 92

Zreika, Salam 197–98
Zubrzycki, Jerzy 117

www.ingramcontent.com/pod-product-compliance
Ingram Content Group UK Ltd.
Pitfield, Milton Keynes, MK11 3LW, UK
UKHW041945140426
5217IPUK00014B/665